Praise for *Micronesian Blues*

"Anyone involved in or concerned about policing in Afghanistan or Pakistan should read *Micronesian Blues* to understand just how hard it is. Bryan Vila's lessons learned, derived from hard experience, apply in these countries as much as they did in Micronesia: make a sustained commitment, choose the right trainers and trainees, understand language and culture, and above all appreciate that change takes time."

Ryan Crocker
Former U.S. Ambassador to Iraq

"*Micronesian Blues* is a must read for every cop and soldier involved in training police abroad. The anecdotes and lessons learned are as relevant today as they were 25 years ago, and the writing is crisp, direct, effective and entertaining."

David H. Bayley, Ph.D.
Distinguished Professor of Criminal Justice
State University of New York, Albany
Author of *Changing the Guard: Developing Democratic Police Abroad*

"Flawless! Bryan Vila provides an engrossing account of his adventures starting up police agencies in Micronesia as well as key insights into cross-cultural law enforcement training. *Micronesian Blues* is the book I wish I had read prior to my deployments in support of Operation Iraqi Freedom and Operation Enduring Freedom. Vila's lessons learned are spot on, as are the policy prescriptions that flow from them."

Major Joe Hansen, OIF I, OEF VII
Former Battery Commander and Civil Military Advisor
3BCT/10th Mountain Division, Dara Pech district
Kunar Province, Afghanistan

Praise for *Micronesian Blues*

"An engaging and personal insight into crime and culture in the Pacific tropics we tend to imagine as idyllic."

Bing West
Assistant Secretary of Defense in the Reagan Administration
Author of *The Strongest Tribe: War, Politics, and the Endgame in Iraq*

"Bryan Vila spent six years training police in a foreign culture, giving him a unique perspective on how to make international police training effective. As a result, the stories in *Micronesian Blues* aren't just entertaining—they're insightful, and should be required reading for anyone thinking about undertaking such work."

Harvey V. Hedden
Executive Director
International Law Enforcement Educators and Trainers Association

"*Micronesian Blues* provides a comprehensive outline for success that should be required reading for all U.S. law enforcement personnel currently involved in cross-cultural police training, especially in Iraq and Afghanistan."

George K. Roberts
Special Agent (Ret.)
U.S. Naval Criminal Investigative Service

". . . a funny, breezy, richly anecdotal account of a cross-cultural adventure. I found it that most elusive of manuscripts—a page-turner."

Police Chief Anthony V. Bouza (Ret.), Minneapolis
Author of *The Police Mystique* and *Police Unbound*

Praise for *Micronesian Blues*

"*Micronesian Blues* should be required reading for everyone involved in the business of international policing—including policy-makers in Washington, D.C., private subcontractors, police operators and trainers working overseas, and the military officers who work with them. It's also a great read for anyone who just likes a good travel adventure."

Alexis Artwohl, Ph.D.
Internationally recognized police trainer/consultant
Co-author of *Deadly Force Encounters*

"*Micronesian Blues* is an engaging read with important cultural insights. The authors demonstrate that by listening and familiarising themselves to cultural nuances, law enforcement officers will be granted deep access to the communities they serve. The ten lessons at the end of the book are a great template for future humanitarian endeavours."

Dr. Kriton Glenn
De-escalation/Cross Cultural Specialist
Director of Cross Agency Projects
Australia

"*Micronesian Blues* offers a rare insight into U.S. efforts to assist emerging countries with developing their own professional democratic police forces, why this work is so important, and how understanding the culture of the host country can impact the potential success of a training program. *Micronesian Blues* is also laced with humor and the excitement of facing danger in a foreign country—and Vila's personal commitment to the mission and the people of Micronesia shines through."

David Butzer
Assistant Chief of Police (Ret.)
International Policing Consultant

Praise for *Micronesian Blues*

"*Micronesian Blues* is a thoroughly entertaining read, and I'd recommend it to anyone who wants to understand what it takes to be an effective police officer, trainer, or leader. Many of the lessons Bryan Vila learned about policing during his six years in Micronesia apply to community policing and police training here in the U.S. given our increasingly diverse and complex nation, just as much as they do to cross-cultural police training assignments abroad."

Gregory B. Morrison, Ph.D.
Associate Professor of Criminal Justice and Criminology
Ball State University
Former Senior Instructor at Jeff Cooper's American Pistol Institute
Author of *The Modern Technique of the Pistol*

"*Micronesian Blues* offers a compelling and engrossing portrait of how people with intellectual curiosity, a spirit of service, and a willingness to learn on the fly can make a difference. Bryan Vila's stories of his experiences doing police work in the South Pacific and his presentation of the lessons he has drawn from them provide intriguing insights into what our nation can do to assist the development of sound police services around the globe."

David A. Klinger, Ph.D.
Associate Professor of Criminology and Criminal Justice
University of Missouri-St. Louis
Senior Research Scientist, The Police Foundation, Washington, D.C.
Author of *Into the Kill Zone: A Cop's Eye View of Deadly Force*

MICRONESIAN BLUES

The Adventures of an American Cop in Paradise

In fondest memory and with deepest respect,
we dedicate this book to
Janet Craley, Jim Grizzard, Denny Lund, and Jan McCoy.

MICRONESIAN BLUES

The Adventures of an American Cop in Paradise

by Bryan Vila
as told to Cynthia Morris

Paladin Press • Boulder, Colorado

Micronesian Blues:
The Adventures of an American Cop in Paradise
by Bryan Vila as told to Cynthia Morris

Copyright © 2009 by Bryan Vila and Cynthia Morris

ISBN 13: 978-1-58160-716-1
Printed in the United States of America

Published by Paladin Press, a division of
Paladin Enterprises, Inc.
Gunbarrel Tech Center
7077 Winchester Circle
Boulder, Colorado 80301 USA
+1.303.443.7250

Direct inquiries and/or orders to the above address.

PALADIN, PALADIN PRESS, and the "horse head" design
are trademarks belonging to Paladin Enterprises and
registered in United States Patent and Trademark Office.

Visit our website at www.paladin-press.com

Contents

Acknowledgments

Thanks to the wonderful folks at Paladin Press, including publisher Peder Lund and editorial director Donna DuVall, who first saw the potential in *Micronesian Blues*; Barb Beasley, who did such a great job on the book's design; and last but not least our project editor Jon Ford, who has been a pleasure to work with and has become a friend in the process. We appreciate their professionalism, responsiveness, attention to detail, and good humor.

We also want to thank our advance reviewers and numerous other colleagues and friends whose insightful comments, criticisms, suggestions for improvement, and/or technical assistance helped us make *Micronesian Blues* a better book. They include Patti and Bob Arthur, Alexis Artwohl, David Bayley, Greg Belenky, Anthony Bouza, Sally Burchfiel, Dave Butzer, Ryan Crocker, Dan and Ginny Darrell, Kriton Glenn, Bobbi Grizzard, Joe Hansen, Harvey Hedden, Lois and Steve James, Michelle Katz, David Klinger, Jodie Knox, Ben Krauss, Otwin Marenin, Jim and Kate Meeker, Jason Moore, Greg Morrison, Michael Morse, George Roberts, Joanne Savage, Bill and Kiki Stinnett, and Bing West.

Special thanks to our families for their unwavering encouragement and enthusiasm for this project since its inception.

We are especially grateful to the many Micronesian officers who helped Bryan learn invaluable lessons about cross-cultural policing that have echoed throughout his careers as a cop, federal agent, policy-maker, and academic.

And finally, we honor the service of the American cops, soldiers, and police trainers around the globe, who strive every day to make the world a safer, more just and stable place.

Authors' Notes

Cyn and I wrote this book together. Actually, Cyn did most of the writing—I just told her my stories, often as we walked and talked with a tape recorder on. Ever the journalist, she would pose questions, probe for details, and work to find her way through my blatherings to a coherent, linear tale. So, to the extent that you enjoy *Micronesian Blues*, Cyn gets the credit. To the extent that you find yourself wondering, "What kind of knucklehead would do that?"—you have me to thank.

The events recounted here are all based on actual events, and true within the limits of my recollection nearly three decades after they occurred. Dialogue has been re-created, of course, but it reflects my memories of what was said and by whom as accurately as possible.

Many names have been changed, some characters are composite portrayals of more than one individual, and numerous people were left out of the book due to space limitations and other reasons.

In addition, the names of some of the islands themselves have changed since I lived and worked in Micronesia. Ponape is now Pohnpei, Truk is now Chuuk, and Palau is often called Belau.

Finally, in all fairness to the men and women of Air Mike (now Continental Micronesia)—and would-be travelers to the far Pacific—I would point out that travel in the region has improved a great deal since the "Island Hopper" flights back in the late 1970s and early 1980s. All of the major Micronesian runways are now paved, although I'm told an occasional pig or dog still wanders onto the tarmac.

Bryan Vila

Several years ago, back when Bryan and I were new friends who sometimes got together for coffee, he said, "Someday I'll have to tell you about my experiences training cops in Micronesia."

I was intrigued, but we were both busy—Bryan was a junior professor with heavy research and teaching demands, and I was an overworked university research writer in an understaffed office—so the subject didn't come up again for a long time. When it finally did, I was hooked by the end of his first story and knew I had to get this stuff down on paper.

But out of what I initially envisioned as a funny collection of tales from a remote part of the world, a bigger picture began to emerge. As I listened to Bryan's stories, it became clear that not only had he played a role in a fascinating yet little-known part of history, he had also gained a lot of important knowledge about effective cross-cultural police training during his six years in Micronesia—knowledge that ought to be shared. So, with any luck, you'll find this book both entertaining and informative.

Bryan's right—I did the majority of the actual writing of the book. But I assure you, the stories themselves are all his. So are many of the more colorful turns of phrase. Believe me, I couldn't make this stuff up if I tried.

Cynthia Morris

Preface

Thirty years ago, I quit my job as a street cop in the ghettos and barrios of Los Angeles to become a police trainer in the far Pacific islands of Micronesia.

Why? That's a long story for another book. The short version is that after nine years on the job I was burnt out, and a new adventure in a tropical paradise sounded like just the right cure. When the opportunity came up I jumped at it, and six weeks later I was on a plane headed west.

Here's all I knew about Micronesia when I got on that plane back in 1978. Actually, it's probably more than I knew at the time . . . .

* * *

Micronesia is not one island but many. About 2,000 of them, in fact, scattered across a vast region of the Pacific Ocean about the size of the United States. Most of these islands are so tiny that the total landmass of all 2,000 combined is smaller than the state of Rhode Island. But together, they've unwittingly played a role in the economic, political, and military affairs of numerous countries—including the United States—for nearly 500 years.

Micronesia was "discovered" by explorer Ferdinand Magellan, who claimed the islands for Spain in 1521. Spain kept them until the late nineteenth century, when Guam was taken by the United States after the Spanish-American War, and Germany bought the rest of the islands for a song. The Germans were primarily interested in copra—dried coconut meat used to make oil for soaps and cosmetics—which meant that apart from the establishment of some schools and health services, they left the locals pretty much alone. Germany held on to the islands until World War I, but when they lost that war the League of Nations gave the islands to Japan, along with a mandate to protect and develop them and help bring the people to "civilization." The Japanese were very serious about development until shortly before World War II, when they began fortifying the islands and placing the Micronesians under military rule.

During the war, my father and a lot of other GIs—mostly Marines and sailors—took the Micronesian islands away from Japan through a long and bloody series of battles that left many thousands of Americans, Japanese, and Micronesians dead by the time the war finally ended in 1945.

After the war, there was a substantial and heated debate back in the States over what should be done with Micronesia. The Navy wanted us to take the strategically important islands as spoils of war. But the folks in the State Department, who opposed the idea of increased colonialism, argued strongly against annexation.

Eventually, a compromise of sorts was reached. The United Nations was formed in 1945, and in 1947 it gave the islands to the United States as a strategic trust territory. Under the trusteeship agreement, the United States was given the right to develop and fortify the islands in the interest of international security. However, the islands officially belonged to the United Nations, not the United States, and it was expected that they eventually would become independent and self-governing.

With that agreement in place, the United States set up a military base on Kwajalein, conducted some intelligence activities, and ran a few CIA training camps for Chiang Kai-shek's Kuomintang guerrillas here and there in Micronesia during the fifteen years or so that followed. We also blew up a couple of atolls, Bikini and Eniwetok (now Enewetak), during nuclear testing in the Pacific Proving Grounds—a Cold War decision that displaced a lot of folks for a lot of years and resulted in contamination that we've paid hundreds of millions of dollars to clean up. But by and large, we left the local people as they were and tried not to screw things up for them any more than we—and everyone else before us—already had. In our effort not to contaminate the local culture, we even went so far as to put an anthropologist at the right hand of every administrator of every district in Micronesia. This well-intentioned policy has been uncharitably characterized as the "zoo theory."

Things went along pretty much that way until 1961, when John F. Kennedy became president. Despite the trusteeship label, it was obvious to him that the Micronesian islands were essentially colonies of the United States—a real embarrassment in view of the fact that, like the United Nations, he was pushing for worldwide decolonization.

At around the same time, the UN sent a visiting mission out to Micronesia. The mission report harshly criticized the lack of economic, social, political, and educational development in the islands and recommended "greater and speedier effort" toward Micronesian independence. So now the problem facing the Kennedy administration wasn't just that we still had these islands, but that we had them and hadn't done much of anything with them—or for them—in a long time. Cultural conservation had meant no progress.

Kennedy's solution was to begin pouring serious amounts of money into the islands. The money went primarily for education—which Kennedy viewed as the key to economic, political, and social progress—and for health care. The motivation behind the plan was largely humanitarian, although as critics have pointed out, it also was in America's best interest to "win Micronesia's hand" in the hope that the leaders and residents of the islands would vote to maintain a permanent relationship with the United States after they had attained independence. After all, these tiny islands cover an immense and strategically important region of the Pacific.

The push for Micronesia's development and sovereignty continued to gain momentum even after Kennedy's assassination in 1963. The Congress of Micronesia was formed in 1965 to help the islands become self-governing, giving many newly educated Micronesians a chance to participate in their political future. In 1966, the first of many Peace Corps volunteers were sent out to help the islanders along on their way to independence. And top experts like John Kenneth Galbraith, a professor of economics at Harvard and adviser to presidents Kennedy and Johnson, were brought out to the islands as consultants. The goal of these folks was to help the Micronesians figure out what it was they wanted to become—whether it was independent countries, territories of the United States, commonwealths with the United States, or something else. It truly was government in the making.

Contrary to what some people believed at the time, most Micronesians *wanted* change. They embraced the idea of progress and a more modern lifestyle. They wanted better schools and higher education for their children. They wanted access to consumer goods, and the money to buy them. They wanted television. In short, they didn't want to be left behind while the rest of the world headed into the twenty-first century.

One of the things the Micronesians needed to take their place among the independent nations of the world was a more modern system of laws and law enforcement. That's where I came in. I was told that my new job as a police specialist for the U.S. Trust Territory of the Pacific Islands would include training police, designing law enforcement programs, and a little "saddle up" time here and there, whenever things went sideways. The goal was to help each group of islands develop new laws that fit with their traditional ways but still met the challenges of modernization, and to help them become capable of enforcing those new laws on their own.

Frankly, the job sounded like a paid vacation in paradise. Was I ever wrong. With six different governments, twelve different cultures, and nine different languages to deal with—along with more than a few riots, rapes, and murders—policing in Micronesia turned out to be as challenging as anything I had ever done as a street cop in L.A. or a Marine in Vietnam. Yet living and working there was one of the most rewarding experiences I've ever known. It was also the adventure of a lifetime.

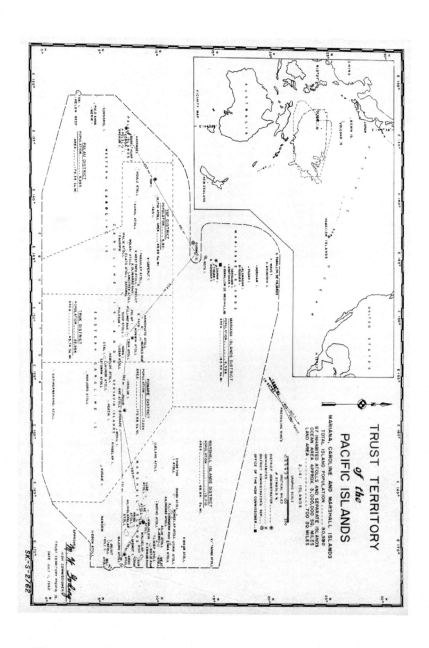

CHAPTER I

Island Hopper

June 15, 1978

I cinched my seatbelt down tight, grabbed both armrests, and hung on for dear life as the plane banked sharply to the right, then continued its descent on our final approach into Saipan. The old couple next to me were likewise braced, white-knuckled, and staring straight ahead. The woman's lips were moving slightly, as if she was reciting a prayer.

Flaps swung down and the pitch of the engines dropped an octave as we lost altitude. I looked out the window and saw nothing but dark blue ocean beneath us, lightening rapidly to shades of green as we approached the island. I took a deep breath and held it in preparation for landing. Not a crash landing—at least I hoped not. Just another typical adrenaline-pumping, smash-down landing on an unpaved Micronesian runway.

I'd been through six of them since the Island Hopper—an Air Micronesia Boeing 727 with reinforced landing gear—left Honolulu more than twenty-two hours earlier. Johnston, Majuro, Kwajalein, Ponape, Truk, and Tinian. What an experience! Especially that first landing on Johnston, where I'd had no idea what to expect.

It was *slam* down and flaps up, braking all the way. We landed so hard the oxygen masks fell down and several of the overhead storage compartments popped open. Babies squalled, while most of the adults just sat there in stunned silence, staring numbly at the carry-on baggage that had tumbled down into the aisle.

On every island but Johnston and Kwajalein, which were military bases and off-limits to civilians, we'd had about an hour on the ground. The plane would slide to a halt on the coral runway next to a thatched-roof terminal, and those of us whose legs weren't shaking too badly from the landing would get off for a few minutes to stretch them and to look around.

I'd wander about in the humid darkness among the crowds of people who came to greet the plane. Even though it was the middle of the night during most of the journey, there were people everywhere, every time we landed. Everyone seemed to know everyone else, and they'd greet each other with leis and floral crowns called *mar mars*, speaking in languages I'd never heard before. I'd watch them curiously, bewildered by the newness of it all, yet relishing the edge of a new adventure.

At most of the airports, there were pretty young women selling Coke, cigarettes, and local handicrafts. Many of them wore faded missionary dresses with high ruffly collars, puffy Cinderella sleeves, elastic waists, and full skirts that went down past their knees. At first glance they looked quite prim—but then I noticed that most of them had unzipped their dresses all the way down to their waists in back to let out the heat, and wore nothing underneath.

I didn't blame them. It was stiflingly hot, even in the middle of the night. I was wearing jeans, running shoes, and what I had thought would be a very cool, short-sleeved nylon shirt. But you know, you get out into the tropics and you find out that there's only one fabric if you want to be cool, and that's cotton. One hundred percent, don't-give-me-poly-anything cotton. Period. That shirt was so hot, I might as well have been wearing long underwear.

I'd buy another pack of cigarettes, and sometimes a Coke,

even though I didn't care much for the stuff, and then it would be time to get back aboard the crowded, smelly Boeing 727.

The smell had gotten worse toward the end of the journey—and not just because all of us on the plane were pretty ripe with sweat and travel grime. We'd been traveling for hours, with no place to dump the heads along the way, and they had begun to overflow. Every takeoff brought blue slimy sewage spilling out of the forward head, sloshing down the aisle. Every landing sloshed sewage out of the rear head and sent it flowing down the aisle in the opposite direction, like some evil-smelling tide that shifted with the currents of the flight. It was so bad I found myself wishing I'd worn waders instead of running shoes. *Thank God this is the last leg*, I thought, as I continued to brace myself for the inevitable jolt.

It didn't come. This time, with just the barest chirp, the wheels touched down and we coasted smoothly to a gentle stop. Amazingly enough, the Saipan runway was paved.

I let out the breath I'd been holding, exhaling loudly with a profound sense of relief that the journey was finally over.

* * *

It was mid-morning when I stepped off the plane on Saipan, my new home.

By now, I was almost used to the sudden burst of hot, heavy air that greeted me as I started down the stair ramp of the travel-weary 727 amid a bustle of Japanese tourists. The air in Micronesia is so moist and soft you can feel it on your skin, and there's this overwhelming smell to it—a heady combination of coconut husks and mosquito coils and insect repellent and plumeria and salt from the sea.

I followed the tour group into the old airport building, which wasn't much more than a tin shack back then. We waited for about twenty minutes, until three pickup trucks overflowing with luggage and other cargo pulled up to the back entrance of the building and a crew of workers began heaving the baggage off the trucks into a big pile. I retrieved my bags from the bottom of the heap, went through immigration and customs, then lugged my suitcases outside and stood under the shaded eaves next to the curb, wondering what to do next.

I guess I'd just assumed that Jim Grizzard would be there to meet me at the airport. It was two months since I'd met him in the walnut-paneled bar of an upscale hotel in Pasadena. He'd been the funny little guy in the aloha shirt and chinos at the end of the bar, regaling a group of people with one hilarious story after another. I'd been the dapper cop dressed in a gray herringbone polyester bell-bottomed suit, maroon knit shirt with long collar points, broad paisley necktie, and two-tone platform shoes. (Hey, it was the seventies. We all dressed like shit.) The coincidence that Jim worked for the Justice Improvement Commission on Saipan, where my dad had fought and almost died during World War II, had been enough to draw us together in conversation. Four or five martinis later, when he'd mentioned that there was a job opening for a police specialist on Saipan, I'd been hooked.

It wasn't just that I was burnt out and in search of a new adventure. Another reason the job appealed to me was that I'm basically an optimist, and I didn't want to give in to cynicism like many of my fellow officers. I'd become a cop back in 1969 because I wanted to help people—maybe even be a hero with a small "h". But in the ghettos and barrios of Los Angeles where I worked, people were afraid of cops. Most of them tolerated us as a necessary evil, but they certainly didn't regard us as heroes. We were more like an occupation army in a war zone. Deep down, I hoped this move would give me a chance to finally wear the white hat I'd been searching for since I'd joined the Marine Corps when I was seventeen.

So I'd said yes, and now here I was, my nine-year career

with the sheriff's department behind me and God only knew what stretched out in front of me. Waiting. Jim, with his dark tan, droopy mustache, bad comb-over, and smoker's cough, was nowhere in sight.

Finally, a high-pitched, nasal voice behind me asked, "Bryan?"

"Yeah?" I replied expectantly. I turned to find a sparrow-faced ectomorph—about five-foot-six and 120 pounds—with a mustache, thinning ginger-red hair, and freckles. He was wearing an untucked aloha shirt with a pack of Chesterfields in the pocket.

"I'm Denny Lund."

"Denny? Hi. Good to meet you," I said, doing my best to hide my surprise. My new boss was nothing like I had pictured. According to Jim, Denny had run security on the Alaska pipeline and headed the state of Alaska's criminal justice planning agency before coming to Micronesia as administrator of the Justice Improvement Commission. I guess I had been expecting the Hollywood version of the adventurous type. Denny seemed quiet and unassuming—shy, even.

"How was your trip out?" he asked.

"It was amazing," I said.

Denny chuckled and nodded, tipping his head down a little and covering his mouth behind his hand to hide a row of half-rotty teeth. "Yeah, it's quite an experience. Especially the first time. But you'll get used to it." He paused and chuckled again, like maybe he was remembering his first trip to Saipan. "Well, have you got all your stuff?" he asked me.

"Yeah, I think so."

"C'mon then," said Denny. He led the way as we lugged my suitcases and carry-on gear out to the car. "Sorry Jim couldn't be here to meet you," he said over his shoulder as we walked. "He's at a training session on Ponape this week."

Denny's car was an old, beat-up Subaru station wagon

with giant rust holes all over, a muffler that was just barely hanging on, and windows that didn't work on one side. It was filthy beyond belief—even worse than the cars I used to see when I worked in the ghetto. This, I soon learned, was the norm here. There were a few jeeps and some trucks, but most of the islanders drove cars that were shipped over from Japan, and because of the humidity and salty air, rust was the most prevalent color.

I loaded my suitcases into the rear, sweating. It was still morning, but the sun was already blazing, and I was really starting to hate that nylon shirt I was wearing.

"I live on Capitol Hill," Denny said as he slid in behind the wheel. "You'll be staying with me for a couple of weeks until your house is ready. Hope you don't mind."

"No, that's fine," I said. I dumped my carry-on bag on top of the suitcases in the back and got in front. When Denny started the car it made a loud mechanical shriek, but the engine finally turned over and off we went.

"So, when's your wife get here, then?" Denny asked, as he drove the car with one hand and fished out a Chesterfield from the pack in his shirt pocket with the other.

"She'll be here in a couple of weeks. She wanted to visit her folks in Seattle before she came out," I explained.

Denny nodded. "That's good. It'll give you some time to get settled in."

I could tell something was bothering him a little bit. He puffed on his cigarette and looked out the window. "Sometimes Micronesia is hard on families—especially stateside women," he said.

"Yeah, I can appreciate that, Denny. But I don't think it'll be a problem for us," I said. "Susan's lived overseas before. She taught English in Japan for more than a year and really enjoyed it. She's looking forward to this move as much as I am."

Denny nodded again, but he didn't look convinced. It wasn't

until much later that I found out why—his own wife had left him earlier that week.

Swiftly changing the subject, Denny began a running commentary on everything we passed as we drove along the bumpy, rutted road between the airport and his house on Capitol Hill. Frankly, I only had half an ear on Denny's monologue. My attention was too fully captured by the incredibly beautiful natural scenery—dark blue sky scattered with white, billowy clouds, sprawling flame trees bursting with bright orange-red flowers, coconut palms, and plumeria—and the stark contrast of the ugly, dilapidated man-made structures, most of them made of concrete or rusting tin. I kept reminding myself to put my stateside sensibilities aside, but it still looked pretty disreputable.

"The CIA built these houses in the early 1950s when they were training the Kuomintang guerrillas here," Denny told me as we pulled up in front of a gray concrete bunker that apparently was his home. "The nicest thing you can say about them is that they're typhoon-proof. Well, sort of."

There was wood trim around the windows and doors that helped to relieve some of the plainness of the concrete, but the wood was all peeling and termite-ridden, so it didn't help much. The roof was a flat concrete slab, partly covered with scabs of moss and gobbets of tar, with a little slope to let the rain run off. Landscaping was limited to a few big Norfolk pines, tall hibiscus hedges, and a struggling lawn.

Denny parked the car in the driveway. The engine subsided with a gasp and a sigh, as if it had just drawn its last breath. We pulled my luggage out of the back and dragged it into the house. I followed him past the living room, which was furnished with floral-cushioned rattan, and down the hallway to one of the back bedrooms, where we deposited my luggage.

Denny spent the next half hour or so showing me around the house and explaining how various contraptions worked—like the water distiller that was gurgling away in the kitchen.

Then he went back to the office, leaving me to settle in and get some badly needed sleep.

I unpacked first, then headed for the shower, anxious to be rid of nearly two days of travel grime. The water that drizzled weakly from the showerhead was the dark reddish color of rust, but it felt refreshing anyway. I toweled off, climbed into bed, and was dead to the world in less than five minutes.

***

As it turned out, I needn't have bothered to unpack at all. The very next day, after introducing me to everyone at the Justice Improvement Commission office and having me fill out a mountain of paperwork, Denny informed me over lunch at the Continental Hotel that I'd be catching the Island Hopper back to Ponape in the morning.

"Tomorrow?" I repeated, not sure I had heard right. Ponape was 1,200 miles away, and I had only just gotten here.

"Yeah. Sorry for the short notice, but I'd really like to get your take on this officer training program that Jim's at," Denny said apologetically. "It's being run by the FBI and the acting police chiefs for Ponape, Truk, Yap, and Palau. The chiefs are all from Honolulu P.D. We brought 'em over about six months ago to help us get the departments here into better shape."

"How's that working out?" I asked.

"Not too bad," Denny told me. "But not great either, in some places. I mean, we figured they're Hawaiians, they're islanders, so they'd fit right in here, right? Well, Oahu's an island all right, but Honolulu's a big city, and Hawaiian culture is a lot different from Micronesian culture. So the island theory didn't really pan out. Things are going pretty well overall, but there's still lots of room for improvement. I'd appreciate any suggestions you might have about that, once you get more familiar with things here."

"All right. I'll keep my eyes open," I assured him.

"Good, good. That's exactly what I want you to do on this trip," said Denny. "Watch, listen, and get to know people. Learn as much about Ponape as you can. It's real important to get to know the different islands and their cultures when you're working out here. One of the first things I did when I came out was take a tour all the way out to the Marshalls and then back to Guam and down to Yap and Palau. We'll try to get you the same coverage during the next few months."

I nodded, still somewhat taken aback by the thought of traveling again so soon, but at the same time realizing what a smart idea this was. Every veteran cop and soldier knows that one of the keys to success in a new environment is an intimate knowledge of the people and the terrain. Denny obviously understood this, and my respect for him went up a notch.

II

Still seriously jet-lagged from my trip west, I took the first flight to Guam the next morning. From there, I caught the Air Mike flight to Truk and Ponape. The plane—the same one I had been on just two days earlier—arrived right on schedule, and pretty soon I was wheels-up again.

I spent a lot of time staring out the window on the two-hour trip to Truk. It was amazing. There were few clouds over the open ocean that day, and no land in sight anywhere. You could see from one horizon to the other, with absolutely nothing to break the view. No boats, no islands, nothing. Just mile after mile of water. It's hard to comprehend that kind of water. After a while, it starts to feel like you'll never see land again. And then, way off in the distance, there's the tiniest bump on the horizon and you can't help but feel a thrill of discovery.

"Ladies and gentlemen, we'll be landing on Truk in approximately fifteen minutes," the flight attendant said, soon after I had detected the bump up ahead to our right. "We'll be on the ground for one hour before the flight leaves for Ponape. Passengers going on to Ponape who wish to deplane, please be sure to leave an 'Occupied' card on your seat."

We put down with the usual slam-bang landing. I fumbled in the seat-back pocket in front of me, found my "Occupied" card, and placed it on my seat. Then I gathered up my carry-on bag and went down the back stairs in search of some iced tea.

The airport was just as overflowing with people this morning as it had been the other night. I made my way through the crowd to the little counter inside the airport building where they sold cold drinks.

"Hello," I said to the elderly woman behind the counter.

"*Ran annim*," she said.

I assumed this was the Trukese equivalent of a greeting, so I smiled and asked, "Do you have any iced tea?"

"Coke or Pepsi?" she asked with a heavy accent.

"No, thank you. I'm looking for iced tea. Is there any place I can get some around here?"

She sort of tittered and turned and walked off, a splay-footed, heavy walk. She returned shortly with a very pretty young woman, probably her granddaughter.

"May I help you?" the young woman asked in good English.

"Is there some place I can get some iced tea, please?" I asked.

"Sure. Over at the Christopher. They have iced tea."

"Great. Where's that?"

"Just over there," she said, pointing to a blue, low-lying two-story building a block and a half away.

"Thanks," I said.

I checked my watch and saw that I still had nearly forty-five minutes till the plane was due to depart—plenty of time. I hoisted my bag over my shoulder and walked briskly down the road to the hotel.

The bar was open, and a few people were sitting around drinking coffee or Coke.

"Could I get some iced tea, please?" I asked the woman standing behind the bar.

"Sure," she said, and disappeared.

Five minutes later, she still wasn't back. Ten minutes later, just when I was starting to get concerned, she returned with my tea.

I had just taken my first sip when I heard the roar and whine of engines starting up. I checked my watch again. It was still half an hour before the plane was due to take off. *What the hell?*

I slapped a dollar on the counter, ran out the front door and down the street, just in time to see the plane—*my* plane—taxiing down the runway for takeoff. Panicked, I raced into the airport building and up to the Air Mike counter.

"I was supposed to be on that plane," I told the ticket agent, a heavy-set Micronesian woman in her mid-thirties.

"Well, it's gone," she replied complacently.

"I can see that. What happened? When I got here from Guam they said it was going to be on the ground for an hour."

"They got a weather report that there's a storm headed for Majuro. They have to hurry to beat the storm," she said.

"So they just left? Half an hour ahead of schedule?" I said.

"Yes."

"So what do I do? I have to be on Ponape today."

"I dunno," she said.

"Well, when's the next plane?"

"Two days."

"Two days? Isn't there anything else? Could I take a boat?"

She looked at me like I was crazy and shook her head.

"What about a charter? Are there any other airlines that go to Ponape?"

"No. No other airlines."

"What about that little red plane out there?" I asked, pointing to a red Cessna sitting out on the runway.

"Oh, that belongs to PIA. Pacific Island Aviation."

"Are they flying today?" I asked hopefully.

"I dunno."

"Where's their office?"

"They're closed," she said. "But maybe you can find the pilot."

"Great. Where would he be?"

"I dunno. Maybe at the Christopher."

I didn't remember seeing anybody who looked even remotely like a pilot at the Christopher, but I went back over there anyway to look again. There were a couple of somewhat reputable-looking Americans drinking coffee and playing cards in the back of the bar.

"Are either of you guys the pilot for PIA?" I asked.

They both laughed. "No, you want Earl. Earl the Squirrel. He's out there on the patio," said one of them, pointing. "Guy in the shades."

I followed his finger and saw a sixtyish man wearing mirrored aviator sunglasses slouched over a cup of coffee. *Earl the Squirrel? Shit.*

"Thanks, I think," I said.

I went outside and over to his table.

"Are you the PIA pilot?" I asked.

"Yep."

"Mind if I sit down?"

"Suit yourself," he grunted. He had gray hair and a sort of gristly look about him, in spite of his red nose and cheeks, heavy jowls, and paunch. It was pretty obvious that he was nursing a serious hangover.

"Any chance of getting a flight to Ponape today?" I asked.

"I already got a charter," he said.

"Oh? Where are they going?"

"Ponape."

"Have you got room for one more? I missed my flight on

Air Mike and I've gotta get there today," I said.

"Maybe. It's three Japanese businessmen. If they haven't booked anyone else on you can come along."

"Great. How much is it?"

"Hundred and seventy-five."

"Round trip or one way?"

"One way."

"Well, there goes half my budget for this trip," I said.

"It's that or Air Mike."

"All right," I agreed. "When are you leaving?"

"'Bout an hour, depending on when the Japs get here."

"Great. Where do I meet you?"

"You can just hang around here and I'll stop by when I'm ready."

"That's OK, I think I'll wait at the airport," I said. I wanted to wait in full view of that red Cessna. I had already missed one flight today, and I sure as hell couldn't afford to miss another.

"Suit yourself," he said, getting up and tossing a bill down on the table. I followed him out of the hotel and down the road, back to the airport.

"A friend of mine's supposed to be picking me up at the airport on Ponape," I said. "Is there any way to call ahead and let him know I'll be late?"

There was a long pause. "You're new here, aren't you?" Earl asked, giving me a sideways glance.

I didn't answer. I figured the question was rhetorical anyway.

Earl snorted. "Look, everybody misses planes. Your friend'll know what to do. Quit worrying about it. Go wait inside and I'll come get you when I'm ready."

So I went inside the airport and waited. I sat where I could keep an eye on the Cessna—and get a better look at it. It turned out to be an old push-pull, a funny-looking airplane the CIA used to fly in Vietnam. It had an engine in front of the pilot's cockpit, a four-passenger cabin, and then another engine behind the cabin.

The good thing about this kind of aircraft is that it's made for bush flying, so it can take off and land on a very short airstrip. The bad things, in my opinion, outweigh this advantage. For one, you're sitting between two 300-pound chunks of metal that are likely to flatten you into a pancake if you crash. Second, the wing is on top of the fuselage instead of under it, which means that if you go down in the water and somehow survive the pancake effect, you'd have to force the doors open underwater in order to escape instead of just stepping out onto the wing like you would in a plane with the wing below the fuselage—unless you got "lucky" and the plane flipped over on impact. Third, this particular aircraft—like its pilot—had seen better days.

Pretty soon I saw the Japanese businessmen show up and get on board. I didn't wait for Earl to come get me—I headed straight out to the airplane.

"You ready?" Earl asked as he saw me coming.

"Yeah," I said. What could I say? I had to get to Ponape, and there was no other way. Hell, I'd survived Vietnam. I figured I could probably survive Earl the Squirrel.

"Why don't you go ahead and sit up front with me. It's pretty crowded in back," he said.

"Great," I said. I nodded hellos to the businessmen, stuffed my lone bag in along with their heaps of luggage, and hopped up into the cockpit. At least the seat was comfortable.

To his credit, Earl did make a safety check of sorts before we took off. He shuffled around the plane a couple of times, kicked the tires, checked to make sure the fuel was up and that there was no water in it—which can be a real killer in the tropics—spun up the engines and we were off.

Being up front, I soon discovered that there was no fancy navigational equipment on the plane. Earl simply took a compass heading for Ponape and figured our flight time based on distance and prevailing winds. We were about to travel 450 miles across the open ocean to a tiny island that we very well might miss all together if we were even a smidgen off, and that was as sophisticated as it got.

Worse, about an hour into the flight, Earl put the plane on autopilot, tipped his hat over his eyes, and fell asleep. I could see the reflection of his eyes in the corner of his mirrored sunglasses and they were shut tight. He was copping Zs for the next two hours. I just sat there and didn't say squat, but I kept a close eye on all the gauges and a keen lookout for anything that looked remotely like land.

Earl must've had a pretty good internal clock, because as soon as we got within communicating distance of Ponape, he came to. After a few phlegmy coughs and a swig of coffee (at least I hoped it was coffee) from the battered thermos he kept in the pouch next to his seat, he got on the radio with the communications station on Ponape and gave them our heading and ETA. Everything appeared to be in order, and we continued on for the next half an hour or so, until land appeared on the horizon.

As we approached the island, Earl got back on the radio with the communications station and asked them to *listen* for us. Seriously. The cloud cover was so heavy that the control tower couldn't see us, so this is how he typically landed the plane. As soon as they could hear us, Earl started descending in a gradually tightening spiral, homing in on the radio signal from the communications tower.

As we descended, the lagoon finally came into view. From my previous flight into Ponape on Air Mike just two days before, I remembered that the airstrip had been built over the lagoon. One of the other passengers had told me that it's a fairly dangerous place to land, because there's a thirty-foot drop-off at one end that creates a condition called a wind shear where you're flying along level and lined up with the airstrip and all of a sudden, just about the time you get over the runway, the air drops out from under you and you start to fall. The pilots know about it and have to correct for it, but it's always a little hairy because there's no way of knowing how far you'll drop.

My confidence in Earl was not great, but I figured that anyone who flew here regularly must be pretty familiar with the conditions. So I was just starting to think I might actually survive this flight when I noticed a cloud of heavy black smoke smudging off to the side of the airstrip where some yachts and sailboats were moored.

Earl saw it, too. "That's my sailboat!" he yelled. "That's *my* fucking sailboat on fire! Son of a bitch! I built that boat with my own hands!"

Then he tipped the Cessna to starboard to get a better view. That's when the turbulence began. We were at the midpoint above the end of the airstrip and likely to encounter the wind shear any second now.

"Earl, fly the plane!" I yelled.

Too late. We hit the wind shear and the plane dropped suddenly, like an elevator car with a broken cable. I braced myself, expecting to eat it any second, but somehow Earl just set the damned thing down, amid all the sluing and thrashing about, shut it off, opened the door, and ran off toward his sailboat without another word to me or his other passengers.

My legs were just a little shaky. I undid my harness but took my time getting out of the plane. I pulled the curtain back to see how the businessmen were doing, but they seemed pretty unimpressed. Maybe they had thought the sudden drop was normal, or maybe, being in the back, they hadn't had the same bird's-eye view I had just had of how close we had come to crashing.

I gathered up my stuff and headed off toward the airport terminal. There was Jim, his back to the bar, a Budweiser in one hand and a cigarette in the other. He was tan as ever, stringy hair plastered across the top of his head, and a big grin on his face.

"Well, welcome to Micronesia, Bryan," he said, slapping me on the back.

"You see that landing?" I asked.

"Yep."

"What an asshole," I said. I caught the bartender's eye and ordered a Budweiser. "Sorry I'm late," I added.

"Hey, don't sweat it. You're here, aren't you? What happened anyway?"

I told him and he laughed. "Yeah, like I said, welcome to Micronesia."

CHAPTER 2

Keystone Kops
and Elephant Snot

The cars on Ponape were just as beat up as they were on Saipan, and the roads were worse. Jim and I bounced up and down pretty wildly, even at fifteen miles an hour, as we drove along the Sokehs Causeway to the Cliff Rainbow Hotel.

But the scenery—wow. I was impressed by the beauty of the place. I mean, Saipan is tropical, but Ponape is lush.

The Cliff Rainbow Hotel was tucked away in the jungle, surrounded by banana trees and guava trees and papaya trees and palm trees and acacia trees. It was a two-story hotel made of concrete block. My room was small—kind of like a monk's cell—but it was comfortable enough. The whole place smelled musty, but then, everything smelled musty in Micronesia.

"Why don't you take it easy for the rest of the day—settle in a bit," said Jim. "I'll stop back at the college for what's left of the afternoon session, then meet you back here for dinner later."

"Great," I said. "I sure could use the break."

"Yeah, the place takes a little getting used to at first, but you'll catch on," said Jim.

After Jim left I unpacked, then took a shower and a nap. I was really drained, and the mid-afternoon heat and humidity weren't doing much to boost my energy.

* * *

I woke, several hours later, to the thump of disco music. "What the hell?" I said out loud. This was the last place I expected to hear that crap. It was already dusk. I dressed, splashed some water on my face, and headed downstairs to the bar—a central area furnished with picnic tables under a big thatched roof.

The music got louder as I approached, and there was some sort of group dancing going on in the bar. *Oh God, the Latin Hustle.* My head was already swimming from the heat and humidity, the jet lag, and the newness of the place. And now, to top it all off, here were Micronesians and Americans and Japanese and Chinese and Germans and Belgians all learning to do the Hustle in the middle of the Ponape jungle, as one disco tune after another played at full volume on a rusty old jukebox. I stood there staring for a while, dumbstruck, until I finally remembered what I was there for and went looking for Jim.

I found him back in a corner of the bar, his usual beer and cigarette in hand, watching the dancers with an amused expression.

"Hey, there you are. Pull up a beer," he said in greeting. He waved to the bartender, who brought me a Budweiser.

"Thanks. But I think I'm gonna need something stronger than this," I said, nodding to my beer. "Do they do this every night?"

"Yep. *Saturday Night Fever* sweeps Ponape. Pretty weird, eh?" Jim said, shaking his head.

"Weird? It's like something out of a Hunter S. Thompson novel," I said.

I met a lot of people that night and I drank a lot of beer, but not enough to get me out on that dance floor—at least, not that I remember.

II

The next morning I met Jim at the hotel restaurant—a sort of makeshift building with a tin roof and the same kind of picnic tables as in the bar. Breakfast fare here was rice and sashimi or bacon and eggs. The bacon and eggs plate sounded great, and ever the optimist, I ordered it. Of course, my style of traveling always had been that if you get the trots you get the trots, so go ahead and eat and drink what you want, and don't worry about it. The operative words here are "had been." You learn pretty quickly in the islands, like I did that first week, that there are some things you've just got to avoid if you know what's good for you. After that, I ordered rice and sashimi for breakfast whenever I traveled.

After breakfast, we drove to work in Jim's rental car, rocking and bouncing all the way through the narrow jungle roads, past people and houses, until we finally arrived at the police station. Like most of the buildings in Micronesia, it was low and flat and roofed with rusty tin.

"I thought I'd take you in and introduce you to the troops before they go out on patrol. Then we'll head over to the college for the training session," Jim said as we got out of the car.

"Great," I replied, following him into the station.

The "troops" were hard to take seriously, especially to someone coming out of the L.A. County Sheriff's Department via the U.S. Marine Corps. They were wearing ratty dark blue trousers with gold stripes down the sides, rumpled light blue shirts with little corroded badges above their left breast pockets, and white bus driver-style policeman hats with patent leather visors. Some of them wore socks with their shoes and some of them didn't, and some wore zoris—rubber flip-flops—instead of shoes. I had never seen uniforms that bad, not even on Vietnamese army reservists. (But I'd soon learn—the hard way—not to let my stateside prejudices blind me to their potential as cops. In this environment, appearances counted for nothing.)

Jim introduced me around briefly, then we walked over to the Community College of Micronesia, where the training session was being held. On our way to the classrooms we passed the administration building and a collection of low, flat concrete structures that served as dormitories for the students. Just past the dormitories was a basketball court, where several young men were playing. Most of them wore raggedy jeans and either no shirts or thin-strapped T-shirts with lots of holes in them. And most of them—racing back and forth on hot asphalt and jumping and shooting and playing good basketball—were barefoot. The ones who weren't barefoot were wearing zoris, for chrissake, and it didn't seem to be slowing them down one bit. Tell *that* to your kids when they ask for another pair of Air Jordans.

The college design was similar to that of the dormitories—a series of narrow little single-story concrete block buildings. When we arrived, class was already in session. There were about thirty-five students in attendance—Micronesian cops who had been flown in from all over the Trust Territory. Jim and I took seats in the back of the room.

"That's Mark Dugan," Jim said, nodding toward the lecturer, a medium height, round-faced guy in his early forties. "He's FBI. The guy with him is Alan Pierce, the police captain out of Honolulu who's running the expatriate program here."

The air conditioner was roaring and it had started to rain—huge drops that were making a deafening racket as they pelted down on the tin roof. From what I could hear over the din, I gathered that Mark and Alan were teaching search and seizure law. It was an excruciatingly boring and highly technical class, and I seriously wondered about the wisdom of using fancy terms like "curtilage"—which refers to the area of a person's property surrounding the actual dwelling that is considered to be part of the dwelling—when half the cops in the room could barely understand English. But I kept my mouth shut. I was only there to observe at this point.

After the first class, Jim took me up and introduced me to Mark and Alan and to Steve "Kimo" Panolo, another Honolulu P.D. cop who was working as the acting police chief on Truk. Kimo was about six-foot-six and 250 pounds of huge, impressive bronze muscle.

"You the guy from LAPD?" Kimo asked.

"Sheriff's Department," I said.

"Right," said Kimo. "Look, you guys ever do role-playing exercises in the classes back there?"

"Sure," I said.

"Great. I could use your help," he said. "I'm teaching a class on report writing in about ten minutes, and I've got this role-playing exercise all set up for them. I was gonna have one of the other Honolulu guys do it with me, but it would work better with a stranger. You game?"

"Why not?" I said. It beat the hell out of sitting through another class with nothing to do.

"All right," said Kimo. He pulled me aside and gave me the setup.

The exercise Kimo had in mind is one that's pretty standard in academies all over the world. First you create an incident that takes the students by surprise, then you test their ability to remember the details of what they just observed. The idea is to impress upon them how important it is to constantly pay attention to every detail of their surroundings.

We waited until halfway through his class, when people were desperately trying to stay awake and take notes, to spring it on them. Kimo was up at the front of the classroom lecturing when I burst in the back door.

"Kimo," I yelled, striding up the aisle between the chairs full of stunned students. "You son of a bitch! I told you to stay away from my sister!"

When I got almost to the front of the room, I reached under my shirt, pulled out the .38 loaded with blanks that Kimo had given me, and shot him three times. Kimo crashed to the floor in front of the class, and I turned to run.

Now, the way it's supposed to work is that Kimo gets right back up as soon as I leave and explains to the students that they have fifteen minutes to write down a detailed account of what they just witnessed, including a full description of the suspect—me.

The problem was, neither Kimo nor I had stopped to think just how different people in this part of the world really were, or what their reaction might be. They'd had no experience with role-playing exercises, so to them this was real. And before Kimo could get up to explain, all five of his officers from Truk jumped up and took off after me, intent on avenging their "dead" chief.

I started running as fast as I could, with the entire herd of Trukese policemen thundering down the hallway behind me. It was like something out of the Keystone Kops, but believe me, I wasn't laughing. They were unarmed, but they were all really big—squat, broad-shouldered, and 220 pounds or more. If they caught up with me, they could—probably would—tear me apart with their bare hands.

Adrenaline pumping, I raced out into the square courtyard surrounded by the long, low classrooms and quickly scanned it for an escape route. I remembered that the way out of the courtyard to the administration building, where I might find help, was through the basketball court. But as I turned to head that way, I slipped on the slick, rain-soaked asphalt and fell ass end over teakettle. I was back up and running in a flash, but now the Trukese officers had gained ground.

As I reached the basketball standard I grabbed the pole and swung around to the left, accelerating into a cut between two buildings, past a plumeria bush and into a gravel lot where several rusty old cars were parked. The concrete administration building was just across the lot, and one of the doors was wide open.

As I hauled ass toward that open door, I could hear loud panting and the heavy flip-flopping sounds of five pairs of zoris on big square feet right behind me. I made it through the door and turned to slam it shut behind me with both hands. Too late. A thick brown arm shoved it back open. As I scanned the room, desperately searching for cover, I saw Mark Dugan and Alan Pierce, who were inside taking a coffee break. They were both staring at me with puzzled looks on their faces.

"What the hell—" Mark started to ask.

Before I could answer him, the Trukese police officers shoved their way through the narrow doorway and headed straight for me.

"What the hell are you doing?" Mark yelled at them. "Leave him alone!"

The Trukese officers ignored him and kept coming at me. I ran across the room and got behind a heavy table. It wasn't likely to do much good, but it made me feel a little less vulnerable.

"Whoa, guys," Alan said, putting himself between them and me. "What's going on here?"

The officers either didn't understand or weren't in the mood to talk. They pushed past Alan and began to close in on me, ranting and raving in Trukese. Just when I knew I was screwed, Kimo showed up—a little belatedly, if you ask me.

"Hey," he growled in his deep Hawaiian voice. "Enough."

That got their attention, and all five officers immediately turned to see Kimo standing there, unharmed. Eyes wide, shocked to see their leader alive, they finally backed down, and between the four of us, Kimo, Mark, Alan, and I managed to explain the situation, in spite of the fact that the officers didn't speak much English and none of us spoke Trukese.

As the afternoon of training wore on, I thought ruefully about how easy it was, when you came from a spit-shined policing world, to forget that these raggedy-ass cops were still *real* cops, not raw recruits. The Trukese officers lacked formal training and had never been exposed to role-playing exercises, but they sure knew what to do when one of their own was attacked. I made a mental note to myself to remember that—*and* to not participate in any more role-playing exercises until the Micronesians were much more familiar with our training practices.

III

"Hey, wanna go get a beer someplace?" Mark Dugan suggested that evening as he was packing up his training materials after class.

"Sure. Where?" I asked.

"I dunno. Where are you going, Jacob?" Mark asked the Ponape department's assistant chief, Jacob Akapita. "Is there a good place around here to get a drink?"

"I'm going to go drink some *sakau*," Jacob said quietly.

"Oh yeah, I've heard about that stuff," said Mark.

"What is it?" I asked.

"It's the local drink," said Jim. "They make it from this root they pound."

"I've heard it's a drug of some sort—a hallucinogen," said Mark. "But apparently it's legal here."

"So what's in it?" I asked again, my curiosity piqued.

"I don't know. What's in *sakau*, Jacob?" said Mark.

"It's just—*sakau*," said Jacob.

"Well that explains it," Mark said dryly. "So where do we try this stuff?"

"Come with me. I'll take you."

We all piled back into the car and drove down the road past Kapingamarangi Village and toward Kolonia.

It was twilight when we got to the bar, an outdoor establishment on the outskirts of town surrounded by sort of a half-high bamboo fence. It wasn't anything like the kind of bars I was used to back home. It was more like a pigpen. Well, maybe not that bad, but I mean, people were sitting on a dirt floor and holding their beer cans between their bare feet. Many of them were hawking and spitting on the ground like they had a bad case of the flu.

We followed Jacob in—Jim and Mark and I and one other agent, whose name was Scott something-or-other. Jacob found us a spot that was a little cleaner than most, and we sat down on the ground around a low wooden table.

Pretty soon a young woman came around to our table.

"*Kaselhelia*," she said. "What can I get you?"

"Budweiser and *sakau*," said Jacob.

The waitress giggled, looking around at us, and repeated, "Budweiser and *sakau*?" We all nodded. She giggled again and left.

A few minutes later, she returned with five cans of Budweiser on a tray. She set the tray down on the table and we passed them around.

"It's good to save some beer to drink after the *sakau*. It helps wash it down," said Jacob.

We tried not to drink our beers too quickly, even though we were all pretty thirsty. The *sakau* was sounding more ominous all the time.

But it didn't arrive right away. We finished our beers and ordered another round, smoking and drinking quietly. People all around us were hawking and spitting, hawking and spitting. Mark looked a little disgusted and Scott looked downright ill. Jim seemed amused.

About halfway into our second beers, the waitress arrived with one coconut shell and a galvanized bucket full of grayish brown slop. She dipped the coconut shell into the bucket, filled it and handed it to Jacob, who handed it to Mark Dugan. Mark eyed it suspiciously, with a "What the hell have I gotten myself into?" expression on his face.

"Now, you have to close your eyes when you drink it because the fumes can blind you," Jacob told him. (They can't, I later learned, but that bit of folklore is just part of the custom that goes with drinking *sakau*. I think they just tell you that to keep you from looking at it—otherwise, no one would ever drink the stuff.)

Mark took a deep breath, closed his eyes, put the cup to his lips, and went for it. He started gulping, got it about halfway down, then started to shudder and stop.

"Now don't stop, Mark, don't stop," Jim coached. "Keep drinking. Just finish it off. If you stop, you're gonna puke it all over."

Mark took one more convulsive gulp and the rest of it just sort of swallowed itself down. He handed the cup back and reached for his beer, taking it in long chugs. He didn't say a word.

"Who's next?" Jim asked, grinning.

"I'll have some," I heard myself saying.

"Atta boy," Jim said, patting me on the back.

The waitress poured me a cup. It looked viscous and slippery, and it had an earthy smell of mud and roots with kind of a sharp, almost flinty edge to it, probably because there's so much coral in the soil there.

I didn't pause—I knew if I did, I wouldn't go through with it. I closed my eyes and knocked it back. The whole thing went down in one glob, sort of like eating oysters for the first time. (Since then, I've heard it characterized as "snails in a blender" and "elephant snot." I'd have to say the latter is probably the more accurate description.) The minute it was down I had this urge to throw up. Like Mark, I chased it with about half a can of Budweiser.

"Here, Jim, you have some," I said, handing him the coconut shell.

"Yeah, I'll have some. I always like this stuff," Jim said.

I thought he was joking, but he took a cup and drank it down like an old hand. Jacob drank next. Scott didn't want any, but we all harassed him till he finally tried some. We finished our beers and ordered another round.

"Do you feel anything?" I asked Mark.

"No. Do you?"

"No. Hey Jacob, how much *sakau* do you have to drink before you feel anything?" I asked.

"Oh, six or eight cups."

"Six or eight cups? Holy shit!"

"Well, I'm not gonna drink any more of that crap," said Scott.

"What happens if you drink that much of it?" I asked.

"It makes your body fall asleep," Jim interjected. "Your mind stays alert, but your body's off in la la land."

"So it's like what—having an out of body experience or something?"

"Yeah, maybe," Jim said.

Our waitress came around again with the bucket. Everyone had another except Scott, who flat out refused this time, no matter how we cajoled. It wasn't quite as bad to get down the second time, especially now that we were working on our third beers.

"So, what are we going to do tomorrow?" I asked.

"Thought we'd do some firearms training. We've just about got the range set up," said Mark.

"Great. What program?"

"Just a basic familiarization course," he said. "It's the best we can do for now, because most of the weapons here are too old to be safe. We couldn't even get some of them open—the rounds were completely corroded in the cylinders. But we managed to find about ten revolvers that are good enough. We'll have to rotate them among the men."

"That's going to be a pain in the ass, isn't it?" I asked.

"You complainin' already, Vila?" Jim said.

"Hell no. Not me," I said, taking another swallow of beer. "Good."

The bucket came around again, and all of us but Scott had

another round. After that one, I started to get a little bit of a strange feeling. I mean, my limbs were all there and I could move my legs and wiggle all my toes, but I didn't much feel like it. My body felt heavy and separate, but my head was still pretty clear, except for the beer I had drunk.

"How do they make this stuff, anyway?" I asked. I noticed that my lips were a little numb, too.

"Well, here in the *sakau* bar they use an old washing machine," said Jim. "I saw them do it once. They fixed the wringer on the thing so it'll crush the juice out of the *sakau* root. Then they catch the juice in a big tub and drain it off."

"That sounds appetizing," Mark said, making a face.

"Yes, but that's just the way they do it in the *sakau* bars," said Jacob. "Usually, *sakau* is prepared by hand in a special ceremony."

"What kind of ceremony?" I asked.

"Oh, many different kinds. Sometimes we have *sakau* ceremonies to honor people. Sometimes they're used in negotiations or to settle arguments," said Jacob.

"Yeah, it's a real important part of the culture," Jim added. "You'll do better here if you learn to drink *sakau* properly and respectfully."

Jim didn't look over at Scott, but we all knew what he was thinking. He was right. Scott's reluctance to participate, while understandable, instantly cast him in the role of outsider—which is not a good thing to be when you're trying to connect with people from another culture.

We sat there for a while longer, passed around another pack of cigarettes, and had another beer. Eventually Jim suggested, "Let's go get some dinner."

"Yeah, OK," said Mark. "Can you drive, Scott?"

"I think I better," he said pointedly, as the rest of us staggered a bit toward the rental car.

We went to dinner in town and then afterward, we headed

back to the Cliff Rainbow, where the Disco Dannys were out in full force again, dancing to the Bee Gees under the lanai.

CHAPTER 3

Cheese Grenades and Kamikaze Geckos

The week after I returned from Ponape I moved into my house in Dandan, near the Saipan airport. It was small and unimpressive—a one-story concrete block house furnished with the usual Trust Territory rattan with floral print cushions. But it was rent-free, and it was mine.

Susan arrived from the States that same week, tired and bedraggled after the long trip on the Island Hopper. Despite my calm assurance to Denny that she would do just fine in Micronesia, I have to admit that I was relieved when she didn't flip out over the rustic setting.

Instead, the first thing Susan did after she arrived was set out to make our dilapidated little concrete house a home. We spent hours moving the furniture from one place to another until it was just right. Then, even though our personal effects wouldn't arrive for another six weeks or so, Susan started decorating. She hung the leis she had gotten at the airport on the headboard of the bed, snagged two small plumeria branches off the neighbor's tree and put them in a Coke bottle vase on the dining room table, and yanked several sprouted coconuts out of the front yard to bring some greenery inside. It wasn't much, but it was enough of an improvement to make her happy—for the moment, at least.

After Susan got settled in, we bought a car for $400. It's

hard to believe that any car could be in worse condition than Denny's, but it was. It was rusted so badly it's hard to tell what it had originally started out as, other than some sort of economy sedan. But it worked, and pretty reliably, too. We spent a lot of time in that car during the next few weeks, exploring the island and frequently getting lost in the process.

Everywhere we'd go, Susan would collect more things to decorate the house with. She made up for the lack of shopping opportunities on Saipan by searching for pretty seashells, driftwood, and big glass fishing net floats as we walked along the beaches, and by gathering plants from the jungle to add to the inside greenery.

I was impressed by her creative decorating strategies and dutifully helped with her treasure hunts. But I was far more captivated by the constant reminders of World War II that riddled the island. Driving along Beach Road at low tide, you could see wrecks of tanks and amphibious vehicles sticking up above the water in the lagoon. In Susupe and some of the other towns, there were a lot of old bullet-pocked concrete pillboxes, where Japanese soldiers had fought to the last. And noodling around on weekends in the many caves on island, we'd sometimes find old helmets and gas masks, and occasionally even a partial skeleton.

On the north end of the island was Banzai Cliff, where hundreds of Japanese soldiers and civilians had jumped to their deaths rather than be captured by the Marines during the war. In the parking lot there was a small monument to those who had died, and everywhere you'd look close to the edge of the cliff there were flat Japanese prayer sticks wedged between rocks, along with miniature sake bottles and sometimes a cigarette pack or burned-out stick of incense.

On the opposite end of the island from Banzai Cliff was the beach where my dad had landed with the first wave of Marines. I'd go there by myself sometimes and look out across the sand and water, trying to imagine what it must've been like for them—

pitching up and down for hours in scores of flat-bottomed landing craft as they circled, waiting, and then turning toward shore on command like a line of sitting ducks. Hearing the chatter of machine guns and the mortars booming in the water. Hitting the beach under fire, then trying to sprint through the deep, soft sand loaded down with machine guns, ammo, and rations.

I once tried to find the place where Dad had been overrun. It'd been a sugar cane field during the war, but as far as I could tell it was just an overgrown jungle area now. The Japanese had thrown four grenades into the fighting hole he shared with his assistant gunner, killing the A-gunner and leaving my father for dead. It was two days before he was rescued and another three days before he got any medical treatment. He once confided in me that the only thing that had kept him alive was his rage at having survived so much, only to be left with the hopeless cases in triage for so long.

During all the years Susan and I lived in Micronesia, I never could get my dad to come out to visit. I had thousands of airline miles to pay for his trip, but he never took me up on the offer. He'd sound excited at first, but then something would always come up to prevent him from coming. Finally, he admitted to me that he never, ever wanted to see Saipan again.

* * *

When we weren't out exploring the island, Susan and I were settling into our new lives. She had landed a part-time job with the Trust Territory (or the TT, as it was commonly called), training island girls to become secretaries. So when I wasn't off traveling, we'd typically go up the hill to work together each day.

Our ten-minute commute along Back Road was a helluva lot better than the hour-and-a-half commute each way in bumper-to-bumper traffic back in Southern California. With the exception of an occasional typhoon, the weather was beautiful, plus the sunsets were grand and you could walk for miles on pristine beaches without seeing another soul.

Still, there were plenty of new hardships to make up for the ones we had left behind. For example, the lack of simple everyday things that we take for granted in the States made life in Micronesia challenging. The power would go out. The water would go out. The phones didn't work. And there was never any toilet paper in the bathroom at work. I grumbled about it—we all did—but you know, I didn't really mind that much. It was all part of the adventure.

Hell, even buying groceries was an adventure on Saipan. There were only two stores on island that sold groceries—Joeten's and Town House. Neither of them even came close to being what we'd consider a supermarket in the States.

In Joeten's, freight pallets stacked high with huge sacks of rice and other dry goods made the narrow aisles of the food section even narrower. There was canned food from Australia and Japan, including tinned butter, mackerel, whale meat, tuna, and corned beef. And there were cases and cases of Spam. The islanders really loved Spam—it was a taste they'd acquired from the GIs during World War II. To the day he died, my dad wouldn't even consider eating Spam—most veterans of that war developed a distinct distaste for the stuff—but the Micronesians thought it was quite delicious.

The eggs at Joeten's always looked stale and rotty, and dairy products were almost nonexistent. There was usually some recombined milk available. It was shipped to the islands in powdered form, and they'd mix it at a local factory. I'd had it at Denny's house a couple of times and it tasted terrible, so we never bought it. There was also something named "Real Milk," which was ultra-high-temperature treated milk that came in aluminum-lined cartons. It tasted terrible, too.

There were almost always frozen turkey tails for sale in the meat department, along with frozen beef from Australian range cattle that had absolutely no marbling whatsoever. I mean, it was tough. But it made great chili meat because you could cook it for two days to get all the flavor out of your spices into it, and by that time it was just starting to get tender enough to eat.

Most of the foods that came from the United States were outdated by a year or two or more. We'd check and see that the month was right, get all excited, and then we'd realize that the year was 1975 or 1976, and this was 1978. Prices were high, too. Canned goods typically were about 20 percent more than you'd pay in the States, and bulky goods like toilet paper and paper towels were astronomically expensive—three, maybe four times more than in the States. In shipping, it's cubic feet that count.

Town House was even smaller than Joeten's, with a similarly poor selection of edible food. It had a dairy counter, at least, with some very old, very green cheese. Once when we were there, Susan picked up a container of ricotta to check the date and it exploded all over her. There was rotten ricotta everywhere, and it stank to high heaven. So much for our plans for lasagna.

Town House also had a produce counter, but little produce to speak of. There were a few half rotten oranges, lemons and limes, some yams and some coconuts, but not much else. It was pretty grim pickings. Years later they finally organized a farmer's market on Saipan, but it wasn't until shortly before we left in 1984.

The meat department at Town House, like Joeten's, had lots of Spam. There also was some hamburger and chicken. But you couldn't get fresh fish. There we were on an island in the middle of the Pacific Ocean and we couldn't get fresh fish. At least not in the stores. The Micronesians sometimes sold tuna from an old pickup truck down on Beach Road, but the fish would all be packed tail-up in the back of the truck, without ice, and they were stiff as boards. We didn't know how to cook them and quite frankly, it didn't seem like a very good idea.

As time went by, we gradually learned what to stock up on

and what to avoid. Our staples were hamburger and chicken, which were always outdated but not too bad. A bag of rice and a bag of weevily flour that we'd have to sift carefully before using. Canned tuna and mayonnaise for sandwiches. Stale bread and hamburger buns. Coffee, even though it was very expensive there. Canned vegetables and canned milk for coffee. And plenty of Budweiser—one of the few things that was almost always in good supply.

There was no TV, no movie theater, and nothing worth listening to on the radio on Saipan back in 1978. There was a newspaper—the *Pacific Daily News* from Guam—that we typically got a day late, and the *Marianas Variety* came out every couple of weeks, but that was about it.

Instead, for home entertainment, we had geckos. There were geckos everywhere inside the house. At first we thought it was pretty strange to have these funny, slick-skinned lizards scampering inside the house on the walls and ceilings and all over. But soon, like everyone else in Micronesia, we were hooked on watching them.

I especially enjoyed the antics of the young geckos who were still learning the art of ceiling hunting and would, with all the grace and patience of a feline, slowly stalk a moth while hanging upside down from their suction-cup toes, then do a final scamper to get within striking distance, freeze, and leap for their prey. Gravity would take over and they'd fall on their heads on the floor and lie there stunned. Eventually, they'd get up and run off, having learned that one does not leap while hanging upside down from the ceiling.

Our other main sources of entertainment on Saipan were eating and socializing. There were a lot of feasts and dinner parties to help break up the monotony of daily life—and daily diets. Everything typically was potluck, and most of us would go all out. We'd ship in ingredients from the States, or bring back goodies from trips to Guam and other places to share with everyone else. At the end of the feasts, we'd each take some of the leftovers home.

It was at those dinner parties that Susan and I met most of the other Americans living on Saipan. It was an interesting group—there were doctors and lawyers and judges and engineers and businessmen. In fact, one of the things that often surprised people from home the most when they'd visit me in Micronesia was that the expatriate community wasn't just a collection of beach bums—there were a lot of intelligent, adventurous folks who really could do things. Sure there were some flakes—there were some classic flakes—but mostly there were creative, energetic types who wanted to accomplish something while they were still young enough to enjoy it.

If you were good at what you did and if you were willing to be flexible, Micronesia was a wonderful place. There wasn't the enormous cultural inertia that we have in the States. If you had a good idea, you could sell it to other people and run with it—charge with it—as creatively as possible. And sometimes you could really make things better. That was the most seductive thing about Micronesia—being able to matter. It made the hardships of living there much easier to tolerate.

CHAPTER 4

The Betel Nut Express

After giving me some time to settle in, Denny sent me traveling again, this time to the southwest, to the island of Yap in the Western Carolines. It was September, I think, although it's hard to remember for sure since the weather is pretty much the same all year round—about eighty degrees and absurdly humid.

I was eager to be on the road again. Saipan was a fascinating place to explore, and even the simplest basics of daily living there could be an adventure in themselves, but I had spent way too much time sitting behind a desk these past couple of months for my liking, and I was starting to get restless.

Of course, I tried not to look too eager about the trip in front of Susan. We had known when I took this job that it would involve a great deal of travel, but we'd foolishly envisioned sailing together from island to island as I did my work. That dream was quickly deflated by the reality of the vast distances between islands. Flying together from place to place was out of the question, too—each round-trip ticket cost half a month's salary. So mostly I traveled, and Susan stayed behind on Saipan.

She had already become good friends with Jim Grizzard's wife, Bobbi, and there was a large network of "left behind" spouses on island at any given time, so at least she had a social life and things to do while I was gone, in addition to her work.

MICRONESIAN BLUES

* * *

I took Air Mike to Guam, and then on to Yap—a big, tall, rugged island surrounded by beautiful reefs. We flew over Colonia, the capital city, before circling around to the airport on the southwest side of the island. We came in low, but not too low—there were palm trees at the end of the runway that we had to clear before we could set down—then taxied to a stop in front of a tiny old open-sided airport terminal with a thatched roof.

As I got off the plane behind the rest of the passengers amid the usual masses of people waiting to greet their loved ones, I noticed several things about Yap that were different from any place I had yet been in Micronesia.

First, the air was much drier here. It was immediately apparent—one of those things that you pay attention to when you live in the tropics and that I had unconsciously become sensitized to already. It wasn't arid by any measure, but compared to the heavy, overbearingly moist heat of Ponape and Saipan, it was quite pleasant.

Second, most of the women, both young and old, were topless. Jim had already told me a little about Yap back in Pasadena, and Denny had confirmed that Yap was the most traditional of all the Micronesian islands, so I wasn't too surprised to see them dressed in nothing but grass skirts, but it was still a little disconcerting at first. (Imagine a big family picnic with sisters, wives, grandma, and great-aunt Tillie topless and you'll get the picture.) In similar fashion, many of the men wore only the traditional loincloth, called a *thu*, which looks sort of like a large white bulky diaper.

Third, everybody, from the toddlers on up, had a big wad of betel nut in their jaw. I had seen betel nut before. People chew it in lots of places in Southeast Asia, including Vietnam. It's sort of like chewing tobacco. It's a stimulant, and it also has nicotine in it so it works as a worming agent, which is important in that part of the world because most people have intestinal parasites. But I had never been anywhere where even the *kids* chewed it. They literally cut their teeth on it here, and it showed. I mean, the Yapese have these enormously muscled jaws—almost triangular—from chewing betel nut all their lives. And they all have dark red lips, because betel nut turns lips and teeth and everything else it comes in contact with red. It's pretty disgusting, really. There was red spit everywhere. Grinning, I now realized why the Air Mike jet that serviced Yap and Palau was nicknamed the "Betel Nut Express."

Rifin Manglay, the Yapese assistant police chief, was waiting at the airport to meet me.

"Are you Bryan?" he asked quietly. Instead of a *thu*, he was dressed in a shirt and pants. But, like everyone else, he had a wad of betel nut lodged in the side of his mouth and carried a woven betel nut basket made of pandanus—a plant with long, fibrous leaves similar to the yucca.

"Yes. Hello," I said, attempting to match his hushed tone. "You must be Rifin."

"Yes," he replied. "Chief Takagi couldn't be here today, but he said to tell you that he'll meet you tomorrow morning and show you around."

Ray Takagi was the acting police chief on island—a Hawaiian who, like Kimo Panolo, had been in Micronesia for several months now.

"Great. That's just fine," I said. It was Sunday, and I had been hoping to have the afternoon to myself to explore anyway.

I went through immigration and customs with Rifin at my side, but we didn't talk much. It seemed a little strange to me at first—I was accustomed, as most Americans are, to filling up empty space with idle conversation. But it wasn't the uncomfortable silence of two strangers struggling to find something to talk about. It was just, well, quiet.

After I had gotten through the formalities and collected my

luggage, Rifin drove me north to Colonia in the police jeep. He drove slowly and cautiously, despite the fact that there were few other cars on the road. It was a very long—and very quiet— drive. Along the way, I discovered that Rifin was not only a man of few words, but was also rather jumpy. He didn't seem nervous, exactly, but he startled easily, especially at any loud noise. Like when a rock thrown up by the tires of a passing truck clanged against the side of the rusty police jeep. Most Yapese, I soon learned, are sensitive this way.

Finally, we came to a stop out in front of the Rai View Hotel. It was a small place, sort of half traditional and half modern. At the front desk, I learned that I would have to share my room with a stranger.

"I'm sorry. We have very few rooms, and many people traveling," the clerk said in response to my look of obvious surprise.

I had never in all my life heard of such a thing and was sorely tempted to refuse the room. But I didn't want to risk offending anyone straight off the bat, so I agreed to take it. There was only one other hotel on the island, so I didn't have much choice anyway.

"I have to go back to work now," Rifin said in his quiet and concise manner. "Will you be all right?"

"Sure, I'll be fine," I told him. "Thanks for picking me up at the airport, Rifin."

"Maybe I could come by after work?" he offered tentatively.

"Great," I said. "Why don't we meet in the bar for a drink?"

"OK. I'll see you later, then."

Rifin got back in the jeep and headed to the station, and I trudged up the stairs to my room. It was pretty rustic, with only one bathroom to share between every two rooms, but it was clean, and it had a pretty view overlooking the estuary and bay.

I was relieved to see that there were two double beds in the room, so at least I wouldn't be sharing a bed as well as a room with a total stranger. I was also relieved to find that my roommate wasn't in at the moment. I plopped my bags down on one of the beds and headed for the shower—always a real necessity after a long flight on Air Mike.

II

That evening, after a day spent exploring the island a bit on my own, I went downstairs to the Rai View bar. I was on my second beer when Rifin arrived.

"Come, I'll introduce you to some friends of mine," he said quietly.

He led me over to a couple of guys who were sitting on the deck outside overlooking the water and said, "Bryan, this is John, and this is William. John teaches at the school and William works at the hospital. Bryan is the new police specialist from TT."

John and William smiled and greeted me quietly. Both were Yapese and looked to be about my age or a little younger. Rifin and I sat down, and John brought out his woven pandanus basket. It was shaped like a small canoe, thin and long, with a delicate fringe along the bottom and ends.

"Have you ever chewed betel nut?" he asked.

"No," I said quietly, once again slipping into the gentler rhythms of Yapese conversation.

"Do you want some?"

"Please. I'd like to try it," I said. More and more, I was discovering the importance of participating in the local culture and customs. It helped set me apart from the endless stream of bureaucrats and tourists who flowed in and out of Micronesia every year. "How do you do it?" I asked.

"You have to be very careful. Some Americans get really sick the first time," Rifin cautioned.

"Don't worry. I grew up chewing tobacco," I said. "This can't be too much different."

John smiled and reached into his basket, bringing out a

45

branch with five or six thumb-sized nuts on it. He broke off a nice medium-sized one that was a brilliant, grassy green, with a fibrous husk like a coconut, and handed it to me. Then he handed one to Rifin and one to William and took one for himself.

I waited and watched the others. First, they rubbed them between their fingers to remove any of the excess husk on the stem end of the nut. I did the same. Then they put them between their enormous, red-stained teeth and cracked them. I put mine between my smaller, whiter teeth and cracked it in half. Then John reached back into his basket and brought out a beautiful little baby coconut shell that had been polished and intricately carved into what looked like a saltshaker, with a tiny cork in the top. He and the others each shook some white powder out of the coconut and onto the inside of their halved betel nuts. I took the coconut last.

"Be careful, it'll burn your mouth," said William.

"What do you mean? What is it?" I asked.

"It's lime," said John.

"Lime? What kind of lime? You mean like citrus fruit?"

"No, no, not that kind of lime," said John.

"Well where does it come from, then? How do you make it?" I asked.

"It's from coral. You take the coral and you put it over the fire. After a while it turns into lime and you grind it up into powder," said John.

I thought back over basic chemistry and realized they were talking about quick lime, the kind of stuff we used back in Vietnam in a one-holer toilet, or poured on a corpse to reduce it to bones. That stuff was nasty. But the Yapese were all eating it and they were still alive, so I figured what the hell, I might as well try it. Although I did go a little easy on the lime powder.

Next, John brought out four pepper leaves. We each took a leaf, and John showed me how to roll the betel nut inside it.

You first tucked the leaf into the center of the nut halves, then folded the halves back and rolled the leaf around the nut.

"Now you put it back between your teeth and bite down on it," he said, tucking the green wad into his cheek.

I followed suit, biting down hard. Surprisingly, it tasted nice. A bit sharp and pungent and grassy, but nice.

"How is it?" John asked.

"It's really good. Thank you," I said.

They all smiled at me approvingly—drooly, red-toothed betel nut smiles. (The red color must be the result of some reaction between the betel nut and the lime, because neither one is that color alone.) I grinned back, equally drooly. And for the next couple of hours we sat together quietly and chewed, watching the sun go down and periodically spitting over the railing into the tidal estuary below.

III

The next morning, Ray Takagi picked me up at the Rai View. Ray was tall, polite, and fairly reserved. Whether he had always been the latter, or the Yapese culture had already begun to rub off on him, I didn't know for sure.

"I thought I'd take you over to the police station and introduce you around, then take you to some of the different villages," he said, shaking my hand.

"Great," I said.

The police station was just down the road from the hotel. It was the same kind of one-story, tin-roofed building as the Ponape police station.

"I should warn you, things are a little hectic around here right now," Ray said as we parked in front of the station. "We've had one officer shot and a couple others stabbed in the past few months. We figure we've got to increase surveillance and backup, so we've hired a bunch of new recruits. A lot of them are still pretty green—and they could all use some inten-

sive firearms training and stuff. I was hoping you might be able
to help me with that while you're here."

"Sure, I'd be glad to," I said, following him into the police
station.

Most of the officers on duty that morning were out on patrol. The few who were manning the station were young—some
of them looked barely eighteen—and dressed about as poorly as
the officers I had met on Ponape.

I was surprised to see that one of the new officers was a
woman, Teresa Robert. She was the first female officer I'd met
in Micronesia. But she wasn't Yapese. She was from Palau, the
next island south, and unlike the Yapese women I had seen, who
tended to be rather shy and quiet, Teresa was a strong, outgoing
young woman who'd look you directly in the eyes when she
spoke. She was about as tall as most of the men, and very attractive. She got along just fine with the male officers, and like
them, she seemed eager and very, very earnest.

After meeting the officers and touring the small station, I
had some coffee in Ray's office. Then we got back into his jeep
and headed out to explore Yap.

"There are six main villages on Yap," Ray told me as we
drove up the main causeway toward the Coast Guard station on
the north end of the island. "Most people live communally—so
there's a lot of togetherness—but they also take their privacy
very seriously. That means you don't just go walking down the
road into someone else's village. If you want to enter a village
on foot, you carry a branch of some sort of greenery as a sym-
bol of your peaceful intentions. Then as you approach the village, someone will come to greet you, and you must ask
permission to enter the village."

"What about if you're driving through?" I asked.

"Well, you don't need permission if you're driving
through, but you do have to remember to drive very slowly.
You can't really drive anything *but* slowly around here—the

roads are in terrible shape near all the villages."

"Even worse than the rest of the island, you mean?" I asked, not sure that was possible.

"Oh, yeah. One of our biggest problems is vandalism on the roads near the villages," Ray explained in a sort of exasperated tone. "Public works goes out to gravel and grade them four, maybe five times a year. But when the roads are in good condition, people drive through the villages faster. The villagers don't like the noise, so they go out and dig holes in the road to slow things down. We keep trying to stop them from doing it, but we haven't had much luck."

I had to suppress a grin. I didn't want to say anything because Ray seemed clearly vexed by the situation, but frankly, I thought it was pretty enterprising of the villagers. It sure beat posting speed limit signs that nobody follows.

We drove along for a few miles, the jungle to our left and the mangrove swamps to our right. Just when the road started to get worse, Ray pulled over onto the shoulder and stopped the jeep.

We got out and each plucked a hibiscus branch from the jungle foliage before walking up the road toward the village. Before long we reached a crossroads, where a narrow path paved with coconut husks led to a large, thatched-roof house situated on a sandy beach near the water. We started walking more slowly, branches in hand, up the path. The coconut husks were soft and spongy underfoot.

"That's the local meeting house, called a *faluw*, up ahead," Ray told me.

As we neared the meeting house, one of the villagers noticed us and came down the path to greet us. He was a very thin older man, with spindly legs, bent shoulders, and a sort of caved-in chest. He was wearing a *thu* and had a huge wad of betel nut in his left cheek.

"*Mogethin*, Joseph," said Ray, bowing slightly. "This is my guest, Bryan Vila, from TT headquarters. May we enter?"

"*Mogethin*, Ray," the old man replied, bowing back. "Come." Ray walked behind Joseph the rest of the way up the path to the meeting house and motioned for me to follow behind him single file, as is the custom on Yap. We passed by a group of bare-breasted women weaving betel nut baskets and a *thu*-clad man carving a model canoe out of mangrove wood. Small children eyed us curiously, and free-ranging chickens clucked and scurried out of our path as we approached.

Joseph led us into the *faluw*, where we were invited to sit, then offered betel nut, drinking coconuts, and coffee. Ray accepted a coconut, while I opted for a steaming cup of strong black coffee.

It was much the same in each of the six villages we visited that day. We'd stay and chat for a while—or sit and smile with those who didn't speak much English—drinking coffee or coconut milk and chewing and spitting, and then go on to the next village. It took a while for me to catch on that Ray was doing much more than merely taking me on a sightseeing trip. He was teaching me local manners and building a gentle bridge of hospitality between me and the people of each village that would serve me well on my future visits to Yap. In just one afternoon, he had helped me become an insider there.

***

The sun was just starting to set as Ray drove me back to the Rai View. "Hey, while you're here, would you mind doing an arrest techniques class for me?" he asked casually.

I had absolutely nothing prepared and no materials with me to teach the class, but I figured I could probably manage to put one together in a few days. "Sure," I said. "When?"

"How 'bout tomorrow morning?"

"Great," I replied with a smile, stifling a groan.

So, after what had already been a pretty full day, I sat down in the bar that night with a couple of beers and planned a half-day course on arrest techniques. And I taught it the next morning. I was quickly learning that seat-of-the-pants was the way a lot of things were done in Micronesia.

IV

During the rest of that week and most of my second week on Yap, I took charge of the firearms training program.

I taught the officers the same pistol range rules we've always taught recruits in the States. I'd say, "Ready on the right? Ready on the left? All ready on the firing line?" And if someone wasn't ready, they'd raise their hand and everyone would wait for them to get ready and then we'd start the procedure all over again. When everyone was finally ready, I'd yell "Fire!" and they'd shoot. It was tedious, but that's the way it's been done since Christ was a corporal.

Hour after hour, day after day, the officers would practice in shifts. By Friday of the first week, I was getting a little punchy. I'd also had a fair amount of beer and some spicy Filipino food at a local restaurant the night before, so I was a bit windy and looking for an excuse.

"Ready on the right?" I yelled. "Ready on the left? All ready on the firing line?" And then, "*Phhffrrtt!*"—I let out an enormous fart.

I thought it would be funny. In just about any stateside police department, everybody would crack up and it would relieve a little boredom and tension all around. On Saipan and Ponape, I had seen people laugh themselves sick over a well-timed fart.

But here on Yap, it was a different story. Rifin and his two lieutenants were appalled and immediately started smacking the young recruits upside the head, demanding to know who was responsible for such impudence. They were completely humiliated that someone had done something so offensive, especially in front of me, the distinguished police specialist from TT headquarters.

I was tempted to keep my mouth shut, but I couldn't let some poor recruit take the blame for what I hadn't realized was a serious faux pas in this society. A little sheepishly, I confessed. I half expected Rifin to smack me, too. But he just looked at me sort of funny, like he wasn't quite sure what to make of it, and went back to his post. Down the firing line, all the recruits were sort of staring down at their feet uncomfortably in an effort to avoid eye contact with me. All except Teresa Robert, who turned to give me a bright red ear-to-ear grin.

CHAPTER 5

Ghosts of Truk

After two weeks on Yap I returned home to Saipan, but only long enough to fill out my trip reports and get a new set of travel orders. By mid-October, I was on another Air Mike flight—this time to the southeast, to the islands of Truk.

The landing on Truk was even more spectacular than usual—we came down with an incredible jolt that threw me forward in my seat, straining against the belt, and then back. But as we screeched down the runway, engines on full reverse, I realized that for the first time, I was starting to feel like an old hand at this. I didn't even grip the armrests any more when we landed.

The plane stopped just in the nick of time, as it always did. I gathered up my carry-on bag, hoisted it over my shoulder, and followed the rest of the passengers off the plane.

As I was leaving immigration and customs, an American I hadn't met before approached me and asked, "Bryan?"

"Yeah," I said.

"Bill Stinnett, assistant police chief here on Truk," he said, smiling broadly and holding out his hand. "*Ran annim*," he added, booming the Trukese greeting in an exaggerated deep voice, like the Trukese do.

Bill was a good-looking guy, about my height, with curly brown hair and a square jaw. He wore the expatriate uniform—aloha shirt, jeans, and running shoes—and exuded an easy-going competence. Sizing him up professionally, the way most cops do when they meet a fellow cop, I knew straight off the bat that he was the kind of guy you'd want to have watching your back when the shit hit the fan.

"*Ran annim*, Bill," I said, gripping his hand firmly and giving it a single, hard, Trukese-style shake.

"*E'fal sum?*" Bill rumbled, the Trukese equivalent of, "How are you?"

"*A'woona*," I replied in similar fashion. In Trukese, it means something like, "I feel strong." I had learned it from one of the Trukese officers on Saipan.

Bill laughed. "Kimo's back at the office meeting with some people, so he sent me to get you," he said. "The car's just over here. Here, let me help carry some of this stuff."

"Great. It's good to meet you," I said, giving him one of my bags and following him to the parking lot next to the airport. "Have you been out here since the start, like the rest of the Honolulu guys?"

"Nope. I just got here about three months ago," said Bill.

"Hey, me too," I said. "Whaddya think so far?"

"Are you kidding? It's paradise," he said, grinning as he gave me the standard American answer to that question. "It's also pretty weird sometimes, but you get used to that shit."

He stopped at an old, rusted Suzuki jeep and tossed my bags in the back, next to a young Trukese man wearing a police uniform.

"This is Katios Gallen, one of our best officers," he said. "He's just back from the States, where he was in college."

"*Ran annim*," I said to Katios, holding out my hand.

"*Ran annim*," he said, shaking my hand in a crushing grip. Katios was built like a fucking tank.

I took my hand back, resisting the urge to check for broken bones, and got in the jeep on the passenger side. Bill jumped in behind the wheel and we were off, bouncing all the way.

We drove far out of town, all the way to the southern end of Moen, Truk's largest island, to get to my hotel. But the Truk Continental was worth the drive. It was beautiful, set out on the end of a spit of land overlooking the lagoon.

"Hey, how 'bout if we go have a beer or something after I drop my bags off in my room?" I said to Bill and Katios after I had checked in, nodding toward the hotel bar just off to our right.

Bill laughed. "Nobody told you?" he asked.

"Told me what?"

"There's no beer here."

"What do you mean? I saw beer cans all over," I said, remembering the litter I had seen along the sides of the road.

"Yeah, I know. But they passed prohibition about six months ago," he said.

"You're kidding," I said. It certainly didn't seem in keeping with the rest of Micronesia, where Budweiser typically was the largest import. "Well, I guess it's not all bad. I mean, most crime's alcohol-related, so I guess it makes your job a little easier, right?"

"Yeah, it ought to, but they smuggle beer in anyway," Bill said.

"And you can't catch 'em?"

"Are you kidding? It's the congressmen and the legislators who are doing all the smuggling."

"Well, why did they pass the law if they didn't want it, then?" I asked.

"That's not exactly how it happened," said Bill.

Katios snorted. "The women passed the law," he said.

"Why? How?" I asked.

"Most of the women here are Baptist or Congregationalist," Bill explained. "They're teetotalers because their church says no drinking. But the men—that's another story. Trukese men are supposed to drink hard and smoke hard and be strong and tough."

"So then how did they ever pass prohibition?" I asked.

"The women set it up, led by the governor's wife," said Bill.

Katios interjected, saying, "They wait, and they have the election on payday Friday, when all the men are drunk. So the women are the only ones who vote that day, and they vote in prohibition."

"And they can't overturn it?" I asked.

"No. It takes a two-thirds majority to overturn, and half the voters are women," said Bill.

"Great. No beer, then," I groaned. "So, what else is on tap?"

"Well, I've gotta drop Katios off at the station right now, but how 'bout if I come back over here afterward and we grab some dinner at the hotel restaurant," Bill suggested. "After that, we can go to the station and I'll introduce you around before the night shift begins."

"Sounds good. In fact, I was hoping I'd be able to ride around with you guys and see what patrol's like here. You think I could do that?" I asked.

"Yeah, I think Kimo'd go for that. I'll ask," said Bill.

He and Katios left, and I unpacked and took a shower.

* * *

I was sitting out on the veranda when Bill returned for dinner, watching an amazingly gorgeous sunset that was just starting out over the lagoon.

"So, what'd Kimo think about my going out on patrol tonight?" I asked as we walked over to the hotel restaurant.

"He didn't think it was such a good idea for you to go out with the men just yet. But he and I will take you around and show you what's going on," said Bill.

"OK," I said, not too surprised. Kimo obviously wanted me to know who was lead dog.

"And there's one thing I should probably tell you about before we get to the station," Bill said.

"What's that?"

"Well, when we first got here, the police officers never patrolled at night."

"Why not?" I asked.

"Trukese mythology," Bill explained. "They believe in lots of different kinds of ghosts here. And the cops, well, they may be these huge hulking guys, but they don't want to be out at night 'cuz they're afraid of them. They think they'll be possessed or something."

"Do all the bad guys feel the same way?" I asked.

"Unfortunately, no."

"So what did you do?"

"First we tried to force them to work at night, but every time we'd check the station they'd all be back there, sitting around drawing pay for nothing. We tried disciplining people—even fired a couple of guys—but it didn't do any good. As soon as nobody was looking, they'd all be back at the station. Or we'd go out and find them all hiding in somebody's house," said Bill.

"You're kidding."

"No, it was pretty embarrassing. But I think we've got it fixed now."

"How?"

"Well, Kimo sprays them with perfume before they go on patrol."

"What?"

"He sprays 'em with perfume," Bill repeated. "You ever notice at the airport here when people are leaving that folks spray them all over with perfume?"

"Yeah. I always wondered what that was all about."

"It's supposed to help ward off evil spirits," Bill explained. "So Kimo had this stewardess girlfriend of his bring him some cheap perfume from Honolulu. He told the policemen that it was magic and that it'd protect them at night. So every night after roll call he sprays them all with perfume before they go out on patrol. And presto! No more problem."

"They believed him?"

"Yep. True story. So don't blow it, OK?" said Bill. "I mean, you can't laugh or smile or anything while he's doing it. They take this real seriously."

"Hell no, I won't blow it," I promised, wiping the grin off my face. Humorous as it was to us, coming from a culture without such superstitions, I thought it was a pretty creative solution to a tricky dilemma.

***

After dinner, we got into Bill's jeep and drove back to town. It was almost dark by the time we arrived at the police station. Kimo was up at the front desk when we walked in the door.

"Hey, Kimo, how's it going?" I said.

"Going good, going good," Kimo said, crushing my hand in his grip. "Just got my jail training all set up. Look at this. I've started a new discipline program." He waved some paperwork in front of me.

"What's that?" I asked.

"Well, you know, I used to have big problems with prisoners in the jail beating up the jailer and stuff. But it doesn't happen any more," Kimo said, grinning proudly.

"What did you do?"

"Easy. I instituted a boxing program. Anybody who commits any infractions, they've gotta put on the gloves and go two rounds with me," said Kimo.

"Well, no shit, Kimo. That'd be a pretty good deterrent," I said, chuckling.

"No, no, it's real. I don't just beat the crap out of them. I show them how to box for real," Kimo said. "The idea is to build some self-esteem and let 'em show they're tough, and at the same time show 'em they aren't as tough as the police."

"I have to hand it to you, Kimo. It's not a bad idea," I said.

"It's a *great* idea," he corrected me. "Come on, I've gotta do the roll call."

Bill winked at me and went into his office. I followed Kimo into the briefing room, where twenty-some uniformed officers were at ease, talking and laughing.

Kimo motioned to me to join him at the front of the room, which resembled a classroom with a chalkboard at the front, several long tables facing the chalkboard, and uncomfortable-looking plastic chairs.

"Roll call," Kimo yelled. The officers took their seats—dwarfing the small plastic chairs. I recognized several of them from the training session on Ponape. They were still eyeing me warily, as if they expected me to pull out a gun and shoot Kimo any second.

"Listen up, men," said Kimo. "This is Bryan Vila, the new police specialist from TT headquarters. He's going to be helping us with training, so I want you to take care of him while he's here."

I smiled and nodded. Then, getting the distinct impression from Kimo that I was no longer wanted up front, I took a seat.

Kimo went through the roll call, then gave the officers their orders for the evening. One group was to patrol the area near Xavier High School, another was to keep an eye on the village just past the Continental Hotel, where there had been a fight the night before, and so on. It was pretty much the same routine followed by every cop shop in the States when a new shift begins.

When he was finished with the briefing, Kimo called the officers to attention. They lined up single file at the front of the room while Kimo inspected them, and they looked good—it was pretty obvious that Kimo had told them to be on their best behavior to impress the visiting guy.

Then, after the inspection, Kimo called, "Right face." The

officers all turned right in unison, and Kimo marched them out the front door. And as they marched by, he sprayed each one with two strong bursts of some of the most noxious perfume I had ever smelled.

II

On a Friday evening toward the end of my stay on Truk, Bill and Kimo and I were sitting around at the Truk Continental bar drinking iced tea, chatting and watching the sunset over the lagoon.

"Hey, how 'bout if we go diving tomorrow?" Kimo suggested. "You wanna go inside that old sunken Japanese sub?"

"There's a sub?" I asked curiously.

"Yeah, the I-169. It's off limits to tourists—we finally had to padlock it 'cuz a couple of divers got killed in there last year— but I've got the key to the lock," said Kimo.

"Sounds like fun," I said. "What do you say, Bill?"

"I'm in," he said.

"Good, good," said Kimo. I couldn't be sure, but I thought I detected a faint smirk on his face. "I'll have one of my men stop by and pick you up around seven."

***

Phil, one of the newer recruits, picked me up the next morning and drove me out to meet Kimo and Bill. They were waiting for me at the police boat—a fancy new model I was sure Kimo must've picked out himself.

"Morning, Bryan," said Bill, passing me a cup of coffee from a thermos.

"Hey, Bill."

"You ready, Bryan?" Kimo said.

"Yep. What kind of equipment have you got?"

"Six tanks, four regulators. Should be plenty," he said.

We got in the boat and headed out into the huge Truk lagoon. Phil drove the boat and Kimo navigated while Bill and I sat back, drank coffee, and enjoyed the morning. It was a beautiful day—but a little overcast, with a bit of a chop to the water.

"We're getting near the spot," Kimo shouted after about thirty minutes. "Look for a sheen on the water."

"There it is," said Bill, pointing northeast off the bow of the boat. I followed his finger with my eyes, squinting, and saw the shimmering on the surface from the oil that still seeped up from the wreck, decades after its demise.

"Lemme take a compass heading," said Kimo. He fiddled for a minute with the compass, then said, "Yep, that's it."

"How deep is it?" I asked.

"It's on a slant. The bow's at about a hundred and twenty feet," said Kimo.

Shit, I thought, *that's pretty deep*. Eighty to a hundred was about my limit for recreational diving. But I didn't say a word—not in front of Kimo. This was a test. Cops don't accept anyone new on their turf until they see what they're made of.

We ran an anchor line, then hung a tank with a regulator for decompressing down at about twenty feet.

"It shouldn't take us much more than twenty minutes to decompress," said Kimo, figuring it out on the dive chart he kept in the boat. "At that depth, one tank should be plenty to share."

"How much time will we have on the bottom?" asked Bill.

"About ten or fifteen minutes," said Kimo. "Here's what we'll do. We'll go right down the line to the bow. When we get to the bow, I'll open it up and we'll go inside and have a look around. Bryan, you'll have to stick close to Bill and me 'cuz we were only able to find two flashlights."

"No problem," I said, trying to sound nonchalant.

We checked our tanks and regulators carefully—the gear was usually pretty good in Truk because diving was so popular there, but it still paid to be extra careful. Then we stripped to our jeans and went over the side. And down we went. And down and down and down. Even in the clear waters of Micronesia, 120 feet below gets pretty dim. There were four- to five-foot sharks all around us, and I was really having to work hard to slow my breathing by the time we reached the hatch.

The bottom was dead and desolate, as if the sub, when it sank, had destroyed everything around it. And there it lay, silent and still forever, slowly eroding until one day it would become part of the nothingness here.

A large chain was hooked around the forward hatch, held in place by a padlock. Bill and I trained the flashlight beams on the lock while Kimo worked the key into it, popped it open, took the chain off, and opened the hatch.

Japanese subs are small. To get inside, we had to take off our scuba tanks and trail them behind us as we squeezed in head first.

I followed into Kimo's light, and Bill came behind me. As we entered the cabin and settled in, feet down again, the water became thick with sediment—the remains of old, decomposed bodies—that was getting stirred up by our fins. It was eerie, this thick, brown darkness. At that moment, I could see why the Trukese believed in ghosts.

The three of us were facing each other in these really tight, tight quarters. Kimo thumped himself on the chest, pointed at Bill, and motioned that they were going to go back out and astern, to the rear hatch, then come back through the sub to get me on their way out. I wasn't too thrilled about the idea, but I sure as hell wasn't going to let Kimo see me flinch. So I nodded in agreement and they left me, taking both lights with them. Suddenly I was alone in pitch darkness in a sunken Japanese sub at 120 feet.

* * *

It was really claustrophobic in there. My gear was half off, trailing in the muddy snow that was all that was left of the sub's crew. And I didn't even want to think about the sharks that were everywhere in the Truk lagoon—and might have found their way into the sub.

As the minutes ticked by, I got to thinking about what would happen if Kimo and Bill got hung up and didn't make it back before my air ran out. Could I find my way out of the sub with no light? Could I squeeze out without getting my gear snagged, and even if I did, could I find the line back up to the tank we had hung off the side of the boat for decompressing? It wouldn't do any good to get up and then die from the bends, 650 miles from the nearest decompression chamber on Guam.

I thought about all of this. I thought about panicking—it would've been easy to go bat-shit crazy trapped down there in the dark—but it wouldn't do any good. So I made a conscious, rational decision not to panic. Instead I waited, checking the luminous dial on my watch every couple of minutes and keeping a close eye on my air pressure.

I forced myself to breathe gently—not too little and not too much—trying not to use up too much of my air and hoping I wouldn't start getting nitrogen narcosis like I'd had once back when I was training porpoises for the Navy at Point Mugu. By the time my air got down to well under a thousand pounds, I was getting ready to say to hell with it, take my chances, and start heading back up in the dark by myself.

Kimo showed up at just that moment—the absolute end of my comfort zone. Bill was following behind him, and the three of us went back up through the hatch, sealed and locked it, then started back up to the decompression tank, blowing gently all the way.

We hung off at the decompression tank, passing the regulator back and forth and keeping an eye on the sharks that were circling us. A thresher here and a hammerhead there—all fairly small, but interested enough in us to be a potential problem.

I wanted to chew Kimo out when we got back to the boat, but I didn't. I wasn't about to give him the satisfaction of knowing his "test" had rattled me. Besides, I'd had a pretty good time, now that it was over.

CHAPTER 6

The Con Con

It was early February—at the end of a long day spent poring over a mountain of paperwork in my office on Saipan—when I got an urgent call from Denny, who had been at a conference on Guam all week.

"Bryan, I need you to go to Palau on tomorrow's flight to testify at the Con Con," he said.

"What's a Con Con?" I asked.

"Their Constitutional Convention. They need someone to testify on capital punishment and incarceration at a hearing the day after tomorrow. I can't go—I've gotta be in Honolulu—so you're up," he explained.

"Jesus, Denny, their *Constitution*?" I said, a little intimidated.

"Yeah, they're in the process of writing it," said Denny. "It's a big deal for them, so I need you to give this your best effort."

"Of course I will, Denny," I assured him, trying to sound confident.

"Make sure you look at the big picture on these issues," Denny continued. "They've been getting a lot of advice from heavy hitters, people like John Kenneth Galbraith and Harrop Freeman, so they'll be expecting some fairly sophisticated expertise on these topics."

Nothing like a little pressure, I thought. Galbraith was a Harvard political economist who had served as ambassador to

India during the Kennedy administration—I'd read two of his books in grad school—and Freeman was a well-known attorney and human rights activist. If they'd already been getting advice from the likes of these two, what could *I* possibly tell them?

"Are you sure I'm up for this?" I asked Denny skeptically.

"Yes, I am," he said matter-of-factly. "Just put your practical knowledge to work. You've been a cop for ten years. You know as much about this stuff as anyone—at least from a law enforcement point of view. And that's what they need to hear. Just think it through, and you'll do fine."

"OK, Denny, I'll give it my best shot," I promised, silently hoping I didn't make an ass of myself.

* * *

I had never been to Palau before, but I knew it was just about 300 miles southwest of Yap. The two islands are neighbors by Micronesian standards, so I assumed that they might be fairly similar, culturally.

Was I ever wrong. Aside from chewing betel nut, I soon found that the two cultures have almost nothing in common. For example, the Yapese are quiet, while Palauans are fiery orators. The Yapese are peace-loving, but Palauans love a good argument. The Yapese are slow-paced, but Palauans are full-speed ahead. And while the Yapese are pretty somber most of the time, Palauans have a great sense of humor.

There was nothing subtle about the differences between the two islands—from the stateside clothes and loud laughter to the energetic bustle that pervaded the tall, timber-framed airport, they were apparent from the moment I stepped off the plane and went through the usual routine at customs and immigration.

"Yeah, Palauans are different, all right," said Gil Alvaro, Palau's acting police chief from Honolulu, when I brought up the subject. We were waiting to catch the ferry on the way from the airport on the south end of Babelthuap to the Continental Hotel on the island of Koror, the capital of Palau. "I've been having a helluva time with the cops here. They've got ways of doing things left over from the old days of Japanese rule that just don't fly under our Bill of Rights."

"Like what?" I asked.

"Like—well, see that bridge?" he said, pointing to a quarter-mile long, fifty-foot high bridge under construction to the right of the ferryboat stop. "That's the new Koror-Babelthuap bridge. Last week I caught some of my officers dangling a suspect over the side of it by his ankles to get him to talk."

"What'd he do?" I asked.

"He and some friends had been drinking down by the old water tower. Somewhere along the way, somebody pissed on somebody else's shoes by mistake, and they killed him. Bashed his head in with big chunks of concrete. My cops arrested one of the kids with blood splattered all over his shoes and pants, but they couldn't get him to give up his friends, so they took him down to the bridge."

"And he talked?" I asked.

"Abso-fuckin-lutely," said Gil. "People around here know that the Palau police mean business. Hell, I've caught them beating prisoners with rubber hoses and using torture—like making suspects kneel on a broomstick for hours—to get confessions out of them. I've tried to put a stop to it, but old habits die hard, especially when they get such good results."

"Yeah, but you know, I think this is one of those times when we've just gotta say 'screw their culture,'" I said. "They swore an oath to uphold their new laws, and they need to know that if they break them, they're gonna go to jail just like everybody else."

Gil nodded and laughed a bit ruefully. "I hear you. Let's just hope we don't end up with the whole police force in the slammer."

MICRONESIAN BLUES

***

The Palau Continental was set atop a lushly jungled knob of
land overlooking a glassy mirror of a lagoon dotted with tiny
rock islands that looked like tree-topped mushrooms.
Gil waited for me while I checked in and dropped off my
bags. Then we got back in his jeep and headed out for lunch.
Gil took me to a place called the Japanese Cafe, where we or-
dered sashimi, rice, and a couple of Budweisers.
"Hey, you wanna check and see if Salvador Idechong is in?"
Gil asked me with a sly grin.
"Who's he?" I asked through a mouthful of sushi.
"The leader of the opposition party here," Gil said. "His of-
fice is just right upstairs."
"Sure, why not," I said. I figured it couldn't hurt to get the
anti-American viewpoint while I was here. So far, most of the
Micronesians I had met had been very pro-American.
After we finished our lunches, Gil took me upstairs to Idechong's office above the restaurant. Going upstairs is pretty impressive anywhere in Micronesia, where there aren't many
two-story buildings because of the typhoons.
Idechong's office was equally impressive by Micronesian
standards. The outer lobby area had wall-to-wall carpeting,
hardwood paneling, and a gorgeous secretary behind a high-
quality wooden desk. Gil, who obviously knew her well, kidded
around for a few minutes before asking if Idechong was in and
if we could see him.
"Sure, I'll check," she said, flashing a pretty red smile as
she passed me on her way to Idechong's private office. She
knocked softly and entered; then after a couple of minutes she
returned with Idechong's right-hand man, Moses Katosang.
Gil introduced us and explained that I was on Palau to testify
at the Constitutional Convention and had wanted to be sure to
pay my respects to Idechong while I was here. He laid it on a

bit thick, but Katosang seemed pleased and more than happy to oblige.

"Come on in, Bryan, let me introduce you to Salvador," he said. "Gil, I hope you don't mind waiting out here."

"Fine by me," Gil said.

I followed Katosang into the office, where Salvador Idechong sat behind a huge mahogany desk. He was a trim man, tall for a Palauan, with dark skin and thick, curly black hair. His eyes were hidden behind tinted glasses. His expression was solemn and stern.

Katosang introduced me to Idechong in Palauan, then turned to me and said, "Bryan, this is Salvador Idechong."

"Hello, sir," I said. "I—"

But before I could get in another word, Idechong began to speak in Palauan. Actually, he pontificated, with Katosang translating every three or four sentences. As he spoke, I got the distinct impression that this was a well-rehearsed speech that he had given many other times, to many other visitors.

"Mr. Vila, we're a small and developing country. We've been overrun many times—first by the Germans, then by the Japanese, and now by the Americans. For more than one hundred years, we've had foreigners running our affairs. We don't have much choice. We're a poor country, without resources or sophistication. We need a great deal of help, but we need to do things our way. We don't need people telling us how to run our country or how to run our lives. We have our own ways of doing things, and we've tried hard to maintain our culture."

His speech went on and on, and Idechong was such a good orator that I might ordinarily have been moved by it. But something about Idechong just didn't ring true to me. His office was too plush. He was wearing $250 Gucci loafers and a gold Rolex. And his trousers were wool worsted—he'd have to send them all the way to Japan just to get them dry-cleaned. I didn't doubt that Palau had its problems, but Idechong seemed to be doing just fine, thank you, and his whole routine about the poor, simple islanders and the big, bad Americans seemed like a bit of a put-on to me. I also later learned that he spoke perfect English, so having Katosang interpret for us had just been another bit of posturing on his part.

I mentioned these observations to Gil when my audience with Idechong was finally over and we were on our way back to my hotel.

Gil laughed and said, "Yeah, I was wondering if you'd pick up on that. You wouldn't believe this guy. He talks a good show, but the truth is, he's probably done more to exploit his own people than the Germans and the Japanese and the Americans combined. See, what Salvador does is if you're some poor guy who wants a flashy new pickup truck but can't afford it, you go see him for a loan. If you've got a piece of land he'll say, 'OK, but you've got to put the land up as collateral. As long as you pay me off, you keep your land.'"

"But of course, you don't pay him off—he's counting on that—and now he owns your land," I interjected.

"Exactly," Gil said. "So now Salvador owns damn near all the land on the island. In fact, he was Palau's first millionaire."

II

The next morning, I spent three hours answering questions and offering opinions before the Palau Constitutional Convention's Committee on Civil Liberties and Fundamental Rights. Bonifacio Basilius, a well-respected elder statesman of Micronesian politics, was the chairman.

Most cops—especially those of us who've had to deal with murderers, rapists, and child molesters on a regular basis—tend to support the death penalty. And most of us probably see incarceration as a similarly simple issue—as in, the longer these assholes are locked up, the better. Once I'd thought through it, though, I was surprised at how complicated things got on an island where the people you were locking up or executing were sons and brothers and neighbors rather than just anonymous scumbags. The intimacy of Micronesian policing—and Micronesian life—didn't allow the kind of disconnection from offenders that urban cops use to buffer themselves.

By the end of my testimony, I was feeling pretty impressed with myself for coming up with recommendations that melded traditional island mores with the needs of impending statehood, and for testifying at a constitutional convention. It was a heady change from where I'd been just a year earlier, supervising street cops in East L.A. But Chairman Basilius brought me back down to earth when he directed me to submit a typewritten statement paraphrasing my testimony by the next morning—especially after I realized I'd be doing all my own secretarial work.

"Mariko, will you find Mr. Vila a place to work and help him with whatever he needs?" Basilius said to his pretty young assistant. "I'd like twenty copies of his statement for the committee tomorrow morning."

She smiled and nodded, then gestured for me to come with her. As I followed, I couldn't help appreciating her lithe, swaying grace. There's something about the way Palauan women carry themselves that reaches deep down inside a man. Sort of like hearing a French woman talk about even the most mundane things. I found myself instinctively standing a little straighter, a primal stir I relished for a moment before forcing it into the background.

Don't drool, Bryan, I thought. *You're married, remember? Besides, she's probably some senator's wife.*

Actually, as I found out during the next six hours hunched over a low desk banging awkwardly at an old Underwood manual typewriter, her husband was only a congressman. I was absorbed in trying to turn out the essay, but every time Mariko stopped by to see how things were going or to chat for a moment, it was impossible not to notice the glow of her freckled bronze skin or the way the light glistened on her short, soft hair, or . . . *concentrate, dammit!*

And so the afternoon went until I gave the lengthy document a final edit around five-thirty. "I think that's it," I told Mariko.

She showed me to the Xerox machine, which was housed in a narrow windowless room, and asked, "You know how to use this?"

"Sure," I replied.

She nodded and said, "OK then, I'll come back in about fifteen minutes."

Standing beside the Xerox machine, I was leaning back at the waist and kneading the screaming muscles in my lower back when Mariko walked back into the room.

"Here they are," I said, handing her a neatly collated and stapled stack of documents.

"Thank you," she said, standing close in the tiny room. "I know that Boni will be happy to get these."

I followed her out into the hallway and watched as she locked them in a cabinet. She turned and stated, "Your back hurts." Then she took me by the hand, tugging toward the door and said, "Come. I'll fix it for you."

We walked up the dank stairway out of the basement of the congressional building into the pastel early evening light. Most of the workers were gone by then. Motioning to a soft grassy spot on the large quad around which most of the government offices were arrayed she said, "Come on, lie down."

My mind no longer on political and legal philosophy, I did as she said, noticing for the first time how revealing her sleeveless cotton blouse was as she knelt down beside me, then bent over to push on my shoulder. "Roll over on your stomach."

I lay there with my face in the lawn while she knowingly massaged my neck, shoulders, and back, dreamily watching through nearly closed eyes as the occasional small insect bumbled its way through a forest of grass. After about a hundred years or so, she stood and kicked off her zoris. I turned my head toward her and began a feeble attempt to rise. She pushed me back down with a foot that was surprisingly trim—even from that angle—then began walking on my back.

Up and down, side to side, she kneaded and prodded. Not saying a word.

It was twilight when she stopped and knelt beside me. Rolling over halfway, I propped my head on my hand and said, "*Mesulang. Mesulang.*" Thank you. Thank you.

Looking seriously into my eyes from inches away, she said, "I think we need to go someplace else."

The pleasant clean scent of betel nut and pepper leaves wafted on her breath. Unable to break her gaze—not wanting to—I dug deep for whatever dregs of professionalism might remain in my blood-starved brain. "What about your husband?" I asked.

"That doesn't matter," she replied with a trace of a pout.

I was breaking the rhythm, violating the tenuous cross-cultural bridge she'd built, and I knew it. I wasn't quite sure how to handle the situation. I didn't want to offend her. And I have to admit, I was tempted. But even as my moral compass wavered a bit—OK, swung wildly—I remembered a warning Denny had given me back when I first arrived on Saipan. Apparently, while Micronesian women often are willing to share their attentions with strangers, Micronesian men tend to be pretty proprietary. "They'll forgive you if you steal their money or even if you take their property," he had said, "but not if you mess with their sisters, wives, or daughters."

"*Mesulang,* but I can't," I said regretfully.

Her face unreadable, she rose fluidly, slipped into her zoris, and sauntered away.

OK, good job, I thought, proud of my restraint. I rolled into a crouch, brushed myself off, then walked back to my rental car with a sense of self-righteousness tinged with a hint of regret. I was becoming all too aware that if I wasn't careful, travel and infidelity could easily become partners.

**

I was lying in bed trying to read, no longer feeling the least bit righteous, when there was a little *knock, knock, knock* at my hotel room door. I didn't get up to answer it right away, figuring it must be someone who had the wrong room.

But my nocturnal visitor was persistent. After a few moments, there was another *knock, knock, knock*, followed by a soft, unfamiliar female voice asking, "Can I come in?"

Somewhat baffled, I pulled on my swim trunks and went to the door. Opening it just a crack, I peered out warily. There on the doorstep was one of the waitresses from the hotel restaurant—the one who had served my dinner earlier that evening.

"Is something wrong?" I asked.

"No," she replied softly. "I came to spend the night."

"I'm sorry, what?" I said, sure I must've misunderstood. I mean, I'd been propositioned before, but never twice in one day, seldom so unexpectedly, and never by anyone who looked so sweet and innocent as this fresh-faced young woman. She couldn't have been even twenty.

"I like you. I've come to spend the night with you," she said matter-of-factly, tilting her head with a half-smile.

I blinked, swallowed, smiled politely, and declined her offer as gently and graciously as possible. After I closed the door on her confused frown, I went back to bed and my book, once again feeling proud of my restraint.

Unfortunately, virtue doesn't always lead to a good night's sleep. After tossing and turning for several hours, I finally got up at around 4 AM to take a cold shower.

The water was off.

III

A little punchy from lack of sleep, I crunched up the long coral-gravel drive leading to Palauan District Administrator Tom Remengesau's residence.

Arriving at 6 PM like the formal invitation—which had been hand-delivered to me at my hotel the day before—had said, I found that things were just beginning to get set up. I had yet to learn that in island time, "six" meant eight, or maybe even nine o'clock. As the first guest, Tom greeted me effusively as he fastened the cuff links in his fancy, embroidered Filipino *barong*. Turning to one of the pretty young women who were setting up tables and arranging seats in a leisurely bustle, he said, "Please get Mr. Vila a beer, Kieko." She went to a cooler full of ice and brought me back a cold San Miguel.

Between the fatigue and the heat just a few degrees north of the equator, it went down very well. So did the next one, and the one after that.

By the time the rest of the guests had arrived and we all sat down for dinner, I was feeling witty, relaxed, and fully in sync with the tides of the universe. But one more San Miguel on an empty stomach and I'd have been on my lips.

There were ten or more of us at the long table, all waiting in eager anticipation as the island delicacies were passed around. First came the pupus—*lumpia* (Filipino egg rolls), rumaki, and sushi—which were followed by a marinated salad and a cold papaya soup.

Just as I was starting to regain a bit of ballast, the main course was served. The Palauans around the table were unusually intent as three big tureens were brought out. As one of the young women began to serve Tom, who was seated to my right, he said, "No, let Bryan have the best piece. This is his first Palauan feast."

I smiled, warmed by his graciousness. With a flourish, she dipped into the thick coconut broth with a large ladle and dished the top half of a fruit bat onto my plate.

Fur, teeth, eyes and all, it looked like a drowned Yorkshire terrier that had been caught in Monsieur Guillotine's doggie door. Its grinning rictus dared me to partake. I didn't have a clue where to start.

Grinning back gamely, I pushed the poor little fellow around on my plate for a bit. The other diners were watching me surreptitiously, dying to know which I'd do first, puke or pass. Kieko saved me, leaning close as she served a side dish. "You can eat it all. It's good, really," she murmured in my ear.

"*All?*" I mumbled into my napkin.

"Everything."

Watching the other guests, I dug in, surprised that the narrow little wing bones were no more substantial than a hollow pretzel. Once you got the gag reflex under control, it tasted like chicken.

Smiling, Tom leaned over and said, "The head's the best part. Go ahead, give it a try."

Smiling back over a mouthful of leathery torso, I nodded, thinking, *I'd rather eat its furry little asshole.*

CHAPTER 7

They Call Me "Cheep"

In March of 1979, I was appointed chief of police for the tiny island of Kosrae—population 5,000.

Under the U.S. administration of Micronesia, Kosrae had been a municipality of Ponape. But the Kosraeans were a different people with a different language, a different heritage, and a different dominant religion from Ponape. So as the islands began to develop into nations, Kosrae became a separate district, and later an independent state within the Federated States of Micronesia. As with any major change of the sort, the transition was not without its problems—one of which was the Kosrae Police Department.

When the island had become independent from Ponape, so had its police station. And once they were no longer a substation of the Ponape police, the Ponapeans pulled out all of their officers except one older man, Nikontro Pelep, who had lived there forever and was married to a Kosraean woman.

The Kosraeans had done what they could to reorganize the department and appoint new leaders from the ranks of their own officers on the force. But the new police chief had died soon after his appointment. The next in line for the position—a lieutenant—had been fired for malfeasance, and the only other potential candidate—a sergeant—had been forced to retire for medical reasons. In short, things were a mess. So the High Commissioner and Denny had decided to send me in for a few months to do what I could to help.

Susan still had a couple more weeks to go on her latest class of secretaries, so I initially went out alone. Frankly, I was eager to leave. We'd been going through a rough patch since I'd gotten back from Palau, and I figured we both could use a break from each other.

It was my fault. I should've just kept my big mouth shut. But, in the spirit of honest and open communication, I'd told Susan about the attractive young women who had propositioned me on Palau. Worse, I'd prattled on about how virtuous I felt for resisting such strong temptation not once, but twice in one day. She'd gotten redder and redder in the face as she listened to me wrap up with my best seventies psychobabble. When she finally exploded, I'd been surprised to learn that it wasn't enough that I hadn't acted on my urges—just *having* them was a horrible affront.

Three decades later (I'm a slow learner), I can see how it must have hurt her. The constant and often lengthy separations had become a real source of contention between us—and I'd compounded the problem by acknowledging outside temptations. As I tossed and turned on the couch that night, I promised myself I'd try to be more understanding—and more circumspect—in the future.

* * *

Air Mike didn't fly to Kosrae, so I had booked a flight with Pacific Missionary Aviation. After my experience with Earl the Squirrel, I was a little reluctant to fly with another small outfit, and even more so when I caught sight of the motto—"On a Wing and a Prayer"—painted along the side of the plane. But the airplane—a twin-engine Beechcraft with a long nose to hold extra cargo—looked clean and reputable. And the pilot, Peter, was very German and very competent. Just the kind of guy you wanted to fly with over 300 miles of open ocean with no fancy navigational aids.

In fact, Peter was such a competent pilot that I was actually able to relax and enjoy the scenery on the trip from Ponape. Flying low over the water in the Beechcraft, the vast expanse of blue sky and blue ocean melded together so that if I squinted just a little, I could almost convince myself that the plane was soaring through pure blue space, with no up or down.

The first glimpse of land—a tiny dot on the horizon—spoiled the effect, but as always, the change brought a new and incredible beauty. We passed directly over two small atolls—first Mokil and then Pingelap. Peter went down to a lower altitude so we could clearly see the villages and the people of these low-lying atolls. Mokil consisted of a curved string of emerald islets linked by bright sandy beaches—the whole string was perhaps two miles long. And Pingelap, with its two beautiful side-by-side lagoons, looked sort of like a pair of eyeglasses in the middle of the ocean.

Then we were back over the open ocean with no land in sight. Finally, Kosrae loomed on the horizon. The island was lush and green, with long stretches of sandy beaches and two large, pointy peaks that defined what locals called the Sleeping Lady, for obvious reasons. It was so beautiful and serene—like something right out of a picture postcard from paradise—that I felt a great sense of calm and peacefulness wash over me.

In that state, I was wholly unprepared for the situation that awaited me below.

* * *

"You fucking animals! You pigs! What's wrong with you people? You're all a bunch of fucking assholes!"

Talk about your shattered illusions. These sorts of epithets and worse—delivered in loud, shrieking tones by a tall, thin American woman—were the first thing I heard as I stepped out of the Beechcraft. Surrounded by other Americans, who all had the same look of disgust on their faces, she was addressing a group of what appeared to be local officials who looked torn between embarrassment and confusion.

Carson Benjamin, the deputy police chief, was waiting for me at the foot of the airplane steps. He was about my age, medium in height and fairly pudgy around the middle, with big biceps and a slight cast in one eye. Seemingly oblivious to the commotion that was taking place nearby, he gave me a broad smile as he greeted me with several brightly colored leis.

"Welcome, Bryan. I am very glad that you came," Carson said in a gentle, slightly sing-songy voice, taking my hand in his.

"Thank you. I am very happy to be here," I replied, adjusting my tone to his in an unconscious reaction to a different accent and dialect.

Still holding my hand—which I later learned was the custom on Kosrae, even among men—Carson continued to smile and to make the usual inquiries about my trip over. But it was becoming more and more apparent that he wasn't at all unaware of the scene to our left. There was a lot more tension in his jaw than I had noticed at first, and he kept glancing over at the angry group a little anxiously while we talked. Finally, somewhat hesitantly, he approached the subject.

"Cheep," Carson said (Kosraeans can't always pronounce their Fs properly, the way many Americans can't roll their Rs when they speak French). "Cheep, I should tell you, we have a problem here that happened the other day with two of these Peace Corps girls."

"Oh? What is it?" I asked.

"Well, these American girls were raped by two of our boys, and they're very upset," Carson said, looking embarrassed.

"Is that what they're arguing about over there?" I asked,

nodding in the direction of Carson's worried glances.

"Yes."

"So who are all those people?" I prodded.

"Well, some of them are Peace Corps and some are from the Navy and some are from our village council—and that's Governor Nena with them," Carson told me. "Maybe it would be good for you to talk with them, too."

"Sure. Let's go," I said.

Carson and I approached the group, and he introduced me to everyone as the new "cheep" of police. The new Kosraean governor, Jacob Nena, was a handsome man with neatly barbered black hair. He was dressed in the island leader version of a power suit—a muted gray flowered polyester aloha shirt, neatly pressed dark trousers, and black loafers—and he greeted me cordially, if not as effusively as Carson. The Navy representatives were from the top ranks—one was a commander from Naval Forces Marianas and the other was a special agent in charge from the Naval Investigative Service office on Guam. The tall, thin woman among them turned out to be the regional Peace Corps director from Honolulu. She and the other Peace Corps folks with her looked even angrier up close than they had from a distance.

"So, you're the new police chief?" the Navy commander asked me.

"Yes, sir," I told him.

"Good. Now maybe this thing will get handled," he said, barely concealing his disgust for the chaos he had encountered here.

"I'll do whatever I can to work with Carson and get this resolved, sir," I replied coolly.

"*Work* with him?" the Peace Corps director, Nancy something-or-other, interjected. "Ha! They've been at this for two days and they haven't done a fucking thing."

Nancy was all red in the face and splotchy and looked like

she was ready to cry out of anger and frustration.

"Look, Miss, er, Nancy," I began uncomfortably. "I'm sure they're doing the best they can to—"

"Oh puh-lease," Nancy interrupted. "Those animals raped two of my people. And these people," she said, motioning in disgust to the governor and his group, "they're trying to tell me that rape's not such a big deal!"

By the time Nancy finished, she was shrieking at me as loudly as she had been screaming at the Kosraeans earlier. There was obviously nothing I could say that would fix things, and with my sorry diplomatic skills, I knew better than to even try.

II

I had originally planned to spend the day getting settled in before jumping into my new role as police chief the following morning. But under the circumstances, I asked Carson Benjamin to drive me straight over to the police station instead. He was happy to oblige—after a morning spent dealing with a bunch of angry Americans, I think he was eager for any excuse to get away from the airport—so we piled my suitcases and gear into the back of the dilapidated old police jeep and headed out.

The Kosrae police station was located in the jungle on the outskirts of Lela, a small island connected by a causeway to the main island that served as Kosrae's "business district." It had a rusty tin roof with long, overhanging eaves, thin plywood walls that went halfway up, and mesh screening for ventilation that filled in the gap from the top of the walls to the roof. Even the top half of the front door was made of screening. It swung on a rickety hinge and had some inner-tube rubber attached to it to make it pull shut behind you. Inside was a squad room of sorts with some well-worn desks and chairs. And off to one corner was a small chief's office—my new office—that was separated from the rest of the station by a couple of plywood walls.

They Call Me "Cheep"

After giving me a brief tour of the station and adjoining jail facility, Carson Benjamin rounded up several officers—including Marciano and Patterson Salik, the two detectives assigned to the rape investigation—for an impromptu meeting in the squad room.

"So," I asked, perching on the edge of a rickety desk, "what've you got so far on this case?"

"We've got two guys. Two suspects," Marciano replied in clipped, heavily accented English.

"Really? Great. Who are they?" I said, a little surprised by this news, which was certainly contrary to Nancy's claim that the local police had done nothing so far.

Marciano hesitated for just a moment, then rattled off two Kosraean names. One of the last names just happened to be Benjamin.

"Benjamin? Is he related to you, Carson?" I asked Carson.

"Yes. He's my brother," Carson replied, eyes downcast.

Carson's officers suddenly became quite interested in their feet as well. I got the impression that they had all known who the rapists were from the start and were very upset at the prospect of having to arrest the brother of their own leader.

"Do you know where he is?" I asked gently.

"Yes, he's at my house," Carson replied. "The officers know where to find him."

"What about the other suspect?"

"We know where he is, too," said Carson.

I reached over and put my hand on Carson's forearm. "You know, we're going to have to be very careful to make sure we treat everybody the same in this case."

"I know," Carson said solemnly.

"OK. Well let's go pick them both up, then," I said.

We walked out and got into the police jeep. I sat in front with Carson, who was driving, while Marciano and his brother, Patterson, sat in the back. Three more officers piled into the old police pickup truck and followed behind us as we drove back into Lela.

When we got to the house, which was quite nice by Kosraean standards, Carson asked me, "Do you want to come inside?"

"No," I said. "Why don't we just wait here and let the detectives handle it, like we would any other crime."

Carson looked relieved. After all, it was his house, his family, and his brother in there. As the new deputy police chief, this was a terrible loss of face for him.

About fifteen minutes later, the two detectives came out of the house, trailing Carson Benjamin's young brother behind them. Carson said something to him in Kosraean as he walked past us and motioned with his head for him to get into the back of the pickup. He nodded to Carson, eyes slightly downcast, and climbed aboard.

Carson and I got back into the police jeep and followed the pickup down the road a bit to another fairly prosperous looking house. Once again, we waited outside while the officers went in, expecting them to return soon with the second suspect in custody. But after a few minutes they came out alone and said something to Carson in Kosraean.

"What's the matter?" I asked.

"The father doesn't want his son to come with us," said Carson. "He says he will take care of this himself. He'll make restitution."

"I'm sorry, Carson, but we have to make the boy come with us. We need to show everybody how important this is, and that we treat everyone the same," I said.

Carson nodded and spoke with Marciano again in Kosraean. Finally he turned to me and said, "I will talk with them."

Marciano went back into the house and came back with the father. Carson talked with him at the front door of the house for about fifteen minutes, holding his hand and gesturing back toward me and toward his own brother sitting in the pickup truck from time to time. Pretty soon the father went back inside the house, then returned with his son in tow. Patterson handcuffed the young man and then helped him into the back of the pickup truck.

As we drove back through town to the police station, people stopped to watch. They all looked very solemn—I mean, this wasn't the kind of voyeuristic spectacle one sees in the States when something of this sort happens. These people were all family or friends of the suspects, and they were all upset and unsure of how to deal with this.

It wasn't as if the Kosraeans condoned rape. In fact, as part of their development as an independent district, they had recently enacted laws against rape modeled after the California and Oregon penal codes. But that didn't necessarily mean that they viewed it in the same way we do. They acknowledged that what their boys had done was wrong, and they were very embarrassed about it, but they just didn't comprehend the full gravity of the situation from an American's perspective.

It wasn't until several days later that Nancy was finally able to help the Kosraeans see the American victims' point of view. Somewhere in the course of the endless discussions about the incident, the subject of potential consequences of the crime came up. Nancy told the Kosraeans that if either of the young women who had been raped were to find out that she was pregnant as a result, she'd most likely have an abortion rather than bear the child of a man who had done this to her. Well, the Kosraeans were utterly, deeply shocked that anyone would do such a thing. But they finally began to understand the impact of this crime by American standards.

It was an important turning point, both for the Kosraeans and for me. I could now see that it wasn't enough for us to try to understand Micronesian culture; we also had to help them understand our culture better if they were going to successfully adopt more modern laws and ways of doing things.

III

After my first few days on island, the rape investigation began to calm down. The suspects were in custody and overwhelming evidence had been collected against them. Satisfied with the progress that had been made in the case, the Navy and Peace Corps folks had left. Now I could finally get down to the business of training.

My new officers—all eighteen of them—were a diverse bunch, ranging from fresh-faced kids just out of high school to intelligent young men with college educations to older men like Nikontro Pelep, the lone Ponapean officer who had remained on Kosrae.

With the exception of one officer—a taciturn young man who was a friend of the lieutenant who had been fired just before I was sent in—the officers were glad that I had come and eager to fill me in on the situation on Kosrae and the problems they had encountered since the separation from Ponape.

After listening to them, I realized that I was going to have to rethink a lot of the plans I had made back in my office on Saipan. For example, I had been strongly inclined toward doing away with police uniforms and military protocols and the like, because they really didn't seem necessary on a small island like Kosrae, where just about everybody knew everybody else. I had assumed that the officers would welcome this less militaristic approach to policing. But I was dead wrong. They let me know in no uncertain terms that they wanted all the pomp and circumstance they could get. They wanted uniforms and badges, firearms and police jeeps—and they wanted a formal rank structure.

I was initially surprised by their attitude, but then, I hadn't understood the full extent of the losses the department had suffered as a result of Kosrae's secession from Ponape, or its impact on the small department. These were good, hard-working men—both the long-time veterans and the new recruits—who suddenly had been left without leadership, equipment, or train-ing, and subsequently had been reduced to a joke within their community. So they wanted not only structure and training, they wanted the traditional symbols of power and authority and discipline in order to regain their lost prestige.

I could understand the cops wanting all the trappings of power—especially after what they'd been through recently—but what really surprised me was that the community wanted them, too. In my many talks with Kosrae's political leaders, village councils, and women's groups, I discovered that while they wanted offenders such as the young men who had raped the Peace Corps women to be treated with compassion, they also wanted justice and order, and they wanted police officers with uniforms, badges, and weapons.

I'm nothing if not flexible (and in Micronesia, I was learning to be more flexible all the time), so I went to the communica-tions station and got on the radio to TT headquarters right away to see what I could do about ordering new uniforms and equipment. Personally, I wasn't too thrilled about the uni-forms—as the "cheep," I was going to have to wear one, too—but I requested them anyway. I also requested two new Suzuki jeeps, some shotguns, and other basic equipment like nightsticks and flashlights. It was a lot to ask for all at once, but TT knew I was starting from scratch here and ended up approving almost everything I requested.

* * *

Once we had come to a mutual understanding about the style of policing to be adopted and the goals for the department, it was time to tackle the problem of how to train a group of mostly new recruits when half of them didn't speak English.

By then I'd had enough experience with the aching tedium of working through a translator to want to avoid it. I was determined to find a way around, through, over, or under the language barrier.

So, I decided to try a new approach. First, I learned the basics of Kosraean using homemade flashcards for about a hundred key words and phrases. Then I divided the officers into two groups—those who spoke English and those who didn't—and held morning and afternoon classes for them every day in the squad room. I'd teach morning classes to the half of my officers who spoke English and have them translate key concepts for me. In the afternoon, with Carson Benjamin or one of the other English-speaking officers at my side to help when I got stuck, I'd try to teach the same class in Kosraean for the officers who spoke little or no English.

The afternoon classes were a disaster at first—I could tell the officers were only pretending to understand me most of the time, and very little of what I was trying to teach was getting through to them. I soon realized what was going on. Cultural differences were creating an even bigger roadblock to communication between us than language differences. That's because in a small community like Kosrae, as in many parts of Micronesia, there's strong cultural pressure to conform and get along. If people don't understand what you mean, they won't tell you. If you're wrong, they won't challenge you. If they can't do what you want them to do, they'll still say "yes" because they don't want to upset you or hurt your feelings or make you angry.

Well, that attitude just doesn't work when you're trying to teach people. I mean, I needed to know if I wasn't getting through or if I had used the wrong word in Kosraean, and the officers weren't telling me.

With a little creative thinking, I found a solution to the problem. I made a deal with the officers. Instead of the usual, "Me teacher, you students" routine, the teaching and learning would flow in both directions. My job would be to teach them about police work and help them develop policing strategies that fit with their culture and needs. Their job would be to teach me Kosraean, correct my pronunciation and grammar whenever I screwed up, speak up when I wasn't making any sense to them, help me learn their customs, and correct me when I violated them.

They were a little uncomfortable with the idea at first, but eventually they came to enjoy the interaction. Who wouldn't welcome a chance to correct the boss as often as he corrects you? And finally the real learning process began—for all of us.

Of course, there were times when I wished I hadn't tried so hard to make them feel comfortable about correcting me when I made a mistake. For example, I learned early on that wading or swimming in the lagoon was a big no-no on Sunday. Two of my officers caught me neck deep in water one day after church and pulled over in the police jeep.

"Cheep, no. Culture," they told me, shaking their heads and laughing.

I was hot and sweaty and the lagoon was gloriously cool and soothing, but a deal's a deal. So I thanked them for pointing out my mistake and, with what I hoped was well-disguised dismay, hoisted myself out of the crystal blue water and trudged on back to my hot, air conditioning-free abode.

IV

There were no hotels on Kosrae back in 1979, so I stayed at the "Kosrae Hilton"—a house not far from the governor's residence that accommodated up to four guests at a time—when I first arrived on island.

Built on stilts out over the lagoon, the Kosrae Hilton had a tin roof, plywood walls halfway up, and screening the rest of the way that the mosquitoes always managed to find their way through, just like at the police station. Each of the four rooms was equipped with a little folding cot and mattress, a nightstand, and dresser. There was just one bathroom to share among the four guest rooms, but at least the place had indoor plumbing. A stalk of bananas hung outside by the back door, and the little outdoor cooking area had its own water catchment tank because, like everywhere else in Micronesia, the power went off a lot and the municipal water supply was equally erratic. The dining room consisted of a wooden picnic table that sat out on the veranda overlooking the lagoon.

There was even an old wringer washing machine out back. I hadn't seen one like it since I was a kid back in the fifties and my mother had had something of the sort, but I remembered how to use it, and it came in pretty handy since there was no laundry service on island.

It was all very primitive, and terribly idyllic. The only problem was that the goddam roosters crowed all night long.

I've got nothing against roosters in general. I used to go to my grandmother's in the country in Colorado when I was a kid, and it was wonderful. At about five o'clock in the morning, the roosters would start sounding off on the local farms, and it was a peaceful, natural way to wake up. But not here. The roosters on Kosrae would crow all night long, every night of the year.

There was one particularly loud rooster who lived right across from the little corner room I had at the Kosrae Hilton. After several nights of tossing and turning, I finally followed the ruckus to the house next door.

"Whose rooster is that?" I asked the small boy out in front of the house.

"Oh, it's my brother's," said the boy.

"Well, would you ask your brother if he'll sell it to me?" I said.

The boy ran inside the house. "Isaac!" I heard him shout. "Isaac, the *ahset* wants to buy your rooster!" (*Ahset* is the Kosraean word for foreigner. It's derived from the expression, "Ah shit," commonly used by the early whalers who came to Kosrae.)

Isaac, who was about thirteen or so, came out of the house

looking kind of excited. He was a lively boy, with dark brown hair, a devilish smile, and a glint in his eye. A boy I could identify with.

"My brother says you'd like to buy my rooster," he said.

"Yes, I would," I said. "Is he for sale?"

"I guess so. But he's a very special rooster. Very tough," said Isaac. "He's a good fighter." (They still held cockfights for entertainment on Kosrae at the time.)

"Great. How much do you want for him?" I asked.

"Well, probably twenty dollars," he said, squinting slightly as he attempted to assess what I might be willing to pay.

"OK," I said, getting out my wallet. I figured it was at least double what the rooster was worth, but twenty dollars was a small price to pay for some peace and quiet as far as I was concerned.

"But you're not from here," Isaac said as I counted out the bills. "How will you get him home with you when you leave Kosrae?"

"Oh, I'm not going to take him anywhere," I said. "I'm going to kill him, and then you can eat him if you want."

"What? You can't kill him!" said Isaac. "He's very special, this rooster. He's my friend. Why do you want to kill him?"

"So I can finally get some sleep around here," I said.

Isaac and his brother exchanged looks and started chuckling. Pretty soon they had me laughing, too.

"Don't worry, you'll get used to it," said Isaac.

"Used to it? How do you ever get used to that racket?"

"You will," said Isaac, still grinning. "I'm sorry, *ahset*, but I can't let you buy my rooster."

***

After that first meeting, where we developed sort of a humorous affinity for each other, Isaac and his brother would come over to tutor me in Kosrean every day after I got home from work. It really helped bolster the language training I was already getting from my Kosraean officers, and I appreciated the extra lessons, despite the fact that Isaac was a particularly tough taskmaster who took great delight in correcting me when I made a mistake. He criticized my pronunciation with gusto and deplored my deep voice.

"Why do you talk like this?" he'd say, mimicking me, exasperated by my baritone utterings. Kosraeans tend to have tenor voices and a light touch with the language that's difficult for foreigners to emulate. I'd try again, raising my voice an octave or so higher, and end up sounding sort of like a cross between Tiny Tim and Julia Child. Isaac and his brother would erupt into a torrent of giggles. I imagine it was the comic relief I provided that kept them coming back each day to teach me.

Even after Susan arrived and we moved into the former district administrator's house, which was just down the street from the Kosrae Hilton, Isaac and his brother would come by. And after three months of his tutoring and help from my officers, I was almost fluent.

Initially, I had seen language as a barrier to be overcome. But it was much more than that. It was the key to everything I did. Making the effort to learn the language not only allowed communication to flow both ways, it demonstrated my respect for the culture of Kosrae—and for each person I spoke with there.

V

By my second month on Kosrae, much of the equipment I had ordered had begun to arrive, including the shotguns, and I decided that it was time for a little firearms training. The officers had been carrying pistols on duty, but the problem was that the pistols weren't functional. Most of them were rusted shut. If they'd ever been fired—which they hadn't—they probably would've blown up in the officers' faces. There were also a few

M1 carbines and some old Japanese rifles in the weapons locker—most of which were just as useless and potentially dangerous as the pistols.

On a lightly armed island like Kosrae, I saw no need for the officers to carry handguns on a daily basis. For one thing, very few incidents requiring deadly force ever occurred on the island. For another, without regular shooting practice, it's impossible to be competent with a handgun in a combat situation. And the department couldn't begin to afford the thousands and thousands of rounds of ammunition it would take to maintain the officers' shooting skills.

Shotguns, on the other hand, are extremely effective and require a minimum of training. You can learn how to use one today, and twenty years from now you can still pick it up and point it at somebody and if they're within twenty yards you'll hit them with it just fine. The shot spreads out when the gun is fired, so it's like shooting a dozen or more pistol bullet-sized pellets in a fan pattern, which significantly increases your odds of hitting your target even if you're not such a good shot. It was just the kind of weapon the Kosraean cops needed for their very infrequent emergencies.

They weren't entirely convinced of this at first, so I decided to take them out into the jungle to try out a bunch of different kinds of weapons and show them by comparison that I was right. I had my .357 with me, a few working revolvers, two M1 carbines from the weapons locker that I'd put into working order, and the new shotguns.

We set up a makeshift firing range using paper silhouette targets stapled onto pieces of plywood and propped against coconut palms, and the officers took turns shooting with my .357 and the revolvers at fifteen yards. As I had expected, given their lack of training and regular practice, very few of them even came close to hitting the targets.

Once I had proved my point that handguns probably

weren't the best way to go for the department, we decided to give the M1 carbines a try.

"Shit. We forgot the magazines," I said, staring down at the old carbines, which were entirely useless without the magazines that held the bullets, which had been left back in the weapons locker by mistake. "Marciano, would you and Patterson go back to the station and get them?" I asked Marciano Salik, the bright young detective who had worked on the rape investigation.

"Sure, Cheep," Marciano said, giving me kind of a funny look.

He and Patterson jumped into the police jeep and drove off. I didn't want to move on to the shotguns just yet—I wanted to save them for last—so while we waited for them to return I had the officers take a few more turns with the handguns.

Pretty soon, Marciano and Patterson came roaring down the bumpy path in the jeep.

"Did you get them?" I asked.

"Yes, Cheep," said Marciano. "But we didn't know which ones you wanted. Are these OK?"

He reached in the back of the jeep and handed me a copy of *Skiing* magazine and a couple of old *National Geographics*. I looked down at the magazines and then back at Marciano and Patterson, thinking maybe they were just pulling my leg to see what I would do. The Kosraeans are big kidders, so I thought it was pretty likely. But they were completely earnest. We all had a good laugh over it after I explained the other definition of a magazine to them, and they headed back to the station to collect them.

The officers did a lot better with the carbines than they had with the handguns, probably because many of them were used to hunting with .22-caliber rifles, which are pretty similar in terms of operation. But when they started shooting with the 12-gauge shotguns, they were really impressed. I mean, those things practically vaporized the cans, bottles, and rusty old car doors that we set on top of palm tree stumps to use as targets. They liked that and conceded that the shotguns weren't such a bad idea after all.

VI

My last day on Kosrae came too soon. Sure, I had done my fair share of griping—mostly to myself—during my time there. Conditions were still pretty primitive at the time, which led to lots of little daily annoyances and frustrations and impediments to getting things done. The linguistic and cultural differences hadn't helped any. And the strong religious presence, which affected many aspects of everyday life, was fairly overwhelming. So was the amount of togetherness on the highly communal island, where Susan and I had had almost no time to ourselves.

Even on Sundays, my only day off each week, my time was never my own. I've never been very religious, but one of the reasons I was able to be effective in Micronesia is that I've always had a strong regard for—and willingness to go along with—different cultures and different ways of doing things. So when the Ponapeans drank *sakau*, I drank *sakau*. When the Yapese and Palauans chewed betel nut, I chewed betel nut. And when the Kosraeans went to church, I went to church. It wasn't necessarily expected of me, an *ahset*, but it was appreciated. It was also one of the main social activities on the island, and a good place to talk to people.

After church, several of my officers would always come over with their families to keep us company. Susan would duck into the kitchen, where she'd open a tin of Australian butter, pull down some ripe bananas off the stalk outside the back door, and whip up some banana bread. The Kosreans thought it was just great, and it gave her something to do while I sat and grinned madly back and forth with everyone.

They'd stay all day, just sitting and smiling so we wouldn't be lonely. It had nearly driven me crazy at first. But eventually, as I learned the language and the culture, the very togetherness I had found so alien and uncomfortable began to turn into a real sense of belonging.

It's not that there wasn't a strong sense of community on Saipan—but it was mostly among the expatriates who worked there. We were sort of a community within a community. But on Kosrae, I had begun to feel like part of the whole extended island family, and there was an unexpected comfort and happiness in that. There were many times during the years that followed—especially during the years after I left Micronesia and worked for the Interior Department in Washington—that I found myself wishing we had stayed on Kosrae and lived in peaceful, uncomplicated tranquility. The opportunity was there—the Kosreans had asked me to stay, and even offered me land as an incentive. But I doubt that TT would've gone for it, or Susan either. She was eager to get back to her job and her friends on Saipan.

So we left on schedule, and amid a fair amount of hoopla. Everyone came to the airport to see us off. The governor and several other dignitaries were there, as well as many of the local folks we had met. They loaded us up with leis and *mar mars* until we could barely see over them, and brought beautiful handmade carvings and other crafts as going-away presents. It was really touching, and made it all that much harder to leave.

I was saying my good-byes to Governor Nena when my police officers arrived. The whole department came marching out to the plane—every man in step, every piece of equipment polished and shining—doing the Queen Anne Salute, a complex drill team maneuver that had been passed down to them from the Marines who ran the police constabulary detachment on Kosrae after World War II. With rifles twirling and hands slapping stocks in unison, it was a picture to warm any drill instructor's heart, if drill instructors had hearts. And boy, did I ever get misty.

CHAPTER 8

The Alaskan Connection

I returned to Saipan feeling more sure of myself than I had since coming to Micronesia nearly a year earlier. The Kosrae State Legislature, the governor, the town council, and several other groups had all written resolutions of commendation for the training program I had put on. Their enthusiastic response told me that even though I was winging it, I was doing something right. The training style and ideas I had implemented had worked. Talk about your confidence boosters. I was riding high, and I launched into my next project with gusto.

It was a brilliant plan, conceived by Denny Lund. His idea was to bring several state troopers from Alaska out to Micronesia to help us conduct a basic training program in the fall. We'd hold the training on Ponape, which is one of the most central islands, and fly in about forty police officers from all over the islands to participate.

Why Alaska State Troopers? What could they possibly know about working conditions in the islands? Actually, quite a lot, when you think about it. In fact, despite the differences in weather and terrain, they probably knew more about the style of policing needed in Micronesia than most of the Honolulu officers TT had brought over the year before. They were used to working with native peoples who have their own cultures and languages and systems of doing things. They were used to dealing with remote areas and vast distances between places. And they were used to handling patrol beats the size of small states, either on their own or with just one or two other troopers. These were the sorts of problems that few big-city cops—including myself and the officers from Honolulu—had dealt with on a regular basis. I figured we could probably learn as much from the Alaskans as the Micronesians could.

***

I spent the summer and early autumn setting up the Alaskan training program—along with my other planning and training duties. It was hard work, first getting the funding and then coordinating everything, made harder by the island's primitive communications systems. It typically took a day and a half just to get a connection through to Sitka, where the trooper academy is located, and then, more often than not, the line would go dead on me halfway through the call. But the Alaskans were patient—like I said, they were used to dealing with such problems—and they were really eager to come out for a few weeks. By late autumn it gets pretty cold and dark in Alaska, and it's not too difficult to convince most Alaskans to go anyplace else that time of year, especially a warm, sunny place like Ponape. So eventually we got the whole thing to come together.

The Alaskans arrived on Saipan early in November. There were four of them: John Karja, the former director of the trooper academy who had just been promoted to assistant director of the statewide public safety department in Anchorage; Jeff Miller, a tall, good-looking sergeant from Bethel, more than 400 miles west of Anchorage; Ted Burkin, a lean, sandy-haired trooper from Kotzebue, a remote outpost nearly 200 miles north of Nome; and Tom Painter, a pale, dark-haired guy from the trooper academy on Sitka. All of them were extremely professional and at the same time almost boyishly gleeful to see the sun.

We stayed on Saipan for a couple of days to get acquainted and go over our plans for the training program, then flew out to Ponape to get started.

* * *

It was apparent from the start that these guys knew their stuff. They knew how to take charge, and how to run a training program. They also knew how to put on a good show. They showed up for the first day of training in their summer-weight Alaska State Trooper uniforms and their Smokey Bear hats, and they looked good—very professional. The Micronesian cops were really impressed.

Things went great up until the morning of the third day of training. That's when a pinkeye epidemic hit, claiming more than half the officers as victims.

Pinkeye is an extremely painful and highly contagious inflammation of the conjunctiva. If you've got the right medication, it's easy to treat and clears up pretty fast. But the clinic on Ponape didn't have a damn thing available, and it would be several days before we could get any medicine flown in on Air Mike. We only had two weeks for the whole training program, so by the time the medicine got there it would be too late.

So there we were—on a shoestring budget with a tight time schedule—and half our officers couldn't see. They were even more disgusted by the whole thing than we were. I mean, they really wanted this training and were determined to get it. Some of them were rinsing their eyes out with coconut milk, which apparently was a local remedy, and one guy even went so far as to scrub his eyes with a soapy washcloth, practically blinding himself in the process.

We had to do something. I wasn't sure what, exactly, but something. I wasn't about to let all those months of preparation go down the toilet. So while John and Jeff and Tom kept the training program going for the officers who could still see, Ted and I drove over to the Joy Restaurant, where everybody on island tended to gather for lunch, to nose around a bit and see if anyone had any ideas about what we could do.

We had just sat down and ordered a couple of iced teas when Martin Felix came in. He was a captain with the Ponape police department—a real fit and serious yet personable fellow with dark straight hair, a big smile, and strong white teeth.

"*Kaselhelia*, Bryan," said Martin.

"*Kaselhelia*," I replied. "How are things?

"OK. How's the training going?"

"Great until today," I said. "Everybody's got pinkeye."

"Yes, half of my officers are off with pinkeye," Martin said, nodding.

"It's probably the half that we've got in our training program," I said. We laughed a little half-heartedly, and I introduced Ted to Martin.

The waitress returned to the table with our iced tea. We ordered one for Martin and three plates of sashimi.

"Martin, we don't know what to do," I said after the waitress had gone again. "There's no medicine on island."

Martin was quiet for a moment. Then he said, "Well, you didn't hear this from me, but there's this doctor at the hospital who has some medicine saved up, I think."

"Really?" I said, perking up a little. "They told us nobody had anything."

"Well, you should go talk to Dr. Henry—"

"Dr. Henry? What does he look like?" I asked.

"He's a young American guy, about your height and kind of slim. Maybe you can get him to give you some of his medicine."

"Believe me, if he has it, we'll get it," I said. "I'm not taking no for an answer."

Ted and I scarfed down our food, got into my rental car, and drove out to the hospital, which was about four miles away.

"Is Dr. Henry around?" I asked the nurse at the main desk.

"Yes. He's back by the pharmacy," she said.

"Where's that?"

She pointed us down past the wards, which were chock-full of patients as well as lots and lots of their family members, who had come to bring them food or just to sit with them. I thanked her and we started down the hallway.

When we got to the pharmacy, the door was closed. I knocked, and pretty soon an American guy opened the top half of the Dutch door.

"Hi. Are you Dr. Henry?" I asked.

"Yeah," he replied, eyeing us both a little cautiously.

"I'm Bryan Vila from TT headquarters on Saipan. This is Ted Burkin, a state trooper from Kotzebue, Alaska. We're working here on Ponape for a couple of weeks, and we've got a problem that I think you can help us with."

"What's that?"

"Well, we've got forty Micronesian police officers here for training—we flew them all in at about seven hundred dollars a head, and we're paying them each another hundred and fifty bucks a week for per diem and lodging—and half of them have pinkeye," I told him.

"Oh, I know. They get a conjunctivitis epidemic here about every four or five years. It's highly contagious—usually sweeps from one side of Micronesia to the other before it runs its course. It hit here a few days ago, and it's already spread all over the island."

"Well, we've gotta do something for these guys or they'll miss the whole training program. Have you got anything you can give me for them?"

Dr. Henry paused for a minute, and I kept looking him straight in the eyes.

"Well you know, I've got a little bit of oxytetracycline ointment—that's the treatment for it—but I don't have enough for everybody on the island," he finally said.

"I don't want it for everybody on the island. I need it for my police officers," I told him.

"I'm sorry, but it's all I've got. I can't just give it to you."

"Why? What are you doing with it?" I asked.

"I'm saving it for an emergency," he told me.

"This *is* an emergency, for chrissake," I said. "We've got a ton of time and money invested in this program. We've got forty police officers who desperately need training, and half of them aren't going to get it if we don't do something."

Dr. Henry didn't say anything at first. So Ted and I just stood there, friendly but firm, both bigger than the doctor and willing to outwait him. He finally turned and walked over to an old foot locker under a table in the far back corner of the pharmacy. He fiddled with the combination on the padlock, opened it up, and took out four little tubes of oxytetracycline ointment. Pay dirt.

"So, how do we administer this?" I asked, taking the tubes from him.

"Just run a small bead under each officer's eyelids. It oughta work within two days if they don't have any secondary infection," he said a little grudgingly.

"Great. Thanks, Doc," I said. "We'll order you some more from Guam to replace it."

"Be sure that you do," he said.

I hadn't exactly made a friend there, but I had accomplished what I had set out to do.

The medicine worked like a charm. Within a day's treatment, most of the officers were well enough to attend classes. Two and a half days later, we were running at full speed again. We had to cut into the weekend and fudge a little bit here and there to make up for lost time, but we managed to get the full training program finished on schedule.

II

In spite of the rough start, the training went well. The officers really enjoyed the program and got a lot out of it. And the people on the island, and for that matter all over Micronesia, had heard about these special trainers who had come all the way from Alaska and were very impressed.

We had all been on our best professional behavior for the past two weeks. We had worked our asses off and smiled until our cheeks ached every day. But now the training was over, and we had a couple of days before we flew back out—time to take in a little local culture. So I suggested that we all go to a traditional *sakau* ceremony over at the Ponape Cultural Center, just south of Kolonia.

I hadn't had a chance to see a real *sakau* ceremony yet, but I'd been curious ever since that first experience at the *sakau* bar more than a year ago. Besides, the troopers were all pretty tough, and I figured if anyone would be game for trying *sakau*, they would.

I was right. They were more than game—they were actually eager to try the stuff.

The Ponape Cultural Center, like most structures in Micronesia that aren't made of concrete or tin sheeting, was a beautiful, open-sided mangrove wood and thatch building. Large enough to accommodate a fairly big group, it was where many traditional feasts and ceremonies were held, often for the benefit of visiting dignitaries.

We arrived at about eleven o'clock, just as the ceremony was about to begin. The room was crowded, both with Ponapeans and travelers from various countries, and there was a soft, sort of hushed air to the place.

The five of us stood quietly with the rest of the group and waited. Pretty soon the chief entered, dressed in ceremonial garb, and took his place at the front of the room. He was followed by several other high-ranking island leaders.

As soon as the chief and town elders had taken their places, the ceremony began. Several large Ponapean men, dressed in grass skirts and wearing *mar mars* on their heads, entered carrying the huge, gnarly *piper methysticum* root with great ceremony and placed it on a large basalt slab in the middle of the room. They bowed to the elderly chief and declared something to him in Ponapean, and then they began beating the root with heavy stone pounders that also were made of basalt.

And for the next half an hour or so, they beat this thing and beat it and beat it and beat it—in different rhythms and counterpoints—and as they did the basalt would ring. By the time they were finished their muscles were bulging and they were dripping sweat all over, including onto this mound of root pulp that was forming on the stone.

They continued to work on the gooey mess, squeezing it and adding water and beating it some more until it was finally the right consistency. Then they stripped out the soft inner lining from the bark of a six-foot length of hibiscus tree. They smoothed it out into a slippery, slimy sheet, then put the mashed-up root on top of it and rolled it all together lengthwise. Finally, two of the men picked up the massive roll—one at each end—and twisted it until liquid began to force its way through the hibiscus membrane. Handing his end across to his partner, the smaller of the two men reverently picked up a halved coconut shell and held it under the *sakau* mass to catch the viscous, gooey juice.

He presented the first cupful with great ceremony to the chief—holding it in two hands, bowing and keeping his head lower than the chief's. The chief took the *sakau* with equal ceremony and drank it in one gulp before handing back the cup, which was refilled and offered to the person of next highest rank. They did this over and over until everybody got some, and then they started all over again with the chief. It's a shared thing, a communion of sorts. In fact, the Catholic

church on Ponape included *sakau* in its communion ceremonies, just as they've incorporated a variety of indigenous
ceremonies into traditional Catholic rites, depending on the
culture they're in.

When it got to my turn to drink, I was glad to have had at
least one experience with *sakau* so I knew what to expect, although this was even thicker than the stuff I had drunk at the
sakau bar. I took one sip and the whole mass just sort of went
schloop-goo down. People nodded approvingly and smiled
when I drank the whole cup instead of gagging over it the way
some of the other foreigners did, which is considered disre-
spectful. The Alaskans all followed suit, without a grimace
among them.

None of us drank enough *sakau* that day to really experience its effects—the ceremony was more about the show and the
traditional experience of *sakau* than getting high (or *puputa*, as
the Ponapeans call it).

It was a good thing, too, seeing that our next stop was the
police station, where the local officers were hosting a feast in
our honor.

As always, there was an enormous amount of food. Bread-
fruit chips and yams and fish and barbecued chicken and rice
and *lumpia*. There were also plates and plates of *fafa*, brought
by the Kosraean officers who remembered my affinity for the
stuff. *Fafa* is taro root that's been pounded for hours with a
coral pestle, then rolled into little balls, wrapped in banana
leaves, and baked in a smoky underground oven called an *ohm*.
Served with a drizzle of sugar cane syrup on top, it's a heavy but
delicious dish. Unfortunately, it's only good when it's fresh. The
next day those little balls of starch are so hard you can use them
to play handball.

We ate mass quantities of food, we toasted the Alaskans
profusely, and the officers loaded them up with crafts and other
gifts as tokens of their sincere appreciation for an excellent

training program. And in traditional Micronesian fashion, the party lasted until the Budweiser ran out, which wasn't until the wee hours of the morning.

CHAPTER 9

The Ponape Jailbreak

It was around one in the morning when the phone woke me up. I was back on Saipan, and Susan was sleeping soundly next to me. I almost didn't answer it, but with the time difference, you never knew who might be trying to call from the States at an odd hour. Groggy, I reached out and groped the bedside table in the dark for the phone.

"*Hafa?*" I mumbled, the Chamorro word for "what."

"Bryan?" said a faintly familiar American voice.

"Yeah?"

"This is Adrian Winkel."

Holy shit, the Hi Com.

"Oh, uh, yes sir, hello," I said, sitting up in bed and reaching for the light on the nightstand.

"Bryan, we've got a problem and I wonder if you could come on up to the house and help me with it," said Winkel.

"What's wrong?"

"I just got a call from the governor on Ponape. He said several prisoners have escaped from the local jail. It's still unclear what all has happened, but it looks like they may have shot a police officer and a civilian," said Winkel.

"I'll be right there," I said.

"Thank you," Winkel said, ringing off.

I jumped out of bed and started to get dressed. Susan was

awake by then.

"Who was that?" she asked sleepily.

I told her what was going on briefly, and she sounded almost as surprised as I was that the Hi Com—a presidential appointee and the highest-ranking official in the Trust Territory—had called to ask for my help. Even after living in Micronesia for more than a year, it was hard to get used to being a relatively big fish in a small pond.

**

The drive up to the Hi Com's house on Capitol Hill seemed to take forever. It was dark out—there were no streetlights on island, even along the more major roads, and the moon was only a crescent that night—but I managed to find my way.

Perched on the northernmost tip of Capitol Hill next to Mount Tapochau—the highest point on Saipan—it was a beautiful large concrete structure overlooking the lagoon and Managaha Island to the west. The lights burned brightly inside, giving the house a deceptively cheerful glow.

I parked the car in the drive alongside several other cars that were lined up outside, went to the door, and knocked. The Hi Com's wife, Isabel, answered.

"Hi, Mrs. Winkel."

"Hello, Bryan, come on in," she said. "I'm glad you're here."

Mrs. Winkel took me into the living room, where the others were seated around a large coffee table strewn with coffee cups and plates of half-eaten sandwiches.

"Hello, Bryan," Winkel said, looking up as I arrived.

"Hello, sir," I said.

"Do you know Resio Moses?" he asked, indicating the man seated next to him on the couch. "He's my director of administration."

"Yes. *Kaselhelia*, Resio," I said.

"*Kaselhelia*, Bryan."

"Since Resio's from Ponape, I thought he might help us understand things better," said Winkel. "And you know Dan High, of course," he added, nodding toward the TT attorney general, who was seated in a high-backed wicker chair across from him.

"Sure. Hi, Dan," I said, taking a seat next to him. "So, what's going on?" I asked.

"Well, we can't get very good communications yet, but from what we know so far, it looks like anywhere from four to seven prisoners escaped from the Ponape jail," said Winkel. "They handcuffed one of the guards and left him locked up in a cell. Then they handcuffed the watch sergeant and shot him in the back."

"How's he doing?" I asked.

"He's in the hospital in critical condition," said Winkel.

"What about the civilian who was shot?" I asked.

"He was a deejay at the local radio station. He's dead," said Winkel.

"A deejay?" I asked. "Why would they kill a deejay?"

"Apparently they thought they were at the communications station and were trying to prevent the police from contacting outside help," said Winkel.

"Oh geez," I said, shaking my head. "What are the Ponape police doing about all this?"

"There's not much they *can* do at the moment. The prisoners took all their jeeps and weapons."

"Great. And nobody's got any other weapons except .22 rifles and .410 shotguns, right?" I asked. (On Ponape and most of the other islands, these were the only guns allowed to civilians.)

"Right," said Resio.

"OK, well, at least we have some idea what we're dealing with," I said. "How many jeeps are there?"

"Four, but only two are working. They got both of them," said Resio.

"Does anybody know where they're headed?"

"No," said Winkel.

The phone rang.

"This is Adrian Winkel," said the Hi Com, answering before the second ring. "What? What? I can't hear you. I can't hear you."

He hung up, disgusted. "I couldn't hear a word they were saying. Call Gene Stevens, would you, Resio, and have him come up here to the house. Maybe he can do something about this."

Resio took the phone from him and called Gene, an American radio technician who had been the communications director on Saipan for the past couple of years. Gene came up to the house, looking as bleary-eyed as the rest of us, a few minutes later. With his help, we finally got a call through to Ponape.

"It's as bad as we thought," Winkel told us when he got off the phone. "There are six of them. They've got an M1 carbine, a couple of .38 revolvers, some .22 rifles, and a Thompson submachine gun."

"They've got a Tommy gun?" I interjected.

Most people have only seen a Thompson—or Tommy gun—in old gangster movies. It's not something you want to go up against in a gunfight. It's a bitch of a gun, but it's also a bitch of a gun to shoot.

"Yes, apparently," said Winkel.

"Well, I sure hope they don't know how to use the damn thing," I said. "Who's in charge out there, anyway?"

"No one, at the moment," said Winkel. "The governor doesn't know what to do, and we haven't been able to reach the local district attorney, who's in charge of the police on Ponape. The magistrate is off island and their police chief, Kim Yee, has gone back to Honolulu, so Jacob Akapita is heading up the police department on his own."

"So the Ponape cops have got no weapons, no vehicles, and no leadership," I said.

"That's right," said Winkel. "They've asked for our help. You were a police officer, Bryan. What do you think we should do?"

I paused and thought about it for a moment, running various scenarios and potential outcomes through my head the way I used to do back when I was a street cop. Based on that quick assessment, only one solution seemed appropriate to me.

"The way I see it, these guys have a problem," I began. "They're on an island in the middle of nowhere—it's not like they can cross the border to Mexico. It takes a ship or a plane to get anywhere around here. Even if they managed to take a small boat or a canoe to the next island, they know the folks there would recognize them and call us, and they'd be right back where they started. Everybody knows everybody around here, so there's no place for them to go. That means they're likely to be looking for air transportation off the island, and there are only two ways they can get it—either by taking hostages and bargaining with us, or by hijacking an Air Mike jet."

"Do you really think they'd try that?" Dan asked, sounding a little skeptical.

"Well, they don't seem to have any problem with using force to get what they want," I replied.

"That's true," Winkel said, looking even more concerned than he had before. "Resio, when does the next Air Mike flight stop on Ponape?"

"Um, this morning at about eleven, I think," said Resio.

"Should we cancel the flight? Have Air Mike pass the island?" Winkel asked, looking at me.

"I don't think that's a good idea. It would inconvenience a lot of people, and it would send a message that the police are worried, which doesn't look too good," I said. "Besides, it won't help us catch these guys, and the longer they have to wait to try to get off the island, the more desperate they're likely to get."

"Then what exactly are you proposing we do?" Dan asked me.

"Get out there and take care of things," I replied. Turning to Winkel, I asked, "Sir, is there any way I might be able to get a plane out to Ponape within the next couple of hours?"

"It's possible, I suppose," Winkel said, scratching his chin. "I've been talking with Admiral DeMars on Guam, and he says he'll give us any support we want."

"Great. So I could get a lift on a military plane?"

"Yes, I think so," Winkel said. "But only from the base on Guam to Ponape. We'd still need to find you a ride from here to Guam."

"I can probably get you a charter to Guam," Resio offered.

"OK, then," I said. "If I can get out there with some equipment—and if I can get a hold of Bill Stinnett on Truk—I think we ought to be able to prevent a hijacking."

"Just the two of you?" asked Dan. "What about taking along some of the Capitol Hill police?"

"Well you know, I'd really rather keep it small and stick to stateside law enforcement people who know how to work the way I work. If we're going to pull this off, I won't have time to do a whole lot of coordinating," I explained. "But I think I will go ahead and call Jim Grizzard and see if I can get him to go with us. He's an ex-cop, too, so he can back Bill and me up if we need it. He's also a lawyer, so he can talk all the politicians to death and keep 'em out of our hair."

The Hi Com smiled a little bit at that, although he was looking pretty wan and shaky by this time.

"Well, what do you think?" I asked him.

"Let's do it," said Winkel. "Gene, see if you can get through to Wayne Kirby on Guam."

Gene got Wayne, the new special agent in charge of the

Naval Investigative Service office, on the phone. Winkel spoke to him first and told him our plan.

"Have you got an aircraft available that can get our men from Guam to Ponape?" he asked, shouting to be heard over the squawky phone line. "The Air Force has a what? Oh, a weather plane? We'll take it. Thanks, Wayne. Look, I'm going to put Bryan on the phone now. He can tell you what kind of equipment he's going to need."

Winkel passed the phone to me, and I gave Wayne my wish list. Then I called Bill Stinnett, who was the police chief on Truk now that Kimo Panolo had gone back to Honolulu, and asked him to get on the Air Mike flight to Ponape that morning.

Just as I was ringing off, Nueves, the Winkel's maid, came around with a silver carafe of coffee. I took a cup and dialed Jim's number. Jim was groggy but lucid and said he'd be ready to go whenever I got there to pick him up.

I put the receiver down and walked across the room. A wide bank of windows overlooked the lagoon, but it was still too dark to see anything outside. All I could see was the reflection of the scene in the room behind me. Winkel was on the com line, with Gene Stevens beside him, working the equipment. Resio was on the phone, looking worried. Dan was poring over a stack of papers.

"I found a plane," Resio finally announced, still on the phone. "The pilot said he can meet you at the airport in an hour and take you to Guam."

"Great, Resio," I said. "Tell him I'll be there."

I turned to the Hi Com and said, "OK, everything's set. I'm going to go home to get my gear, then I'll pick up Jim and we'll head for the airport."

"Thanks for doing this, Bryan," said the Hi Com. "We'll stay by the phone. Please call as soon as you have any news to report."

"Will do."

I raced back to the house and changed into a dark shirt and pants so I wouldn't be an easy target, then threw some extra clothes in a duffel bag, along with my handgun and some ammo. It was "saddle up" time and I felt alive—more than I had for a long time. This was what I lived for and what I did best. I had all my gear together in under ten minutes and was at Jim's front door in thirty.

"Good morning," I said to Jim as he sort of staggered down the driveway and into the car. "Here's some coffee. And Nueves made us some sandwiches and stuff."

Jim grunted and took the thermos of coffee and the paper bag I held out. We rode in silence out to the airport.

II

Jim was almost awake by the time we reached the airport. Between the strong coffee and the bumpy ride, it would've been impossible for anyone to sleep, even Jim.

We took the charter to Guam and landed there at about 5 AM. Representatives from Guam P.D., DEA, and NIS were all there waiting for us.

None of them had jurisdiction out on the islands so they weren't able to physically do anything about the situation on Ponape themselves, but they were eager to help us out. They had all the equipment I had asked for and then some.

We packed up the gear and they raced us over to Andersen Air Force Base at the north end of Guam, where the weather plane was waiting to take us to Ponape. It was a big four-engine turboprop used to track storms and conduct atmospheric experiments.

Jim and I soon learned that the rules on Air Force planes were a lot different from what we expected.

"Hold on there just a minute," the pilot said, heading us off at the pass as we headed up the back ramp of the plane with our gear. "Is all that stuff unloaded?"

"What?" I said. "I don't know. We just got it. I haven't had a chance to check any of it out yet."

"Well then, do it now," he said. "You can spread it out on the ground right over there."

Jim and I exchanged a look. "We don't have time for that now," I said. "Didn't they tell you this is an urgent mission?"

"Yeah, and you're slowing it down by arguing with me. No weapons come on board this plane unless they've been thoroughly inspected."

"We better do what he says, Bryan," said Jim. "He's got the keys."

"Shit," I muttered under my breath.

OK, it was his airplane so we did it his way, even if it was costing us precious time that we didn't have. We spread our gear out on the ground to the right of the plane and checked through it, piece by piece, while the pilot watched over our shoulders.

"All clear," I said a few minutes later. "How 'bout you, Jim?"

"Same here."

"Satisfied?" I asked the pilot.

"It's regulation, you know," he replied.

"You're right, Captain. My mistake," I said. It was.

We packed the gear back up, followed him onto the plane, and finally took off.

The plane made a horrible racket, like having your head stuck in a diesel engine. *Arrrrrrrrrrrrrrbhhhhhhhhhhhhhhhhhhh-hhhh*—all the way to Ponape.

The trip took about four hours, and by the time we got on final approach to Ponape we still didn't have the slightest idea where the bad guys were. We had no communications equipment of our own to allow us to contact Ponape or Saipan, but we'd received some relayed messages via the military on the plane's radio letting us know that there still had been no sign of them at the airport or anywhere else.

One of our concerns was that the airport was surrounded by

heavy jungle growth, making it easy for someone to hide and ambush the plane once it got past the part of the airstrip that hung out into the lagoon.

"Better warn the pilot," Jim shouted over the roar of the engines.

I nodded and headed to the cockpit, where the captain was busy preparing the plane for landing.

"Look, they may be waiting for us in the jungle along the perimeter of the airstrip, so here's the deal," I shouted. "If we're taking ground fire when we land, you've gotta try and touch down as far down the runway as you can, and as quickly as you can, and then feather it way back. That way Jim and I can just roll out the ramp in the rear and you won't even have to come to a complete stop—you can just keep going."

Now this sounded reasonable to me—a former grunt. But there's a difference between the Marine Corps and the Air Force, which is much more businesslike. I should've known what the captain's response would be.

"Forget it. If we're catching ground fire we're not landing," he yelled back at me.

"What?"

"You heard me."

"No. Wait a minute. What did we come here for, anyway? There are people's lives at stake."

"There's this aircraft and my crew at stake, too, and I'm the aircraft commander. I say if we're taking ground fire we're not landing."

I finally realized that even though I was in combat mode, to him I was just some civilian with enough pull to get a free ride on his plane. It was no use arguing with him, so I went back to the cabin and took a seat next to Jim.

Fortunately, we didn't take any ground fire.

III

We landed at the airport about half an hour before the Air Mike flight was due in. Jacob Akapita was there by himself to meet us. He pulled up to the Air Force plane in a rental car, since the police jeeps had both been taken.

"Hi, Jacob," I said as I came down the back ramp lugging the gun bag with all our gear inside. "Where is everybody?"

"Hi, Bryan. Hi, Jim. I'm glad you could come," said Jacob, taking the bag from me and loading it into the trunk of the car. "Captain Felix is with the rest of the detectives at the station. They think they may know where the prisoners have gone. Somebody called in and said they've gone out toward Uh."

"How reliable is the tip?" I asked.

"We aren't sure yet," said Jacob.

"Which means we better be ready here just in case," I said.

"Yes, I think so. All of them may not be going to Uh. Just some of them," said Jacob.

"OK then, we're all set. Thanks, Captain," I yelled to the pilot. He waved and nodded from the cockpit, glad to be rid of us, I'm sure.

We piled into the car, drove to the main airport building, and went inside. The usual crowds were waiting there to greet the Air Mike plane, but there was a tense feeling to the place—not the relaxed atmosphere that's the norm on Ponape. We talked to a couple of officers who were on regular duty at the airport, but neither of them had seen anything suspicious all morning.

"Hey, Jim, look who's here," I said, as the governor strode into the terminal. "Can you go find out what's going on with him? As far as I know, no one's been able to reach him since he called the Hi Com for help last night."

Jim nodded and ran over to the governor. I watched as they talked for a couple of minutes, and then the governor went and got in line at the ticket counter.

Jim trotted back, panting a little, and said, "He's going to Guam."

"He's what?"

"I know, I couldn't believe it either," said Jim. "He said he wishes he could stay and help us, but he's got a meeting on Guam."

"Well, is the district attorney available yet?" I said.

"No. Mr. Atlee won't open his door. He's afraid the escaped prisoners are coming to get him, to take him hostage," said Jacob.

"You can't be serious," I said. "He's the chief law enforcement officer on island. And with the governor leaving—"

"No, it's true. He told us to go away and leave him alone," said Jacob.

"Well, fuck him," I said. "Let's go get the gear out and load it up."

We went back to the car, took the gun bag out of the trunk, and opened it up. Jacob's eyes lit up a little. He seemed both encouraged and a little stunned by all the weaponry.

"I brought the tear gas setup in case they end up barricaded someplace with a hostage, and the sniper rifle in case we get into some sort of a standoff," I said.

"Can you use that thing?" Jim asked, nodding to the sniper rifle.

"Was I a Marine?" I replied, grinning.

Jim took a shotgun, I took an M16, then we each donned a vest, loaded up, and waited. Pretty soon, the Air Mike jet made its first pass like it always did to chase the dogs and pigs off the runway. Then it curved back around toward Sokehs Rock and touched down.

So far so good. No action whatsoever. We kept a close eye on the bush line down on the far end of the runway, but it was clear.

The jet taxied up to the terminal, the stair ramp came down, and Bill Stinnett got off, carrying a long cardboard box with a shotgun and a semiautomatic AR-15 rifle inside.

"Any sign of these guys yet?" he asked us, scanning the scene.

"Nope. Nothing's happened here," I said. "But let's stick around till the plane takes off just to be sure."

We waited until after the Air Mike flight took off without incident, then got into Jacob's rental car and drove to the police station. There was hardly anyone there. The old jailer who had been overpowered by the prisoners was sitting off in one corner of the station looking miserable. A young lieutenant was sitting at the front desk.

He rattled something off to Jacob in Ponapean, and Jacob rattled something back. Then he turned back to us and said, "They caught one of them in Kolonia, hiding at his mother's house. And somebody on the CB just confirmed the tip we got that four of them are on their way to Uh. Captain Felix and the other detectives left about five minutes ago to go after them."

"They what?" Bill said sharply. "I thought they didn't have any weapons."

The lieutenant jumped in and said, "Some of them have their .22s, and Captain Felix has a .38 that he had at home."

"He's not supposed to take that home," Jacob said, scowling.

"Well, he did," said the lieutenant. "Maybe it's a good thing."

"Do you think we can catch up to them with some weapons?" Bill asked.

"Maybe," said Jacob. "We can try."

"Great," I said. "Jim, why don't you stay here and see if you can get in touch with the D.A. while we go after these guys."

"Will do," Jim replied.

"What about radios?" Bill asked Jacob. "Do you have any that work?"

"One, but it won't work from this far."

We took it with us anyway, jumped back in the rental car, and started hauling ass out of town toward the village of Uh with the lieutenant, Jonathon, driving. While we rode, we listened in on the radio, but Jacob was right—the only transmissions we could pick up from this far away were broken and garbled.

We pounded down the slimy green and brown tube of jungle road, sluing wildly as Jonathon fought his way through muddy potholes the size of bomb craters. *Bam!*—we'd bottom out, and then *slap, slap, slap*—the dense vegetation would beat along the side of the car whenever it slid too far to the right or left of the road.

Then, just barely audible over the noise of the car, we heard the sound of gunfire off in the distance. *Crack. Crack. Crack, crack, crack, crack. Crack. Bang. Bang. Crack.*

We really hauled ass after that. Finally, in fractured glimpses through the mud-smeared windshield, I spotted the stolen police jeep and a faded red pickup truck just ahead of us. Both vehicles were stopped off the road, in a small jungle clearing.

When we got to the scene, Martin Felix had his .38 in hand, and a couple of the other policemen were holding .22 rifles. There was one body lying on the ground, face down, and lots of blood. Two prisoners were standing side-by-side, handcuffed to each other, and another was lying in the back of the red pickup truck with his hands cuffed behind him. The stolen police jeep was planted nose-first into a coconut tree, and the stolen police weapons were strewn about on the ground.

"What happened?" I asked Captain Felix.

He just kind of turned away, looking pretty choked up, and the rest of the policemen were serious and subdued.

One of the younger police officers finally started explaining. "We caught up to them, and Santiago—him," he said, pointing to the man who was lying on the ground in a pool of blood, "he turned around and started shooting at us. He shot

at us twice, so we all started shooting, and they crashed the
jeep into that coconut tree. And when we got over here, two of
them were standing with their hands up and two of them were
on the ground. The guy in the truck is shot, and Santiago's
dead, I think."

Santiago lay still on the ground, arms akimbo in that awk-
wardness of death, a .38 near his right hand. I bent over to
check him for a pulse just to be sure.

"Is he dead?" the officer asked me a little hesitantly.

"Yeah, he's very dead," I replied. "Why? Did you know him?"

"He's my cousin," said the officer.

"I'm sorry," I told him. "That's really rough."

"Yeah, but he shouldn't have done it. He shouldn't have
shot at us. We had to shoot back," the officer said solemnly.

"We told them not to shoot," an older officer said emphatically. "Santiago, he saw us coming and he saw we had guns. We
held up the rifles, and we let him know, 'don't shoot.' And he
started shooting. There wasn't anything else we could do. We
had to shoot him back."

"Yes, you did. You guys did a great job," I told him. "You
really handled yourselves well today."

"Yes," the officer agreed, but he didn't look too happy
about it.

IV

Bill, Jacob, and I took the two uninjured prisoners back to
the station in the rental car, while Captain Felix and his men
took Santiago and the wounded prisoner, Frankie, to the hospital in the red pickup.

Jim was waiting for us back at the station, glad to see us
with the recaptured prisoners but disgusted by his own lack
of success. He'd spent more than an hour outside the D.A.'s
house with no luck. The house was buttoned up tight, storm
flaps down, and even silver-tongued Jim hadn't been able to

talk Atlee into answering his door.

"I'm going back over there," he said. "Maybe I can get through to him now that most of these guys have been caught."

After calling to let the Hi Com know that everything was pretty much under control, Bill and I headed over to the hospital to interrogate Frankie. His wounds were relatively minor—he had been shot in the arm and leg with a .22—so we were able to talk to him as soon as the doctor finished dressing them.

Unfortunately, Frankie wasn't saying much that we didn't already know. We were still trying to get something out of him when one of the nurses came in and asked, "Are you from TT headquarters?"

"Yes," I said.

"Dr. Owen wants to talk to one of you."

"I'll go see what he wants," I told Bill.

I hunted around the hospital, and pretty soon I found Shep Owen, an American doctor in his early forties who had been on island for several years. I had met Shep briefly on my first trip to Ponape when I toured the hospital.

"We've got a problem here. I'm going to have to release the body," he told me.

"You mean the dead prisoner? Santiago?" I asked.

"No, not him. The deejay," he said.

"You can't. We've gotta have an autopsy."

"I can't help it," said Shep. "The family's starting to gather out front and they're demanding the body. They're going to raid the hospital and take it if we don't give it to them."

"What?"

"They're Kapingi. It's their custom. They have to bury their dead within twenty-four hours. And they have all these rituals to perform first."

"Geez, what's the hurry?" I asked.

"You ever smell a body in this kind of heat and humidity after twenty-four hours?" said Shep.

"I see your point," I said, remembering grimly. "Well, can you go ahead and do the autopsy now if I hold them off?"

"I can't do the autopsy until I've got a court order through the D.A.," Shep said, shaking his head.

"Then I'll get the order from the D.A. and we'll get this rolling right away."

"OK, but you better get some policemen out here," said Shep.

I found a phone and called the police station to explain to Jacob what was going on.

"You know, if they take the body before we do the autopsy, we won't have any evidence," I said. "Can you get me that court order?"

"The D.A. has to get the order."

"Well, can't you get him to write up the application?"

"Jim says he still won't answer his door."

"What? Why not?" I asked.

"Because we haven't caught the last guy yet," Jacob said.

"Oh, for chrissake!" I said. "Look, tell Jim to keep trying. We really need that order. And can you send a couple of men over here to help me keep the family at bay?"

"I'll try, but most of them are out looking for the last guy. The D.A. says we have to find him *now*, and we have to do what he says."

"OK, Jacob, I understand. Just do whatever you can," I said.

I hung up and went back to the emergency room, where Bill was still grilling Frankie. "You aren't gonna believe this, Bill," I said. I told him what was going on.

"What are you gonna do?" he asked.

"I don't know. We haven't got enough policemen to hold off that crowd. Sooner or later, the family's gonna come and take the body. Maybe I can go talk to them and try to stall them."

"Can't hurt to try," said Bill.

I went outside and tried to talk to the family, but very few of them spoke English. They were wailing and weeping, not angry or mobbish, as I had feared, but they were also very determined. And these were Kapingis—Polynesians—who are very large people. It would be pretty difficult to stop them once they decided to come take the body.

"We must bury him," said one of the older men.

"We're doing what we can. Just give us a couple of hours, OK?" I said.

"We must bury him," the man repeated.

"I understand. But we need two more hours. Only two," I said, holding up two fingers.

He didn't agree, but he didn't say "screw you" either, so I figured maybe I had bought us a little more time.

I went back into the hospital and found Shep Owen.

"How 'bout if you just do the autopsy without waiting for the court order," I said.

"No way. I could lose my license," he said.

"All right. What if I do the autopsy and you just sort of guide me?" I said.

Shep grinned. "Yeah, I could do that," he said.

I went and got Bill, and we followed Shep back to the morgue where they had the poor deejay, Linson Bahingai, laid out on a slab.

"So where's he shot?" Bill asked, looking down at him. "I thought they shot him in the head."

"Look closer," said Shep.

Bill and I bent and looked again.

"Do you see it?" Shep asked.

"Well, he's sort of got a black eye," said Bill.

"That's it," said Shep. "The bullet entered the head through the right tear duct. Instead of exploding the eye, it traveled up just between the eyeball and the bone orbit."

"Is there an exit wound?" I asked.

"Nope," said Shep. "Feel the back of his head."

Kind of gingerly, I started feeling around the back of his

head, at about the same level as his eye.

"No, it's up a little bit higher," said Shep.

I felt higher, and there was a big lump where the skull was bulging out. "So do we have to use a saw or something to get the bullet out?" I asked Shep.

"Well, I don't know. It feels like the skull's fractured enough that you probably can do it with just a scalpel and some forceps," he said, feeling around the skull. "Here." He pushed a rolling tray with some medical equipment and a pair of gloves on it toward me and stepped back.

"OK, well, what do you suggest?" I asked, pulling on the surgical gloves.

"Just cut a cross over the top of the wound and that'll give you a start on it," he said.

I took a medium-sized scalpel from the tray and cut a cross about two inches by two inches over the bulge. I moved the scalp back to reveal the skull, which was shattered. Using a large pair of forceps, I pulled out a chunk of skull, set it aside on the autopsy table, and pulled out another piece, and another, until there was room to feel around inside for the bullet. I found it and pulled it out.

"Have you got any evidence bags, Bill?" I asked.

"You betcha," he said, pulling a baggie out of his pocket and opening it up for me.

"OK, there you go," I said, dropping the bullet in. "You got the time?"

Bill wrote down the time, date, location, and witnesses on the outside of the baggie with a felt-tip marker and sealed it shut.

"Now what do I do?" I asked.

"Just suture him back up," said Shep. "I'll go get a needle for you."

He went to a row of cupboards along the back wall of the morgue and brought back a surgical needle and thread.

"Am I going to have to testify about all this?" he asked, one eye closed as he threaded the needle.

"Probably not, since we were both here as witnesses, but I should get some data from you just in case," said Bill.

Shep handed me the needle and left me on my own to do the suturing while he answered Bill's questions.

I tried to stuff all the skull fragments back in, but there was one large chunk that wouldn't fit. I didn't know what to do with it. Then I noticed that there was a garbage disposal in the sink pan at the head of the autopsy table. I tossed the chunk into it, turned on the water, and kicked the switch.

Rrrrrrr! The disposal made a horrible gagging, clattering sound, then died.

"What did you do?" Shep asked, running over to the table.

"Well, uh, I had this extra bone and I didn't know what to do with it," I said. "I figured an operating room garbage disposal would be designed to handle stuff like that."

"Oh geez, not skull bones," said Shep, peering into the disposal.

"Sorry, doc," I said.

A nurse poked her head in the door and said, "Doctor, the family's coming."

"Tell them no, we're not ready," said Shep.

"I did. They're coming anyway," she said.

We could hear them down the hall, moaning and wailing.

"You two get out there and stop them. I'll suture him up," Shep said to Bill and me.

"OK. Thanks, Shep," I said.

Bill and I did what we could to keep the family from busting into the morgue, but they were getting restless, and we knew we wouldn't be able to hold them much longer.

Fortunately, Shep was a fast worker. He emerged less than five minutes later wearing a calm, sympathetic smile that was betrayed only by the tiny beads of sweat on his upper lip.

"Please come in," he said, putting an arm around the tall, sturdy woman I took to be Linson's mother. "I'm so sorry to keep you waiting."

Eyeing us angrily, the rest of the family pushed past us and into the morgue. Bill and I heaved a mutual sigh of relief and headed back to the police station. Exhausted, we dropped off the evidence and drove straight on to the Cliff Rainbow.

CHAPTER 10

Runaway Truk

As a result of the Ponape jailbreak, the Hi Com gained a new appreciation for how vulnerable the TT government was while Micronesia was transitioning from a U.S. trusteeship to independent island nations. He also gained a new appreciation for me and appointed me director of the Trust Territory Bureau of Investigation soon after. As part of my new position, I took over the TT's internal audit and security functions and all the police training programs throughout Micronesia, and I was in charge of the Capitol Hill police force on Saipan to boot. I was given a better office and better pay—and Susan and I even got moved to a nicer house right on Capitol Hill.

In the months since then I'd been traveling even more than usual, running police training programs from island to island. I had recently returned to Saipan after a stint on Palau. A deadly and destructive riot had erupted there in September, when some 800 local government workers—including almost all the police force—walked off the job. About 150 of the strikers had taken part in the disturbance, during which Palau President Haruo Remeliik's office was bombed and burned. Armed with more than thirty dynamite bombs, they threatened to blow up the congressional building as well if their demands weren't met. Given the difficulties of communications and travel in Micronesia, it was all over but the shouting by the time I was able to get there. But I did what I could to help calm things down, and by the time I left things had seemed to be at least somewhat under control.

After a week or so spent dealing with angry Palauans, I was reveling in a peaceful evening at home, just puttering around the house while Susan read a book in bed. But as usual, I had the police scanner on, keeping half an ear on the Capitol Hill Police radio traffic while I puttered.

It was around ten o'clock when I heard a sort of frantic, extra-heavily accented voice come on the radio.

"Command Post, this is Officer Landrik. I have an emergency."

My ears perked up—Henry Landrik was a young, relatively inexperienced police recruit from the Marshalls—and I went over to the scanner and turned up the volume.

"This is CP," the night sergeant, José Kamacho, responded. "Officer Landrick, what is the nature of your emergency?"

"There's a cow, CP. There's a cow on the headquarters lawn!" Officer Landrick replied, his voice rising as he spoke.

"Say again, Officer Landrick," Sergeant Kamacho replied.

"A cow!" Officer Landrick screamed into the radio. "It's here on the lawn."

"What is it doing?" Sergeant Kamacho asked.

"It's loose, CP. It's eating the grass. I'm going to shoot it!"

What a fiasco that would be, I thought. I could just see Henry trying to shoot the cow with his rusty old .38. Frankly, I was only somewhat worried for the cow. I figured it was a lot more likely that Henry would miss, the cow would go wild and stampede, and Henry would end up getting hurt.

I got on my radio and said, "Henry, this is Chief Vila. Do not shoot the cow. I repeat, do not shoot the cow. You copy?"

"I copy, Chief. But the cow's right here. It's loose. What should I do?"

"Stand by, Henry," I said. "Stand by, and do not shoot."

Then I got on the telephone and called Sergeant Kamacho.

"José, go out there and find out what's going on with Henry and this cow. See what you can do to take care of it," I said.

"OK, Chief," José replied.

The radio came alive again just then. "CP, CP, this is Officer Landrick. It's moving! I repeat, the cow is moving!"

"Get out there. And hurry, before he shoots something," I told José.

"Yes, sir," said Sergeant Kamacho.

A few minutes later, the phone rang.

"*Hafa?*" I answered.

"Sir, this is Sergeant Kamacho."

"Hi, José. What's happening out there? Is the cow a danger to anybody?"

"No, sir. It's just one of those big cows from somebody's farm down Back Road."

"What's Henry so upset about, then?" I asked.

"Well, you know, sir," José said. "He's from the Marshalls. He's never seen a real cow before."

I paused for a moment and smiled as I realized how ominous one of those great big Santa Gertrudis cows—which look a lot like oversized Brahma bulls—must seem to someone who's lived on a tiny, flat atoll all his life and has only seen cows in picture books.

"He's not still talking about shooting it, is he?" I asked.

"No, sir. I told him I'd get the owner of the cow to come up and get it," said José. "And I made him take the bullets out of his gun and put them in his pocket. I told him he can't reload his revolver until I've got the cow secured."

"Good thinking, Sergeant," I said. "If there are any more problems, you call me, OK?"

"Yes, sir."

***

I put the receiver down and headed for the kitchen to make myself a nightcap—Tanqueray gin with about three drops of vermouth over ice in a water glass.

I carried the martini into the bedroom and set it on the nightstand, undressed, and got into bed next to Susan. I had just started to reach for a book when the phone rang again.

"What now?" I groaned. Somewhat reluctantly, I picked up the phone.

"Hey, Bryan, it's Bill." Bill had joined the Trust Territory Bureau of Investigation three months earlier and had just moved to Saipan with new wife Kiki, who was from Truk.

"Hey, Bill. I sure am glad it's you. I thought it was José Kamacho calling with more problems," I said.

"Why? What's going on?" Bill asked. I told him about Henry and the cow.

"Oh, geez," Bill groaned. "Only in Micronesia."

"Yeah," I said. "But I think we've got everything under control now."

"Well, not everything," Bill said.

"Whaddya mean?" I asked.

"I just got a phone call from President Nakayama," said Bill. Tosiwo Nakayama was president of the fledgling Federated States of Micronesia and the former governor of Truk, where Bill had worked for him.

"At home?"

"Yeah."

"What did he want?" I asked.

"There's been another incident on Truk," Bill said slowly.

"You mean with the Kichy-Lokopichys?" I asked, referring to a powerful clan that had been terrorizing the tiny Trukese island of Wonei for some time now.

"Yeah," said Bill.

"What'd they do this time?"

"Nakayama says they beat a fourteen-year-old boy to death out in front of the Truk Trading Company a couple weeks ago," said Bill.

"They killed some little kid?"

"Yep," said Bill. "In broad daylight in front of God and everybody. There were about ten of them. They beat him with pipe wrenches and crowbars and a bunch of other stuff."

"What on earth for?"

"Well, from what the president said, it sounds like this kid and a couple of his friends from Dublon got into a fight with some kids from Wonei out in the parking lot. One of the Wonei kids ran down to the docks where the Kichy-Lokopichy men were loading up a boat, and they all went back to TTC in their pickup truck to join in the fight," said Bill. "By the time it was over, the fourteen-year-old was dead and his two friends had to be taken to the hospital."

"And nobody stepped in?"

"Nope."

"What about the cops?" I asked, getting up out of bed to pace around the room. "I mean, the station's only what, less than a mile away from TTC?"

"Yeah, well, apparently somebody called the police right away when it first started, but they didn't arrive for more than twenty minutes. By then, the kid's brains were spilled all over the parking lot, and the Kichy-Lokopichys had piled back into their pickup and headed down to the dock to their boat to go back to Wonei."

"Any witnesses?" I asked.

"Just everybody who happened to be out in front of TTC on a Saturday afternoon, which is half of Moen," said Bill. "But nobody's talking. They're all too afraid of these guys."

"Have the cops done anything?" I asked.

"Nope," said Bill. "They haven't even gotten arrest warrants, even though everyone knows who it was who did this. It's just like last summer all over again."

"I'm getting really sick of this crap," I said.

"Yeah, me too," said Bill.

"So, what do you want to do about it?" I asked.

"Whaddya think I want to do?" he said. "I wanna go out there and kick their asses."

"Yeah, that's what I figured," I said. "Me, too. I mean, somebody's gotta stand up to these guys."

"Well, Nakayama's all for it, so we won't have any jurisdictional problems there," said Bill.

"What about Hank Robertson? You talk to him yet?" I asked. Hank was the director of the FSM's Department of Public Safety, which was based on Ponape.

"No, I haven't been able to get a call through to Ponape," said Bill. "But I'm sure he'll go for it."

"How many men does he have that he can bring with him?" I asked.

"Only two, I think," said Bill. "The DPS is still a pretty small shop. But I know there are a few good men on the Truk police force I can recruit to help us out. They can't all be too chicken to help us take on these assholes."

"Let's hope not," I said. "Otherwise, we're talking five of us and more than twenty of them."

"Piece a cake," Bill said.

***

When I got off the phone, I noticed that Susan was looking at me from the bed, one eyebrow raised.

"Lefty's boys have run amok on Truk," I said, attempting to lighten the situation with a bad rhyme.

"Who?" she asked, unamused.

"The sons of one of the local magistrates."

"You're not going to leave again, are you?" she asked. "You only just got back."

"I don't know yet. Probably," I said.

Susan said nothing and turned back to her novel with a pained expression.

Tired of the cold shoulder treatment I got from her now whenever my job called me away, I took my martini into the living room, where I sat in the dark and thought over the problem on Truk.

The Kichy-Lokopichys lived on Wonei, one of the smaller— and tougher—islands in Truk lagoon. The head of the clan— Old Man Lefty, as everyone called him, because he'd blown off his right arm at the elbow while sawing into an old World War II artillery shell to get explosives for a fish bomb—was the chief magistrate of the island. From what we'd heard, the only reason he kept getting elected magistrate—which is sort of a combination of traditional chief, local judge, and head of the municipal police—was that the folks on Wonei were terrified of him and his family. They were Wonei's version of the James Boys.

Back in May, Old Lefty had caught four young men stealing a marijuana plant off the grave of his thirteen-year-old son, who had recently committed suicide. In retaliation, several members of the Kichy-Lokopichy family and the Wonei Municipal Police Department—many of whom were also Kichy-Lokopichys—had taken the young men prisoner and tortured them for four days. They had ripped their fingernails and toenails out with pliers, forced padlocks through their septums, tied them to trees, and beaten them horribly. When they finally were released, two of the four had had to be hospitalized for more than a week.

Bill was still the chief of the Truk State Police on Moen at the time and had done his best to go after the Kichy-Lokopichys and the Wonei police officers. But the four young men who had been tortured refused to press charges—they were too scared of these guys to say anything against them. So was everybody else on Wonei. So Bill had worked his ass off to get enough independent evidence to convince the judge, Ernie Gianotti, that there was probable cause to issue arrest warrants for these guys, even without the victims' testimony. He was successful, and in June, arrest warrants for attempted murder, aggravated assault, and conspiracy were issued for eight suspects. The only problem was, Bill couldn't get his officers to serve the warrants. Bill would send them out to Wonei again and again, but the arrest warrants were never served. He had even gone to Wonei several times himself and tried to serve the warrants, but each time somebody had tipped off the suspects in advance, and they'd either been off island or in hiding.

Bill was still fuming about not having been able to make any headway against the Kichy-Lokopichys and their cohorts.

Hank Robertson was pretty frustrated about the whole situation, too. Technically, the new FSM national government had jurisdiction over all felonies committed within its territory, so Hank and his small group of investigators had tried to help Bill make the arrests. Their luck hadn't been any better.

We couldn't let it slide any longer—not now that they had actually killed a child. It was time for action, and I was glad.

II

Two days later, Bill and I landed at the Truk airport. Hank Robertson was out on the runway to meet us with two of his FSM investigators, Freddy Marar and Lester Killion, both of whom were Ponapeans with stateside educations.

"Well, have you got it all taken care of yet, Hank?" I said in greeting, as Bill and I reached the bottom of the 727's rear stair ramp.

"Nah, we thought we'd wait and share the fun with y'all," Hank said in his dry Texas panhandle drawl.

"So, what do you guys want to do?" I asked. "You wanna go someplace where we can sit down and talk this over?"

"Well, I don't know about y'all, but it's been a long day and I could use a drink," Hank said.

"Yeah, fat chance on Truk—" I began.

"Actually, we might be in luck," Bill interrupted. "That Air Force Civic Action Team is still on island, I think, and they've got beer over at their headquarters."

"Sounds good to me," I said.

"Same here," Hank agreed. "Especially since Stinnett's buying."

Bill grinned a saccharine smile, pointedly raising his middle finger to flick at an imaginary bead of sweat on his forehead. Hank returned the compliment as we piled all our gear into his rental car and then headed out to the CAT team base, about eight miles north of town.

"Why don't you guys wait here a minute," Bill said as we pulled up in front of the CAT team headquarters and got out of the car. "I'll go see if I can find the officer in charge."

Bill walked into the building and came out about five minutes later with a beefy Air Force master sergeant, Stan Graves. There were introductions all around as we shook hands.

"We were hoping that maybe we could talk y'all out of a beer or two," Hank told Sergeant Graves.

"Sure, come on in," said the sergeant.

He showed us into the bar. It was gloriously cool inside. There were a few off-duty CAT team members playing darts at one end of the room, and a jukebox in the opposite corner played country western music.

The five of us settled around a table. Hank ordered San Miguels for everybody and offered to buy one for the master sergeant.

"Don't mind if I do," said Sergeant Graves, pulling up a seat. "So, what are you boys here for?"

"Well, I'm sure you've heard about what happened downtown a couple of weeks ago," I began.

"Yeah," he said, nodding. "You gonna do something about that?"

"'Bout time, don't you think?" Bill said.

"Absolutely," he said. "But I sure hope you people know what you're doing."

"Why?" Hank asked. "What do you know about these guys?"

"Only that they've got themselves some automatic weapons and a shitload of ammo," said Graves.

"How do you know?" Bill asked.

"Well, we'd heard rumors about it, like everybody else," said Graves. "Then, about three weeks ago, a few of us were out on a boat near Wonei doing some fishing and we heard automatic weapons fire."

"Are you sure about that?" Bill asked.

"I did three tours in Vietnam," the sergeant said by way of confirmation.

"Shit," I said. "Could you tell what they had? Or how many?

"Sounded kind of like M16s—definitely not AKs. Two, maybe three of them, on full rock and roll."

"What were they shooting at?" Bill asked.

"I don't know," said the sergeant. "But they must've cranked off five hundred rounds or more just while we were in earshot."

"So what'd y'all do?" Hank asked.

"What do you think we did? We hauled anchor and hauled ass," said Graves. "Look, I've gotta go get back to work. Good luck, gentlemen. You let us know if you need anything."

"How 'bout an M60?" I suggested, referring to a heavy machine gun.

"Sorry," he said. "We're fresh out."

"Yeah. Us, too," said Bill.

The master sergeant poured down the last of his beer, then got up and headed back out to his office. There was a long, uncomfortable silence at our table after he left.

"Well," Bill finally said. "That's not exactly good news."

"Yeah," I said. "There's nothing like being outnumbered and outgunned."

"I take it neither of you has anything automatic?" Hank said.

"Nope. Best we've got, besides our sidearms and shotguns, is a new AR-15," said Bill, referring to a semiautomatic civilian version of the M16 military rifle. "What about you?"

"'Bout the same, I'm afraid," said Hank.

"Well, I don't like being on the wrong end of a machine gun, but maybe if we get lucky these assholes will be so busy spraying the world on full auto that they won't hit a thing," I said, remembering a personal fuck-up from my first time out in Vietnam.

"Yeah, there's a thought," said Bill. "Besides, there's still nothing like a load of buckshot in the middle of the chest to slow somebody down."

We ordered another round or two of beer and spent the next hour arguing the relative merits of shotguns and various other weapons.

"So, where are we gonna stay?" I asked eventually, noticing that it was almost dark outside. "I'm sure these guys have heard by now that we're here, and I really don't want to be stuck all the way out at the Continental, just in case they decide to come over here and try something."

The Truk Continental was on a narrow neck of land pretty far out from town. If anything went down there, we'd be vulnerable to attack from both land and sea.

"Yeah, I agree. Why don't we stay at my in-laws' place?" Bill suggested. Kiki's family owned a small hotel and restaurant out near the airport.

"Do they have enough rooms there for all of us?" I asked.

"Yeah, I think so. And we'll be a lot more secure there than anyplace else," said Bill.

"Sounds good," I said.

We finished our beers, got into the rental car, and headed back into town, past the airport and on to the hotel, where we had a light dinner and an early night.

III

The next morning, Hank and his men headed out to the police station to interview the officers about where the suspects might be and to begin the tedious task of typing up arrest warrant affidavits to present to the judge, Ernie Gianotti. Bill and I figured we'd go talk to Gianotti and the attorney general to see if they had any new information for us, and to let them know that the affidavits were being prepared.

Wanting to present an appearance of strength and authority, we dressed in our camouflage uniforms and matching TT Police baseball caps and strapped on our gun belts. We rented a car from Bill's sister-in-law at the hotel, loaded a couple of shotguns into the trunk for backup, and headed on up the hill to the courthouse.

We were driving through a residential area, just about a quarter of a mile from the courthouse, when Bill shouted, "Hey, stop right here!"

I slammed on the brakes and Bill bailed out of the car and bolted down the side of one of the houses. I pulled over to the curb, took the keys out of the ignition and raced after him, but Bill was nowhere in sight. There was a loud ruckus coming from the house, so I figured he must've gone inside. I ran back to the car and grabbed one of the shotguns out of the trunk, then ran up to the house, shoved open the unlocked front door, and entered.

I was immediately confronted by a large Trukese man with curly black hair and a long, full mustache. He was about as tall as I am and muscular, wearing nothing but a towel wrapped around his waist.

"You can't come in here," he said in good English.

"Get the fuck out of my way," I said.

"Do you know who I am?" he asked.

"I don't care who you are. Get out of my way," I repeated.

"I'm Krispino Singkoro. *Senator* Krispino Singkoro," he said.

I recognized the name as one of the most powerful political leaders on Truk. He was also closely related to the Kichy-Lokopichys, but as far as I knew, he wasn't involved in any of the crimes they had committed.

I didn't say anything—I just jacked a round into the shotgun and looked him in the eyes. He took a half step backward and I started to walk past him, just as Bill came barging up from the back of the house with a cuffed suspect in tow.

"This is one of the guys who helped beat that kid to death," Bill told me. "I saw two of them from the car, but the other one got away."

"Did you check the rest of the house?" I asked.

"Not yet."

"Is there anyone else here?" I asked, turning to Singkoro.

"None of your business without a warrant," said Singkoro.

"Look, if we have to go take these assholes out by ourselves, somebody's likely to get hurt. Do you want that to happen?" said Bill.

"You can't do that. You don't have a warrant," said Singkoro.

"We don't need a fucking warrant," I said. "Now do we go get them or do you?"

"They're in the back room," Singkoro said angrily.

"How many?" Bill asked.

"Four," he said. "I'll go get them."

"We'll go with you," said Bill, shoving his handcuffed suspect in front of him and following Singkoro down the hall to the back of the house. I took up the rear, keeping the shotgun on my hip.

When we got to the back room, there was a rapid exchange in Trukese between Singkoro and the four startled young men we found there.

"Turn around, all of you, and put your hands on the wall," I shouted.

None of them seemed to understand, so Bill repeated the order in Trukese. Reluctantly, they obeyed. One by one, I handcuffed them. Then, without another word to Singkoro, we marched them out to the car.

"So, have you got any ideas about how we're gonna get all these guys to the jail?" I asked Bill, nodding to our five large suspects and then to the small rented sedan.

"Easy, watch," said Bill.

He put the two biggest suspects in the back first, with the smallest of the five squeezed in between them, and then had the last two sit on the laps of the largest two. With close to a thousand pounds in the back seat, the back of the car dragged on the ground most of the way to the police station.

At the police station, we ran into Katios Gallen and Masachiro Simina, two Trukese officers Bill knew we could count on. Most of the other officers—including their new Trukese chief—were doing their best to ignore us and fade into the woodwork. They didn't want any part of this.

"We got these guys at Krispino's house," said Bill. "Katios, do you know them?"

"Sure. I know all these guys," said Katios.

"Can you and Masachiro book them for us? We're supposed to be up at the courthouse right now talking to Judge Gianotti."

"OK, we can do that," Katios said. He and Masachiro uncuffed the suspects, then led them off to the booking room, and Bill and I headed back out to our car.

"Well, we got five of them. That's a start," I said.

"Yeah, but these are all just the little fish," Bill replied. "We've still got a long way to go."

* * *

As we were coming out of the courthouse after our meeting with Gianotti and the attorney general, Bill noticed two young men sitting in a car at the curb. The driver was gesturing furtively to him with exaggerated head motions.

"Hey, I know these two," Bill said out of the side of his mouth. "Why don't you play it cool and I'll go see what they want."

He headed over toward them while I kept walking up the road to our car, about fifty yards away. I sat in the car watching in the rear-view mirror as Bill stooped down to talk to the driver. After about a minute, he raised up and started walking casually toward me.

"These guys are related to the people we're looking for," he said as he slid into the passenger seat. "They say they want to talk with me but they don't want anyone to see them."

"So what do you want to do?" I asked.

"Drive up to the next corner and turn in by those bushes," he replied, pointing.

As I drove, he took off his uniform jacket and gun belt, reaching to put them on the back seat. In response to my raised eyebrow, he explained, "They're pretty goosey about being seen with me and I don't want them to bail. Maybe they'll calm down if I'm not in uniform."

A moment later, the car pulled alongside where we had parked out of sight behind the achote bushes. The driver gestured urgently for Bill to get in.

"Look," Bill said hurriedly as he got out of the car. "Just lay back and cover me. If I have a problem, I'll toss my cap out the window."

"Gotcha," I said.

I watched as he walked over to the other car and got into the back seat. No sooner had the door closed than the car sped off up the hill, spitting gravel and coral dust in its wake.

I waited a few moments, then followed after them, staying back so they wouldn't notice me. I could see Bill's silhouette alone in the back seat and he appeared to be sitting upright and still—as still as anyone can sit riding on a rutted Micronesian road—rather than talking or gesturing about. This was disconcerting, almost as though someone had a gun on him. Things were so edgy on Truk at the time that I was more than a little concerned, even though I could clearly see that he was still wearing his cap.

They continued inland from town for a few miles, down several back roads, and then turned off the road and into a banana plantation.

With considerable difficulty, I followed their tracks through the thick, wide banana leaves. Pretty soon, I saw the glint of the car through the vegetation and realized that they had stopped. I coasted to a stop, trying to be as quiet as possible, turned off the engine, and eased out of the car. I pulled the shotgun out of the trunk, flipped off the safety, softly jacked a round into the chamber, and made my way through the banana fronds.

When I reached a clearing of sorts, I stopped. Bill was standing there facing me, about thirty feet away. The two burly young men had their backs to me and were talking to Bill in loud, angry voices.

"You can't do this," they were saying. "This is not your business. If you don't stop, we'll *make* you stop."

Their voices got louder and louder as they spoke, repeating themselves over and over again, and from their body language I got the impression that they were a little drunk and trying to get up the nerve to jump Bill. It took several moments of watching them gesture before I could account for four empty hands. Either they didn't have a gun as I'd feared, or it was stuck in somebody's waistband.

Bill was doing a good job of looking unimpressed, and his

nonchalance seemed to piss them off even more. After a couple of minutes, he glanced over and saw me standing there with the shotgun. I caught just the briefest look of relief as it crossed his face and then was gone, replaced by a cocky, confident smirk.

"You aren't gonna stop anybody, do you understand?" he said, reaching over and stabbing a finger into one of the young men's chests. "These people are all going to jail. I don't care who they are."

He turned to the other young man and shoved him on the shoulder. The young man swung sideways a bit, and as he did so he must've caught sight of me, because his eyes suddenly got big as saucers. Seeing his expression, his companion turned to look, too.

"Hey, Bill," I said casually, shotgun at my hip. "You got a problem?"

"No problem," said Bill. "Any problem?" he asked, turning to the bigger of the two young men, who was standing nearest to him, and stabbing him again in the chest with a blunt finger.

"No," he mumbled, eyeing my shotgun angrily.

"Good," Bill said, spinning him around and tossing him up against the car with his hands on the hood. He reached around and grabbed the other young man by the collar of his shirt and pushed him up against the car, too. They both immediately started to turn back around.

"Put your hands back on the car," Bill said sternly.

I raised the shotgun a little, and they obeyed.

"So, have you morons got any weapons, or were you just planning on roughing me up the old-fashioned way?" Bill asked as he patted down the larger of the two.

Neither of them answered.

After he finished searching them both, Bill turned them around and said, "Now get in your car and get out of here, both of you. We're going to take care of business. And if we have any trouble from either of you or anybody else, we'll kick your asses first and then take you to jail. You understand?"

Again, neither of them said anything. They just got into the car and drove off down the narrow path through the banana fronds.

Bill turned to me and said, "Well, that was nice to see you standing there."

"Yeah, it looked like you were about to have some fun with those guys," I replied. "Do you think we should've taken them in?"

"Nah. I think it's better for them to go back and tell everyone that we're tough, and that we aren't afraid of them," said Bill. "Besides, we would've had to spend the rest of the day writing reports if we had taken them in."

Grinning, we walked back to the car and headed back to town.

"God, I'm thirsty. Let's stop here and get something to drink," I said, nodding to a store up ahead on our right.

"Sure," Bill agreed.

Every Micronesian island has dozens of these tiny little "mom and pop" places where they take one room of the house, put a few canned goods on the shelves and some soda in a cooler, and call it a store. We parked out front and went in.

"*Ran annim*," the young woman inside said demurely.

"*Ran annim*," I said. "May we have two Cokes, please?"

She nodded. "You're from TT?" she asked as she walked over to the cooler to get the Cokes. "You're here to get those guys from Wonei?"

"Yes. Why?" I asked.

"You need to be careful," the young woman said as she put two cans of Coke on the counter. "Those people, they're very bad. They'll kill you."

"Don't worry. We'll take care of them," Bill said. She didn't look convinced.

As we walked out I said, "Boy, these fuckers really have everybody scared, don't they?"

"Yeah. Everybody here and on Wonei is convinced that

they're too tough to mess with," said Bill. "This is about the fifth person today who's stopped me to tell me to be careful."

"Let's go talk with Hank," I said. "It's about time we made our move, and we need to figure out what to do."

* * *

We met up with Hank and his men at the police station, where they had just received the arrest warrants. Bill asked Katios and Masachiro and another Trukese officer, Conrad Fritz, to join us, and we all headed back to the hotel where we sat down around a picnic bench, drank iced tea, and worked out a plan.

"You know, we can't fuck around here any longer," I said. "The longer we wait, the better prepared they'll be for us."

"So you want to hit Wonei tomorrow?" Bill asked.

"Yeah," I said. "What time do we need to leave here to get to Wonei before sunup?"

"About 3 AM," Bill said. We all feigned groans.

Bill brought out a map, and over the next couple of hours we sketched out what little plan we had. I mean, we had no radios to communicate with each other, and no automatic weapons. About the only thing we had going for us was the element of surprise—we hoped.

Our main tactical problem was that Wonei is a tiny island— only about two miles in diameter. That might sound like a good thing at first, in the sense that it would make our search for these guys a lot easier. But the problem was, no matter where we landed, someone was likely to spot us and run off to sound the alarm. Even a few minutes warning would give them plenty of time to get ready for us. So what we decided to do was to split up our small force. Normally, it's the last thing you'd want to do, but then, nothing about this operation was normal. In this particular situation, splitting up seemed to be the only way to ensure surprise. Katios and I would land on the south side of the island near a small village and work our way north on the main cross-island path. Bill and Hank and the other men would land on the north side of the island, near the main village, and work their way south. By coming at them from both sides, we figured we had a much better chance of nailing their asses.

"Sounds like fun," Hank said, after we had gone over the plan for the third time.

"Let's do it," said Bill.

"You men ready?" I asked, looking at the Micronesian officers.

Dark, hard-looking men, they all nodded in assent, without a single shrug or sideways glance to suggest that any of them thought our hare-brained scheme was flaky. Briefly, I wondered if their faith in our leadership was warranted, or if our positive attitudes were going to get them all killed.

"Well, then, let's hit the rack. We need to get some rest if we're gonna be on those boats at three."

* * *

When I got to my room, which was just down the hall from the little hotel restaurant, I locked the door behind me for whatever good that might do. The doors and locks were both pretty flimsy and wouldn't be much of a hindrance to anyone determined to pay an uninvited visit in the middle of the night. So as an added precaution, I propped an empty Coke can on top of the doorknob, figuring that if anybody came in the door during the night, the can would fall and make enough of a racket to wake me up.

I needn't have bothered. Try as I might, sleep wouldn't come. I went over the plan again and again in my head, trying to anticipate every possible scenario and every possible response.

Usually, this is an exercise that helps me focus and prepare.

But on that night it had exactly the opposite effect. The more I thought things through, the more scared I got. I hadn't felt cold terror like that since Vietnam. I had forgotten what it was like to be really scared, sort of the way you forget what serious pain feels like once it's over.

It wasn't as if what we were about to do was any edgier than lots of the things I had done as a Marine or a street cop. I had been outgunned and outnumbered plenty of times before and won. But there was a hell of a lot more time to think about it this time, just like there sometimes had been in Vietnam, waiting blind and deaf in the dark rain for a night attack. And a lot more time to think about dying—or worse, failing.

We were going to be alone out there, in the middle of nowhere, without any communications equipment or backup. We'd be sitting ducks for these guys if they had gotten word we were coming and were waiting for us with automatic weapons. They could pick us off before we even made it off the boat. Or while we were walking along the jetty, stranded halfway between the boat and shore, without cover or an escape route.

I thought of a dozen different reasons to call off the mission, and seriously considered each one. I was still mulling them over when the alarm on my watch went off at ten to three, and I got up to take a quick shower, brush my teeth, and saddle up.

IV

By the time I finished putting on my gear I was calm and focused, all thoughts of scrubbing the mission forgotten. I was still very aware of the fact that this might be the day I didn't live to talk about, but the paralyzing fear that had kept me awake all night had turned at last to energizing, heart-pumping adrenaline.

In camouflage pants and T-shirt, jungle boots, baseball cap, bulletproof vest, and gun belt, I headed out of my room and down the hall. Bill, Hank, Lester, Conrad, and Masachiro were already geared up and waiting for the rest of us in the dark, empty hotel restaurant. Katios and Freddy were packing up the last of their gear and joined us soon after I arrived. Hauling the rifles and shotguns in a couple of duffel bags, we headed out of the hotel and down the beach to a nearby dock, where two Trukese officers waited for us with the police boats. With minimal talk, Katios, Masachiro, Freddy, and I got into one of the boats, and Bill, Hank, Conrad, and Lester got into the other. We eased out of the dock and into the lagoon at low throttle, making as little noise as possible in the hope of getting out of town before anybody noticed.

As soon as we were about a quarter of a mile off shore, we opened up the engines, cutting across the lagoon at top speed. There was only a partial moon that night, and the usual scattering of clouds, so there wasn't much light to see by. But that meant we'd be less visible as we approached Wonei, and that was good.

* * *

Just as the sky was beginning to lighten a bit, the island came into view up ahead of us. As we approached, I went over the plan one last time with Katios, Freddy, and Masachiro.

"All right. Katios and I are gonna get off on the jetty and head straight for land," I told Freddy and Masachiro. "You two watch out the back of the boat, and if you see us starting to take fire, you shoot at the fuckers to keep 'em down so we can get off that jetty. Once we're ashore, we'll take care of them. If we're hit, you haul ass until you're out of range. Don't come back unless I signal, like this," I said, raising my arm overhead and swinging my hand in several tight circles. "OK?"

"OK," they both replied.

"As soon as you see us get to shore, follow the other boat on around to the north end of the island," I said.

They both nodded.

I turned to Katios and said, "The second that boat touches the jetty, we've gotta move. I'll get off first, and I'll be moving fast. You wait until you see me get about halfway along the jetty, and then you jump off the boat and head after me. As soon as I get to land, I'll stop and cover you until you catch up with me, and then we'll take it from there. OK?"

"OK."

"You feel good with that shotgun?"

"You bet," said Katios, gripping it firmly in both hands.

"Good," I said. "Anybody comes at you with a weapon, blow 'em in half."

As we came closer to the jetty, it was apparent that it wasn't even a real jetty—just a bunch of rocks cemented together that ran out into the lagoon. It was only about a foot wide and about thirty yards long—even worse than the paddy dikes in Vietnam.

Idling in the last couple hundred yards so as not to wake the whole island, we reached Wonei just as the sun started to peek over the horizon. I jumped off the bow of the boat and onto the jetty and, without looking back, started walking quickly. Frankly, I would've preferred to run, but that jetty was awfully narrow. Besides, just in case anyone was watching, we had to show that we weren't worried—that we were confident and capable and unafraid.

It was a long walk, but nothing happened, other than the fact that I puckered about half the fabric of my pants up through my asshole, I was so tense. When I finally got to the end of the jetty, I crouched behind a coconut tree and covered Katios as he made his way ashore without incident. The boat was already backing up, and as soon as they saw Katios get to shore they took off after the other boat, which had been idling a little farther out.

"Which way do we go from here?" I asked Katios. The last thing I wanted to do was get lost on Wonei in the dim dawn light.

"We just follow this path along to the north," Katios said,

pointing. "It goes along pretty close to shore almost all the way to the other side of the island."

"OK. I'll lead. You stay about twenty feet behind me, OK? And don't just watch up ahead—you need to keep an eye out behind us, too," I said.

"Right," said Katios.

"And remember, if somebody starts firing at us, just shoot the fuck out of them," I added. "Don't stop and try to talk to them. Just shoot."

I checked one more time to make sure the safety was off the AR-15, and we started walking at a brisk pace up the path toward the other end of the island. It twisted and turned, sometimes heading up into the dense jungle that bordered the beach, and other times veering back down toward the water.

After about ten minutes, we emerged from a particularly thick patch of jungle as the path once again turned closer to the beach. Three men—each about fifteen yards from the other— were standing waist deep out in the water, crouched down. A woman, likewise crouched in the water, was farther down the beach.

"Are any of them the people we're looking for?" I asked, motioning toward the early morning waders.

Katios looked carefully at each of them and replied, "No."

"What are they doing out there, anyway? Are they fishing?" I asked.

Katios smirked and said, "No. They're shitting."

"Oh," I said, looking the other way.

We walked past them and then past a small group of thatched-roof, open-sided houses. A few villagers were up and stirring already. They eyed us curiously, and a little warily. By walking into the village without an invitation, we were violating one of the most basic Micronesian rules. Not to mention the fact that we were dressed in jungle utilities and fully armed, which had to be a little off-putting, even to the tough Trukese.

"*Ran annim*," said a middle-aged man sitting on the front porch of one of the houses. It was a gruff and serious greeting—with no smile of welcome. But it was obvious that he was impressed to a certain degree by our uniforms and weapons.

"*Ran annim*," Katios and I replied sternly, nodding to him as we walked past.

A couple of older men sitting on the front porch of the next house greeted us in similar fashion, but a young teenage male with them just glared at us.

I glanced back at Katios with a questioning look, then nodded toward the young man. Katios got my meaning, walked over, and barked a few questions to the young man in Trukese, holding his shotgun across his chest with both hands. The young man was intimidated, but trying hard not to show it. His responses to Katios were brief.

"He says it's not this village," said Katios. "None of the people we want live here."

"Do you believe him?" I asked Katios.

"Yes," he said. "I don't see any of them here."

"OK," I said. "Tell him I want everybody to stay in this village until noon today. Nobody goes out on the trail. Tell him I don't want us to shoot any of them by mistake."

I also didn't want any of them running on ahead to tell the Kichy-Lokopichys we were coming, but I didn't ask Katios to say that. No point in giving them ideas.

Katios turned and translated, and the young man nodded and went off to tell the others.

Katios and I continued on up the trail, walking briskly, but trying to watch everything at once. We passed dense taro patches, with their huge elephant-ear leaves, kili palms with fronds veeing directly out of the soil, and banana groves, all of which were still quiet and deserted at this early hour.

OK, I thought. *Any time now.* Since we hadn't met with any resistance on the beach, I figured it was more than likely that the Kichy-Lokopichys were waiting to ambush us around the next blind corner. Or the next.

But one turn after another, one clearing after another, nothing. I hadn't heard any sound of shots being fired from the other end of the island, where the rest of the team should have landed by now, either. It didn't make sense. Where were they?

Then, just as we came to a sharp turn to the right in the trail, two young men came bursting through the vegetation. My adrenaline pumping, I swung the AR-15 around and centered it on them. Behind me, I could hear Katios crouching and preparing to shoot. The two young men screeched to a halt and stood frozen solid on the trail, staring at us with wide eyes.

"*Ran annim*," I rumbled in an overly stern, deep voice.

"*Ran annim*," they both mumbled. They were barefoot and dressed in raggedy T-shirts and faded jeans, and it was obvious that they didn't have any weapons on them.

Katios came up quickly and started to interrogate them.

"Ask them where they're going," I told him.

He said something to them in Trukese, then turned to me and said, "They say they're going to the next village down. The one we just came from."

"Why?"

"To see their auntie," said Katios.

"Do they know the Kichy-Lokopichys? The ones we're looking for?" I asked.

Katios spoke to them again, and at greater length this time. One of them glanced away as he answered, and Katios reached over and grabbed him by the front of his shirt to get his full attention. The other young man started to step away a little bit, so I lowered the rifle just enough so he could look down the barrel of it, and he stopped dead in his tracks.

"Yes. They say some of them live in the next village north," said Katios.

"How far is that?"

Katios asked them. Both young men shrugged at first. Nobody in Micronesia knows exactly how far it is to anywhere. It's just where it is, where it has been all their lives.

Katios asked them again, more forcefully this time, and one of the young men responded.

"He says it's not far, maybe a two- or three-minute walk," said Katios.

"All right. Good," I said. "What do you want to do with these two?"

"I'll send them on down to their auntie," said Katios.

He spoke to them again in rapid Trukese. They both shook their heads, said something back to him, and looked to the north, like they wanted to go up the trail now instead. Katios didn't reply but instead spun one young man around till he was facing south and gave him a hard shove in the middle of the back. He motioned in the same direction with the shotgun to the other one. They both took off down the trail after that, walking earnestly.

We started back up the trail to the next village, through more dense jungle. After a few minutes it started to open up again, and we could see houses and a few people up ahead. I motioned to Katios to wait, planning to have him stay there while I went around through the jungle to the other side of the village so we could come at them from two angles. But Katios misunderstood my hand signal, and as soon as I started to head for the jungle, he proceeded to walk briskly right into the middle of the village. At that point, there was nothing I could do but follow after him.

There were maybe twenty-five or thirty people up and about, including the usual gaggle of kids running around, the youngest ones stark naked and barefoot. Unlike the first village, where the people had been wary but polite, these folks were giving us the stink-eye. Several of the men stood up inside their houses and stared at us angrily, and I figured this had to be the right place.

We continued walking, calmly and determinedly, as Katios looked right and left, searching for suspects he recognized, and I scanned for that first sign of an ambush—the little sound or clue that gives you a chance to strike first and win.

Finally, Katios spotted one of the young men we were looking for, ran over, and grabbed him by the arm. The young man took a half-assed spin kick at Katios, who knocked him flat on his back in response. Then he pulled him up by the back of his T-shirt and shoved him at me before he ran into one of the houses—an open-sided, thatched-roof structure with several people inside.

I quickly slapped handcuffs on my catch and started to drag him along beside me as I headed for the house Katios had disappeared into. I was about ten feet away when another young man came barreling around the corner with a machete, ready for battle. I couldn't butt-stroke him with the AR-15 because I only had my right hand free, so holding it by the pistol grip, I jammed the muzzle of the rifle into his solar plexus. Undaunted, he raised the machete menacingly. Looking him in the eyes, I calmly raised my eyebrows and started to squeeze the trigger. He dropped the machete, and I motioned to him to lie down on the ground.

Just then, four terrified-looking captives emerged from the house, followed by a shotgun-toting Katios.

"These are the guys we want," Katios said, scowling at each of them in turn.

"Are any more of them in this village?" I asked him, keeping my weapon handy and a wary eye on the crowd that had gathered around us.

Katios grabbed one of the prisoners by the upper arm and rattled off something in Trukese. The young man stared at him defiantly and said nothing. Big mistake. Katios jabbed him hard, stiff-fingered, in the gut. The young man fell puking in the dirt. Katios turned to the young man next to him and raised a threatening hand. The young man flinched and began talking, fast. The others nodded vociferously. Katios said something else to them, their eyes grew wide, and they continued to nod.

"No, there's nobody else we want in this village," Katios told me. "All the rest of them are in the main village or on Moen, and maybe some are on Guam."

"All right," I said. "Let's hook these guys up then so we can get them up the road to the main village. But keep an eye out just in case they're lying."

"They're not lying," Katios said confidently, making me wonder just what it was he had said to them.

We patted them down to make sure none of them were carrying any weapons, then cuffed them up by twos—one man's right hand to the other man's right hand—so there was no way in hell they could outrun us if they tried to escape.

"Nice work, Katios," I said, impressed.

Katios's expression remained serious as he nodded in response, but I could see a gleam of satisfaction in his eyes.

Leaving the villagers a little dumbfounded, we headed on up the trail toward the main village. With six guys in cuffs trailing along with us, there was no hope left of a surprise attack should we come upon any of the remaining suspects. I stayed up ahead with the AR-15, still keeping an eye out for an ambush, and Katios took up the rear with the shotgun, keeping the prisoners between us.

After about twenty-five minutes, we passed through another village. The people here seemed a little incredulous—and not at all displeased—when they saw who we had in handcuffs. They didn't smile, exactly, but they looked us in the eyes and said, "*Ran annim*," with the gravest respect as we walked by.

Not long after we left that village, we ran into Bill and Hank coming down the path.

"Howdy gentlemen," Hank said in greeting. "Looks like you've had yourselves a successful morning."

"That we have," I replied. "How 'bout you? Where are the rest of your men?"

"Back at the main village. We've got another six in custody there."

"You have any trouble?"

"Nope," said Bill. "We landed the boats, and everybody came stumbling out of their houses to see what was going on. Those guys were barely even awake by the time we had 'em cuffed up."

"Nice," I said, grinning. "So our men are all OK?"

"Not a scratch," said Bill.

"Who all did you get?"

"Well, we didn't get Aron and Innocente, if that's what you mean," Bill said, referring to two of the magistrate's sons. Innocente Lokopichy was wanted in connection with the kidnapping and torture case, while Aron Kichy, a Trukese state senator, was among the men who were wanted for the murder of the young boy. "Everybody says they're on Guam with Old Man Lefty."

"You find the automatic weapons?" I asked.

"Nothing," said Hank. "I don't doubt that they've got 'em, but we didn't find 'em."

"Neither did we," I said. "Hell, they could be anywhere."

"Well, at least we got most of these assholes, and it looks like we caught 'em with their pants down," said Hank. "Not a bad day's catch, if you ask me."

"Not bad at all," I agreed.

As we headed north to the main village, everybody was out and watching. No one said a word to us as we walked by, but they all looked a little awed, just like the people in the last village had.

We made our way down to the docks, where the Micronesian officers were waiting for us with the rest of the prisoners. Leaving the prisoners handcuffed, we divided them between the two boats, hopped in after them, and headed back to Moen.

* * *

By the time Bill and I returned to Saipan, all twenty-one suspects in the torture and murder cases—including Innocente Lokopichy and Aron Kichy, who were picked up on Guam—were arrested and arraigned. We eventually got convictions on the majority of them, although most of the sentences weren't much longer than ten or fifteen years, even for the assholes who killed that poor kid. But at least we finally did get them, and the folks on Wonei and Moen could rest a little easier now that they were in custody.

So could we.

CHAPTER 11

Lady Hi Com

Soon after I got back to Saipan from Truk, it was time to deal with Palau again. Tensions there were still elevated, and as news of the September riot and bombings spread Washington leaned on Dan High, who was now the acting Hi Com. (Ronald Reagan had been elected president in November of 1980, and as a presidential appointee—Jimmy Carter's presidential appointee—Adrian Winkel had been officially out of a job as soon as Reagan was inaugurated. Dan, who had high-level family connections to the Republican party, had been appointed to serve until Reagan selected a new high commissioner to oversee the Trust Territory government.)

"How can this have happened without you knowing it? Why didn't you do anything to stop it?" the suits in Washington asked him. Naturally, Dan rolled the same questions downhill to me.

"Well, let's see, Dan," I said, a little pissed that he was suddenly trying to cover his ass by laying a new responsibility on me in the middle of this mess. "I didn't have any way to get there because the airport was shut down—the FAA wouldn't let commercial flights land without fire equipment, and all the firemen were on strike along with the cops. Even if I *had* been able to get there sooner, I couldn't have given you or Washington any information because they blew up the communications station—and we still don't have any communications gear."

Stymied, Dan retorted, "Well, start thinking of a way to keep this from happening again." Six-foot-six of lanky Kansas lawyer, he stalked out of my office like an irritable giraffe.

* * *

Despite Dan's warning, I was caught a little off guard when, shortly thereafter, I found myself sitting next to him in business class on a 747 headed for Washington, D.C. He had given me just two hours notice to pack and prepare for a high-level meeting to discuss what to do about the situation in Palau. Thank God it was a long flight.

We got into Dulles at about 10 AM, feeling gritty and sticky after traveling for nearly twenty-four hours.

"The meeting's not till two," Dan told me as we checked in at the Key Bridge Marriott. "I don't know about you, but I'm gonna go up to my room and try to get some rest. Why don't you meet me downstairs at about one-thirty."

"Sounds good," I said, breathing a silent sigh of relief. I hadn't said anything to Dan, but quite frankly, I no longer owned anything even close to suitable business wear for a high-level government meeting. So while Dan took a nap, I grabbed a cab and crossed the bridge to Georgetown to do a bit of hasty shopping.

II

Dan and I took a cab from the Marriott to the Interior Department headquarters at 18th and C—a big old building with monumental architecture that took up two city blocks. We walked past the large bronze doors into the arched hallway, with its large black-and-white tiles checkerboarding off as far as the eye could see. At the near end of the hallway, we took an elevator up to the sixth floor, where we walked down another long, checkerboarded hallway with doors on either side.

One of the doors on the left side of the hallway was open,

and we could hear people talking inside.

"This must be us," Dan said.

I followed him in, trying not to look as nervous—or as tired—as I felt. The room was a pretty typical government conference room. The mahogany table was large, and there were at least a dozen and a half matching brown leather chairs around it. The carpeting was nondescript, but there were several fairly impressive western paintings on the walls. I didn't know it at the time, but they were probably real Frederick Remingtons, on loan from the General Services Administration.

We were a few minutes early. The afternoon session of the meeting, which had begun that morning without us, had not yet come to order, and the illustrious group was still milling about the room. There was a lot of brass—a Marine captain and lieutenant colonel, an Army general, and a Navy captain, all in full uniform—and a lot of suits. I admit, I was a little awed, especially by the brass (what former Marine corporal wouldn't be?), and really glad I had just spent more than two weeks' salary on some decent clothes.

"There's our new lady Hi Com," Dan said, nodding toward the only woman in the room. Short and rather stout, with curly gray hair and a turned-up nose, she looked a little like Mary Worth from the daily comics.

"Oh? Is that a done deal?" I asked. We had all heard rumors in recent weeks that a woman had been nominated for the position, but nothing had been confirmed yet, as far as I knew.

"Just about," said Dan. "C'mon, I'll introduce you."

Dan made a beeline to the far corner of the room, where the woman was chatting animatedly with a rather eccentrically dressed man.

"Well hello, Dan," she said, turning from her companion as we approached to smile warmly and hold out her hand. "It's so good to see you."

"Hi, Jan," Dan said, smiling his best politician smile and

taking her hand in his. "I'd like to introduce you to Bryan Vila, TTBI's chief of law enforcement and security. Bryan, this is Jan McCoy."

Jan looked me directly in the eyes and gave me a firm handshake. She had good command presence—more on a par with the brass in the room than the suits—and I liked her immediately.

"I'm glad to meet you, Bryan," she said.

"It's good to meet you, too, Jan," I replied.

"And this is Pedro Sanjuan, the new assistant secretary for Territorial and International Affairs," Jan said, indicating her rumpled companion.

I did my best to hide my surprise as we all exchanged greetings. I had been out of the country too long to know that the disheveled preppie look was now "in" in Washington.

"Well, I guess I better call the meeting back to order or we're never going to get through the afternoon agenda," Pedro said.

As soon as Pedro took his place at the head of the table, everyone else returned to their seats as well. Jan invited Dan and me to sit with her, near the head of the table just to Pedro's left.

Pedro began the meeting by briefly introducing Dan and me. Then, for the record, he rattled off the names, titles, and affiliations of the others present, as a young male clerk scribbled furiously.

"In light of the latest disruptions on Palau, our goal today is to find some way to bring U.S. assets to bear to protect life and property and maintain political stability in the Micronesian islands," Pedro continued after he finished reading the roster.

"This morning we discussed plans for dealing with riots and other forms of unrest. This afternoon, we need to turn our attention to an inventory of the resources we have available to support those plans. I suggest we go around the room, starting to my right, and see what we can come up with."

And for the next hour and a half or so, each of the meeting participants described the assets they and their organization had to offer in the event of a crisis. For example, the U.S. Marshals Service had a highly trained Special Operations Group that they could send out whenever violent unrest reared its ugly head. The military had transportation, and whatever weaponry that might be needed could be obtained either from Honolulu or the Marine garrison on Guam. The folks from the Department of the Interior went on at length about their ability to act as liaison between the Micronesian governments and the United States, while the State Department didn't have much to offer except anxious predictions about continued and increased conflict.

As the meeting droned on toward four o'clock in the afternoon, without so much as a word from Dan or me, their plan began to take shape. When there was a problem in Micronesia, whoever was in charge there would notify Washington immediately, setting in motion a chain of events that finally—with the approval of the Secretary of State and the Secretary of Defense and probably the National Security Council as well—would activate the U.S. Marshals' Special Operations Group. The group would then form up and fly to Honolulu, where they would board military aircraft and fly to wherever in Micronesia they were needed.

Maybe it was just the jet lag, but I was suddenly struck by the sheer ludicrousness of this plan. And before I could think better of it, I heard myself talking.

"What's your time frame from notification to arrival in Micronesia?"

Heads went together and notes were jotted for a few minutes. Finally, Pedro replied, "About four, maybe five days."

"So almost a week after we call for help, two dozen sweaty, exhausted guys who don't speak the language, don't know the customs, and don't recognize the players will show up in riot gear," I said, a little more sarcastically than I had intended. Dan looked at me sharply. *Damn*, I thought. *Can't you ever just keep your mouth shut, Vila?*

"All right then, Bryan, what do you suggest we do?" Pedro asked.

I paused and took a deep breath. Everyone at the table was looking at me and waiting for a response, including Jan, who was sitting right next to me and eyeing me intently. Feeling like the main course at a barbecue, I looked around the table for a moment, first at the military brass, then shifting to the Department of Justice folks.

"Well," I began. "I've been a Marine in Vietnam. I've also been a ghetto cop in L.A. And I know that if you're going to depend on force to handle a situation, you better be able to deliver it. Fast. Every time. And you better win."

I paused again, looking for a way to describe the problem of using force in the real world to the nonmilitary folks in the room.

"If we depend on something this complicated and fail, everyone will know that the U.S. really isn't capable of maintaining order if things fall apart," I explained. "The truth is, we're *not*, but right now everybody assumes we are."

"So we just throw up our hands and hope nothing happens again in Palau, or Ponape, or Turk?" one of the Marshals Service managers interrupted.

Looking down to avoid grinning over his slip, I replied, "No. We just keep acting like we can project power. We use street smarts. We send a couple of experienced people in to help keep the peace when there's a problem, and we give them decent communications gear and equipment so they *look* like they can take care of business. With a little luck, things'll hold together until the Micronesians are more stable internally."

"With a little *luck*?" said the same manager.

"There's always that in any combat situation," I said, glancing toward a Marine major with a chest full of ribbons. He stifled a grin. "Besides, most people in Micronesia really want peace and order; they're just having growing pains trying to integrate the old ways with the new ones. The appearance of a

U.S. presence gives everyone an excuse *not* to let things degenerate completely when there's a conflict."

There was a long silence after I stopped talking. Finally, Jan turned to Dan, who was seated to her right, and said none-too-quietly, "Now I see why you brought this kid."

Encouraged by Jan's comment, I glanced around the table and saw that several heads were nodding in agreement with me, although many of the suits continued to look fairly skeptical.

I expected a lengthy and perhaps heated debate to ensue. But instead, one of the bureaucrats from the State Department snapped his briefcase shut and announced, "Pedro, it's almost four-thirty, and I've got a carpool to catch."

"Me too," said another, as he prepared to leave as well.

"All right, then, let's wrap it up," Pedro said. "Interior will take the lead on drawing up a plan of action based on your suggestions, and we'll pass it around to all of you for signatures. Is that acceptable to everyone?"

There were nods of assent all around the table, more briefcases were stuffed and closed, and everybody but Jan, Dan, and I got up and left.

As the Washington elite trooped out of the room to catch their carpools, Jan turned to Dan High and asked, "Have you got anything planned for tonight, Dan?"

"Yeah, Jan, I do," Dan said apologetically.

"How about you, Bryan?" Jan asked. "Would you like to join me and a friend of mine for dinner a little later?"

"Sure, I'd love to," I said, a little surprised by the invitation.

"Good," Jan replied. "Where are you staying?"

"Over at the Key Bridge Marriott."

"I'll call and leave a message telling you where and when to meet us, as soon as I know myself. Will that be all right?" Jan asked.

"That'd be great, Jan," I said. "I'm looking forward to it."

The three of us rode down together in the elevator, then

parted at the street as Jan headed off on foot to meet her friend somewhere nearby, and Dan and I hailed a cab to take us back to our hotel.

III

Dan didn't talk much on the short ride to the Marriott, but I didn't get the impression that he was pissed at me for speaking up at the meeting. We were both just tired.

"So I'll see you in the morning then, around eight?" he said as we parted in the hallway at our hotel.

"Right," I agreed.

When I got to my room the message light was blinking. Jan had left a warm but businesslike message asking me to meet her and her friend at seven-thirty for dinner at Maison Blanche on F Street, close to the old Executive Office Building.

A couple hours later, as I stepped inside the restaurant, I was grateful all over again that I had had the time to buy some new clothes, even though they had maxed out my credit cards. The place was quietly elegant, with plush carpeting, baroque furnishings, and a gold rope discreetly clipped across the entrance.

I walked up to the maitre d', a tall, competent looking man in an expensive dark suit and tie, and said, "I'm here with Jan McCoy."

"Of course, sir," he replied, in a tone that made me feel like I might be somebody terribly important. He led me into the dimly lit restaurant, which was full of very well-dressed people who all appeared to feel they were terribly important, too, although in their cases it was probably true.

Jan was sitting at a corner table with a very attractive, honey-blond woman in her mid-forties. As I approached, Jan stood up to greet me.

"Oh Bryan, how nice of you to come," she said warmly, taking my hand. "I'm afraid you just missed Lyn Nofziger. I'm sure he would've liked to meet you."

Frantically racking my brain trying to remember who Lyn Nofziger was, I smiled and said how disappointed I was to have missed him. (Much later, I remembered that he was a Republican party bigwig and personal adviser to President Reagan whose name was in the paper on a regular basis.)

"And this is my dear friend Neal Peden," Jan continued.

Neal rose to greet me, holding out her hand, and said, "Hello, Bryan," in a thick but still understandable Mississippi accent. As we shook hands, I noticed that she had a firm grip and, like Jan, she looked me right in the eyes.

Jan indicated the chair beside her, between her and Neal, and the three of us sat down.

"Neal's the administrator of the RNC," Jan told me. Her tone indicated that this was an important position, so again I made an effort to act suitably impressed while I rapidly ran through my mental dictionary of acronyms, finally realizing that she must be referring to the Republican National Committee.

After giving us exactly the right amount of time to exchange greetings, the waiter came around to ask if I'd like a drink. Noting that neither Jan nor Neal were abstaining—Jan was drinking what appeared to be a double martini and Neal was sipping a glass of white wine—I ordered a dry martini with two olives.

"Well, that was quite a meeting today, wasn't it?" I said after the waiter left.

"Yes, it was," Jan agreed, smiling. "I thought you did very well. I was just telling Neal before you got here how impressed I was with the way you spoke up in there. And frankly, I think you're absolutely right."

I was both flattered and a little embarrassed by the compliment, and mumbled something that I hoped was suitably humble in response.

Perhaps sensing my discomfort, Neal changed the subject. "Well," she said, "it looks like Jan's going to get confirmed as high commissioner."

"Congratulations. That's wonderful news," I said, raising an imaginary glass in salute since my martini had yet to arrive.

"Yes, and it's about time, too," Neal said. "You know, they desperately tried to convince her that instead of heading off to the wilds of Micronesia, she should take over a nice cushy job in Washington as head of OPIC—"

"Not to be confused with OPEC," Jan interrupted with a smile.

"OPIC is the Overseas Private Investment Corporation," Neal explained for my benefit. "They thought it was a much more suitable position for a sweet little old lady like Jan—"

"Well, this 'little old lady' isn't ready to retire just yet," Jan said emphatically. "I've still got a bit of adventure left in me."

"You've definitely chosen the right place, then," I said. "Just living in Micronesia is an adventure in itself. It's unlike anything I've ever experienced before."

"And how long have you lived there now, Bryan?" Neal asked.

"Just a little over three years," I told her. "I originally signed on for two years, but I extended my contract last year for another two."

"You must like it, then," said Neal.

"Yes. Yes, I do," I replied thoughtfully. "What about you, Jan? Have you been out there yet?"

"No, I haven't had the opportunity," she said. "But I've visited a good deal of the rest of the world. More than a hundred cities in fifty-one different countries so far."

"Really?" I said. "Through your work?"

"No. During my retirements," said Jan.

"Your *retirements*?" I repeated.

"Yes," said Jan. "I'm just finishing up my fourth retirement now. And during each of my retirements, I've traveled—mostly by tramp steamer."

"Tramp steamer? Wow," I remarked, impressed. "Where all have you gone?"

Jan smiled, pleased by my genuine interest, and proudly rattled off a list that included all the major continents and just about every region of the world.

"Does your husband go with you on these expeditions, too?" I asked, remembering that Dan had mentioned that Jan had been married for nearly forty years now to the same man.

"No," Jan replied. "I'm afraid Bill isn't much of a traveler. Since our girls were grown, I've gone off on these things by myself, and he's usually stayed home in Oregon. We have thirty acres on the Umpqua River, and he just loves the place."

"Does that mean he won't be coming out to Micronesia with you?" I asked.

"Well, it's pretty hard to pry him away from home and the cabin and fishing for steelhead on the Umpqua. But I think he'll come at least part of the time," Jan said with a smile.

I returned her smile, silently appreciating the fact that this was a woman who was about fifty years ahead of her time.

IV

On December 7, 1981, forty years to the day after the Japanese bombed Pearl Harbor, Jan McCoy arrived on Saipan.

Having said, "Thanks, but no thanks," to a more private ride on a military jet, which was certainly her due as the incoming Hi Com, Jan flew into Saipan aboard the regular Air Mike flight from Guam. But if she had been hoping for a low-key arrival, she was out of luck. Just about everybody from TT headquarters was there to welcome her at the gate.

Being in charge of security for Jan's arrival, I was one of three or four officials—including Dan High, who was now the deputy high commissioner, and Kent Harvey, the new attorney general—waiting to meet her on the tarmac as she came down the gangway, in full view of the crowd at the gate. Jan shook hands with each of them heartily and said how glad she was to be there as each placed a lei around her neck in greeting. Then she turned to me with a warm smile and said, "Oh Bryan, it's so nice to see you again," and gave me a great big hug, right there in front of everyone.

I was surprised, but not at all displeased. Over Jan's shoulder I caught a glimpse of Dan's face as he watched us with a calculating expression, one eyebrow raised. After Jan released me, she took my arm and we started walking toward the crowd at the gate, with Dan and Kent and the others following after us a little awkwardly. As soon as we reached the gate, Jan was surrounded by Americans and Saipanese alike and inundated with more greetings, leis, and *mar mars*. As Jan dealt with the dozens of introductions, I slipped away to check on security. You never knew when somebody might decide that the thing to do to disrupt status negotiations between the United States and Micronesia was to take a whack at the new high commissioner, despite the fact that she was "a sweet little old lady."

I also checked to make sure Jan's luggage was transported directly to her waiting limousine—a silver Mercury Grand Marquis she had paid for herself and shipped out to replace the aging Plymouth that had been used by Adrian Winkel and then Dan High. Then, as the luggage was being loaded into the vehicle, I inspected it thoroughly as well.

When I was finished, I remained at the limo, staying where I could keep an eye both on Jan and the vehicle. Spotting me standing there, Bobbi Grizzard came over to say hello.

"That was quite a warm greeting our new lady Hi Com gave you, Bryan," she said pointedly. "I'd say your career is pretty well made."

Assuming that she was joking, I chuckled a little in response. Not tuned in to the subtleties of politics or social life, I didn't realize that Bobbi was utterly serious, or that she would turn out to be right.

Lady Hi Com

***

In fact, from that day on, just as Bobbi had predicted, my fortunes were up. It's a funny thing how governments work. Up to this time I'd been reporting to the attorney general and had been kind of a minor player in what was going on politically with the leadership in Micronesia. I had been on the "B" list for parties under both Adrian Winkel's and Dan High's administrations, and had considered myself lucky just to be invited for free food and drinks. But all of a sudden, I was in. I was on the "A" list, both politically and socially.

Things happen differently when you're on the "A" list, I soon learned. For example, I'd been saying all along that the Trust Territory's law enforcement function didn't belong under the district attorneys' offices in each of the new governments— or at TT headquarters. It's a conflict of interest, since the district attorney is the prosecuting arm of the law, whereas the police are supposed to be impartial in their investigative and peace-keeping role. It also didn't make much sense from a practical standpoint, because most district attorneys don't know squat about law enforcement.

Well, so far my arguments had fallen on deaf ears. But within a few months of her arrival I mentioned it to Jan, and she listened. She not only listened, she promoted me to a new position where I reported directly to her, and moved my office from the attorney general's wing in the TT headquarters building to the executive wing, just two doors down from her big corner suite.

In terms of pecking order, it was excellent positioning. I had never paid much attention to that kind of bureaucratic bullshit or been interested in playing those kinds of games. But under Jan's tutelage I learned that in government, that kind of stuff mattered. If you wanted to get anything done, if you wanted to get people to listen to you, you had to play the game. So for the next few years, I did.

It was an interesting and often heady time. Under Jan's command, we didn't just complain about problems that needed taking care of—we *did* something about them. We didn't just whine about all the equipment we needed—we went out and got it. On more than one occasion, Jan handed me an airline ticket and a list of names and sent me off to Washington at a moment's notice to make things happen. Talk about cold calling! The first time I knocked on a senator's door uninvited, I almost threw up.

Between Jan's contacts, shameless name-dropping, and a total disregard for the chain of command, I was able to get things done. It really wasn't much different from being a dog-robbing private in the Marine Corps, except that instead of scrounging rations and ammo and used jungle boots from Graves Registration, I was scrounging communications gear from the National Interagency Fire Center, security devices from the U.S. Marshals Service, and lots of surplus goodies from the U.S. military. Now I stood in their offices in a suit and talked them into giving me what I needed rather than just slipping past a sentry in the middle of the night and using a five-finger discount.

But there were some sad times, too, associated with Jan's arrival. A big part of her job was to try to wind down the Trust Territory government. The Reagan administration had high hopes for completing the Compacts of Free Association with the emerging island nations as soon as possible, leaving them to govern themselves without U.S. interference. Initially, the goal was for us to be out of there within two years. It ended up taking a bit longer than that, but along the way a lot of the government offices—like the Justice Improvement Commission, which Denny Lund still headed—were eliminated.

It worked out all right for Denny and his new wife, whom he'd met on a recent trip to the Philippines. Denny had been offered a faculty position in Arkansas, and he was looking forward to the chance to get back to teaching and research and to finish his doctorate from Michigan State. Still, we hated to see Denny leave. He was a person everybody really cared about and respected, and he was sorely missed.

V

I had gotten to know and like Jan pretty well during the first six months or so that we worked together. But I didn't really know what kind of manager she was until I had the opportunity to see how she handled an incident that occurred between a high-ranking official and one of my junior police officers.

I was on Guam one morning, talking with some DEA guys at their headquarters in Agana over a cup of coffee, when one of the other agents came looking for me. "Bryan, you've got a call from Saipan."

That was a little unusual. With phone service being so bad, even between the more developed islands like Guam and Saipan, the only time anyone typically called me when I was on the road was when there was an emergency back home. With some trepidation, I followed him to his secretary's desk and picked up the phone.

It was Bobbi Grizzard, who'd recently taken a job as Jan's executive secretary. "Bryan, Jan wants you back here right now," she told me.

"Why? What's happening?" I asked.

"I don't know. She just said she wants you back here right now," Bobbi said.

"OK, but there isn't a plane back to Saipan until three o'clock this afternoon. Does she really want me to try and hire a charter and fly back right now, or can it wait until I get in on the Air Mike flight?"

"Lemme go ask her," Bobbi said.

A few minutes later, Bobbi returned to the phone. "Jan says she'll see you when you get back this afternoon on Air Mike. And Bryan," she added in a hushed tone, "I don't know what's wrong, but she's really pissed."

"OK. Thanks for the warning, Bobbi. I'll be back as soon as I can."

From the time I got off the phone till the time the Air Mike flight landed on Saipan, I racked my brain trying to figure out what Jan might be angry about or what I had done wrong, but I couldn't think of anything.

When I got back to Saipan, I had one of my Capitol Hill police officers meet me at the airport so I could go directly to headquarters and see Jan. With what I hoped was well-disguised trepidation, I walked down the long hallway of the executive wing to where Bobbi sat outside Jan's office.

Bobbi greeted me warmly, then flipped the intercom and said, "Jan, Bryan's here," which was always kind of silly because Jan could hear Bobbi's voice outside her open door just as easily as she could hear the intercom.

"Come on in, Bryan," Jan replied, without using the intercom. "And shut the door behind you," she added, as I entered her office.

I shut the door and took a seat across from her. Ordinarily I would've greeted her casually and made some sort of small talk, but under the circumstances I thought it was probably best to keep quiet until I knew what she was angry about.

"Something happened last night with one of your policemen," Jan began.

"What? Who?" I asked, only slightly relieved to discover that it was nothing I had done. As the chief of the Capitol Hill police, I was still responsible for whatever it was that had happened.

"Officer Landrick."

"Henry Landrik?" I said, a little surprised. Henry was the young Marshallese officer who had been so alarmed by the cow on the headquarters lawn a while back. He was a little green still, but he was a good, honest officer who always tried hard to do the right thing. I found it difficult to believe he could've done anything to make Jan this angry.

"Yes," she replied sternly. "What can you tell me about him?"

"He's a good officer, Jan," I said. "He still has a lot to learn, but he's one of my best young recruits. He really takes his job seriously."

"Well, he came up to my residence last night at about 11 PM and knocked on the door," Jan told me. "Nueves wasn't going to let him in, but I heard her talking to him so I went to the door to see what was going on.

"He seemed very nervous and upset, but he introduced himself to me and said he had come to see me because you were off island and he didn't know what else to do. I asked him what was the matter, and he told me that he had just stopped Ed Baker for drunk driving. He said Ed was weaving all over the road, so he pulled him over and said he'd drive him home. Ed refused, according to Henry, and told him he'd have his job if he didn't leave him alone, so Henry let him go instead of arresting him. I need to know if this story is true. I want you to get to the bottom of it and tell me exactly what happened."

I could appreciate the problem the incident posed. As director of personnel, finance, and purchasing and supply—which is damn near everything in government—Ed was a high-ranking official on the TT totem pole. As a rookie cop, Henry was somewhere near the bottom rung. Frankly, a lot of managers would've just ignored the whole thing rather than deal with it. I was impressed that Jan wanted me to look into it.

"Will do, Jan," I said, standing up to leave. "I'll get on it right now."

"I want to know by tonight, Bryan," she told me on my way out the door.

I went downstairs to police headquarters and told Captain Tomasino that I wanted one of the officers to go pick up Henry and bring him in so I could talk to him. Then I went back upstairs to Ed's office and asked his secretary if he was in. He was with somebody, but about fifteen minutes later I got in to see him.

I sat down, slouching nonchalantly, and in my best "one *haole* to another" manner said, "I hear you had a little problem last night with one of my guys."

Ed gave me kind of a half smile and said, "Yeah, one of your rookies wanted to make me leave my car at the side of the road and drive me home."

Feigning commiseration, I said, "Oh geez. What for?"

Ed said, "Ah, you know, I was down at the Continental and had a few drinks. I was coming back home and he pulled me over and said I was drunk."

"Were you?" I asked casually.

He laughed and said, "I was making it all right."

"So, did he arrest you?" I asked.

"Nah," said Ed.

"Well, that's good," I replied. "How come?"

Ed laughed again and said, "Because I told him I'd have his ass if he fucking put me in handcuffs."

"Well, you know, he's a new kid," I said. "Anyway, Jan just wanted me to find out what happened. I'll take care of it."

I left Ed's office and went back downstairs to the Capitol Police headquarters. Henry was there waiting for me with Captain Tomasino. Henry was visibly upset, but he had a look of righteous indignation on his face.

"Relax, Henry," I said in greeting. "Come on up to my office and let's talk."

When we got to my office, I closed the door, sat him down, and said, "Look, you just tell me what happened last night. Don't leave anything out."

Henry told me whole story, much as Jan had recounted it. He'd stopped Ed, who'd been weaving from one side of the road to the other. When he went up to the window he could smell booze, and Ed was slurring his speech so badly he could hardly understand him.

"I knew who he was, I knew he was one of the big guys, but he was drunk, and you always tell us we treat everybody the same. Everybody's equal under the law," Henry said firmly, his chin held high as he spoke.

"Yes. Yes, they are," I agreed. "So, what were you going to do?"

"I just wanted to take him to his house so he wouldn't crash his car or hurt anybody," said Henry. "I told him, 'Park the car here. I'll take you home, and then we'll bring the car to your house.'"

"And what did he say?" I asked.

Henry mumbled something under his breath, his eyes downcast.

"Henry, there isn't anything I haven't heard a hundred times before," I told him.

"I don't talk like that," Henry muttered quietly.

"I know. But this is important. You have to tell me."

"He told me, 'Go fuck yourself,'" Henry finally replied.

"OK. Then what else did he say?" I prodded.

"He said he'd have my job in the morning if I didn't just get in the car and get my ass out of there," Henry said. "He wouldn't come with me, and I was afraid to arrest him, so I had to let him go."

"OK, Henry. I think you made the right decision under the circumstances," I told him. "But the next time something like this happens, I want you to call your sergeant for help."

"OK, Chief," Henry said, nodding. "Am I gonna lose my job?"

"No way," I assured him.

***

After Henry left I remained at my desk for a few minutes,

thinking. Jan seemed like a real straight shooter, but Ed was one of her top people, and I didn't know how this was going to go. I figured I'd just give it my best shot, and do my best to make sure Henry came out of it OK. So I wrote up a memo outlining exactly what Ed had said and what Henry had said and took it to her.

Without a word, Jan put on her huge black reading glasses and read the memo while I stood there waiting.

She looked up at me when she finished, removing the glasses, and said, "Thanks, Bryan. I'll take it from here."

"Well, you know—" I began.

"I'll take it from here," Jan repeated, her tone making it clear that our meeting was over.

Bobbi was right. She was really pissed.

I didn't hear anything more about the incident that day. But the next morning as I came into TT headquarters, our office administrator, Janet Craley, pulled me aside and asked, "Well, did you hear the news?"

"What?" I asked.

"Jan just fired Ed Baker. She told him to pack his things and get off island by the end of the day."

I walked into my office, grinning and shaking my head, thinking, *She's got balls like a fucking rhinoceros.*

CHAPTER 12

Home on the (Missile) Range

It was about 4 AM when the phone rang. I lunged at it clumsily, knocking it off the nightstand. I crawled out of bed, fumbling around for the handset in the dark, and finally located the son of a bitch.

"Sorry," I blurted into the handset as I worked to untangle the cord.

It was Jan. "Bryan, it's happening sooner than we expected," she said, referring to our conversation earlier that night. I'd been up at her place until well past midnight, talking about problems in the Marshall Islands in the far eastern side of Micronesia.

I started to ask what exactly was happening, but she cut me off and said, "The sail-in's getting out of hand. They're starting to come up off the beach. I need you to go out there first thing this morning. Dean Aguilar will go with you."

"Good idea," I said, glad to know I wouldn't be winging it alone. Dean was a new State Department officer on Saipan who seemed pretty competent so far. "Do you want me to come up there right now for the briefing?"

"No, why don't you just come by for coffee before you and Dean take off, and we can coordinate things then. What time does the plane going that direction leave?"

"Seven-thirty, I think," I said.

MICRONESIAN BLUES

"OK, fine. I'll see you here at six," Jan said, and rang off.
Frankly, the situation on Kwaj would've been sort of comi-
cal if the stakes hadn't been so high. Several hundred Marshallese folks, who normally lived on a tiny islet called Ebeye,
had sailed across the lagoon to the top-secret U.S. military base
on Kwajalein and were camped out there on the beach. Men,
women, and children, all barbecuing and having one big picnic—and cleverly putting the skids on an important set of missile tests that President Reagan was depending on as part of his
Strategic Defense Initiative.

Things were getting hot and heavy with the Soviets during
this last phase of the Cold War, and it was essential for us to
convince them that we could win a nuclear exchange, if it ever
came to that. One of the key elements was our new MX system—an intercontinental ballistic missile system that would
allow a single missile to deliver warheads to several different
targets at once. Using dummy warheads, the tests of this deliv-
ery system were scheduled to happen any day now—with the
unarmed missiles launched from Vandenberg Air Force Base in
California and targeted to touch down in Kwajalein's huge lagoon. But of course the tests couldn't happen unless the area
was evacuated so no one would get hit by debris.

Normally, the Marshallese complied. Many of them worked
at the U.S. military base on Kwajalein—which had been there
since the late 1940s, when Micronesia first became a trust territory—and relations were typically cordial. However, as the U.S.
trusteeship neared its end, these nice, peaceful, mild-mannered,
barefoot folks had raised a very interesting legal issue. Their
newly emerging national government had recently granted the
United States a long-term lease on Kwajalein for a lot of
money. The problem was, the Republic of the Marshall Islands
didn't own Kwajalein—these people, who had been displaced
to overcrowded Ebeye for more than thirty years and weren't
happy about it—were the rightful owners of the atoll. More-

over, their new nation had no law of eminent domain, which meant that it had no right to seize their property because of some compelling national interest and lease it to the United States. The Kwajalein landowners argued, therefore, that the lease money should be paid to them, not to their national government. But the United States couldn't pay the money directly to them because the U.S. only dealt with other nations. And the new Marshallese government wasn't about to turn over the money to them, because it had other plans for it. So, in a very reasonable way, the Kwajalein landowners had decided to reoccupy their land, which the U.S. wasn't legally renting from them. And now they were leaving their picnics at the beach and walking across some of the most highly classified pieces of United States real estate in the world.

Christ, I thought, *what a clusterfuck*. I just hoped they didn't have some overzealous officer in charge of things out there. The last thing this problem needed was some tightass bureaucrat making the crisis worse than it already was. I mean, the Marshallese are peaceful people—you have to be peaceful to live on a flat little atoll, crowded up against the same people forever—but they aren't meek. In fact, back in the old days, sailors really feared the Marshall Islands. There's never enough protein on a low-lying atoll, and the Marshallese were known for inviting them for dinner—literally—if they washed up on their shores. These folks could still get tough if they were pissed.

* * *

I pulled into the Hi Com's driveway at 6 AM. Before I could knock on the door, Nueves, who had worked for Adrian Winkel and was now Jan's housekeeper, greeted me with a warm smile and a cup of strong black coffee in her hand. Dean pulled up right behind me and Nueves hurried us both into the kitchen, where she poured him a cup as well.

Dean had only been on island about a month. He was always a little unsettling to be around. At first glance, he seemed like your typical career foreign service officer—he spoke three languages fluently and was comfortable in a tuxedo. But he was also a bookish scholar and a former second-chair flutist with the Philadelphia Symphony. And if you looked even closer, behind the wire-rimmed glasses and the slight stature, what you saw was a highly competitive athlete. Saturday mornings on the basketball court, he was as aggressive as the toughest boonie dogs on island. I didn't know Dean very well, but I was pretty sure he'd prove to be competent in just about any situation.

A few minutes after we arrived, Jan came bustling in. Despite the early hour and our late night before, she was her usual, effusive, good-natured self, looking for all the world like somebody's grandmother at Christmas. She sat us down and proceeded to stuff us with bacon, eggs, toast, fresh squeezed orange juice, and more coffee—all expertly prepared by Nueves—as she gave us our marching orders.

The bottom line was, despite the disagreement between the Kwajalein landowners and the Marshallese and U.S. governments, that missile range had to be operating, and fast. Jan was counting on us to go make it happen.

II

Saipan to Guam. Guam to Truk. Truk to Ponape. At about two-thirty in the afternoon, we finally landed on Kwajalein. As soon as the plane pulled up alongside the terminal and the door opened, two military police officers boarded the plane and asked for Dean and me by name. After they checked our IDs, they took us off the plane before anyone else and we followed them down the gangway and into the tin-roofed terminal. The MPs walked us past customs and immigration to an unmarked door, where they handed us over to a lieutenant who bustled us directly off to headquarters.

The long, low military building was made of cinderblock that had been covered and recovered with many coats of paint over the past thirty years. The lieutenant showed us in, and we followed him down a long corridor to a conference room where eight or nine other men appeared to be waiting for a meeting to come to order. We took the seats he offered to us, nodding in greeting to the others around the table, and waited with them.

Someone shouted, "Atten-hut," and everyone rose around the table. Out of old habit, I found myself standing at attention along with them.

"At ease," said the tall, athletic-looking colonel who entered the room. You could see the West Pointer in him even before you saw the military academy ring on the third finger of his left hand.

"Good afternoon, gentlemen. I'm Greg Webber," he said, introducing himself to Dean and me immediately. "Thank you for coming out."

"Hello, Colonel," I said, shaking his hand. "I'm Bryan Vila from TT headquarters, and this is Dean Aguilar from the State Department."

Greg shook Dean's hand, then turned to the lieutenant who had escorted us from the airport and said, "Let's have a status report, and get these gentlemen up to speed."

I didn't want to hear what I heard next. The lieutenant reported that early that morning, the protesters had marched up from the beach, apparently intent on coming onto the military base. The local police force—which was composed mostly of security officers from Global Enterprises, an American contractor that handled logistics for the military facility—had intercepted the protesters on their way to the base. One thing led to another, and the American rent-a-cops had ended up arresting several of the protesters for trespassing, including Imata Kabua, who was a local senator and the head of the Kwajalein landowners' group, and a few of the Marshallese traditional leaders. They were all being held at the local jail.

Now, I knew enough about Marshallese culture to realize that this was a big mistake—particularly arresting the traditional leaders. Those folks were considered royalty—people didn't even *touch* them without permission—and a Marshallese police officer wouldn't ever dream of arresting them. I looked over at Dean to see if he was thinking what I was thinking, but he was playing stony-faced diplomat, his expression unreadable.

"Thank you, lieutenant," Greg Webber said when the lieutenant concluded his report. "John," he said, turning to his executive officer, "what's new from the Pentagon?"

"They've recommended that we turn the water off to discourage the protesters on the beach, sir," he said.

Greg looked across the table at the director of public works. "Steve, what's your take on that from a public health standpoint?" he asked.

"If we turn the water off, sir," Steve said, "we'll end up with a cholera epidemic on our hands."

"We've already got a thousand people shitting in the lagoon. What difference does it make if we shut off the water?" Greg asked.

"Yes, sir," Steve replied. "But if we shut off their access to clean water, they'll start using the lagoon water for cooking and washing. Given the current levels of E. coli, that'd be a real problem."

Greg nodded and looked back at his executive officer. "Keep stalling 'em," he said. Turning back to the rest of us, he said, "All right, if no one else has anything new to report, this meeting is adjourned. Thank you, gentlemen."

As everyone rose to leave, the colonel turned to Dean and me and said, "Would you come with me, please?"

We followed him into his office, and he closed the door behind us.

"So, gentlemen, what do you think?" he asked.

"We don't have much information yet, Colonel," Dean said.

"I think it would be a good idea if we got out on the beach and started talking to people."

"All right. I'll get you a car and driver right away," Greg said.

"Thank you, sir," Dean replied.

Greg nodded. "We've also got some backup on the way. Your idea, I believe," he said, looking at me.

"My—?" I began, perplexed. "Oh, the Marshallese officers, you mean?"

"Yes," Greg replied. "They'll be here on a flight from Majuro in a couple of hours. About twenty of them. Perhaps that'll do some good."

I'd suggested to Jan last night—was it only last night?—that we fly some Marshallese officers out to Kwajalein so the Marshallese protesters would be policed by their own people instead of a bunch of American rent-a-cops. I'd been trying to avoid a potential disaster like the arrests that had taken place that morning.

"That's great news," I said. "Who's command will they be under?"

"Yours?" Greg suggested.

"Well, how 'bout if I just advise them, and we leave their lieutenant in charge," I suggested. "That way it's less an American versus Marshallese thing and more a Marshallese versus Marshallese thing."

Greg nodded, and Dean agreed that it was the best way to handle things.

"All right then. Let me get you a driver, and as soon as you're ready he'll take you around and give you the lay of the land."

* * *

Instead of heading directly down to the beach, we stopped for a quick bite to eat on the base, then asked the driver to take us to our quarters, which turned out to be an old Airstream trailer with lots of tar gooped on the seams to fend off the corrosion from the salt air. It had two bedrooms, a bathroom, and a sitting room. Usually, such semiprivate quarters only went to folks with the rank of colonel or above. Dean and I didn't really qualify, but we weren't complaining. Compared to bunking at the barracks, it was fabulous. Our luggage, which we'd been told to leave when we were so abruptly whisked off the plane and taken to the meeting, was already there waiting for us. Between the lack of sleep and the long flight earlier, it was a relief to wash off some of the grittiness and change clothes before we headed back out for what promised to be a long night.

The sun was hanging low over the lagoon when Dean and I finally arrived at the inner lagoon-side beach of the atoll, where the protesters had gathered. There were wall-to-wall people, most of them sitting on pandanus mats and eating, drinking, and talking. Babies squalled, and women cooled themselves with intricately woven pandanus fans. On first glance, it looked like a typical, albeit crowded, day at the beach. Except when you looked closer, you could see that these people were very upset. They were talking, but it wasn't the casual smiling chitchat, eyes downcast, that the Marshallese normally engage in. They were talking in hushed tones, and there was tension in their eyes.

Dean and I split up to go talk to people, looking for folks we knew, shaking hands, and just generally trying to get a feel for where things were at the moment and what was likely to happen next.

The tension seemed to build as the sun went down. Dean must've noticed it, too, because when we met up again after an hour or two, he had a worried look on his face. "I think something's gonna happen at the jail. You better get over there," he said.

"Are you coming?"

"No. I'll stay here and keep talking," Dean said.

I trudged back up to the road from the sandy beach, found our driver, and asked him to take me over to the jail. As we approached, I realized that I hadn't really had a chance to look at it when we passed by earlier. Frankly, from a defensive standpoint, it sucked. The entire building was faced in glass, and Global had posted its guards, in their Tijuana cop-like uniforms, all around the building. They were standing there at a nice little parade rest, with their feet spread thirty inches apart and their hands clasped firmly behind them in the small of their backs, looking straight ahead. They looked good—nice and official— but with all that glass behind them, there wasn't shit they could do if they got rushed.

A crowd was starting to form outside the jail, but it wasn't your usual crowd of protesters. There were a few tough, committed-looking young men, along with a group of large Marshallese women, each with three or more young children in tow, including infants. It was good planning on their part. The thinking was that they'd take their people out of the jail and nobody would be able to stop them without hurting the women and children.

Things were still under control at the moment, although a few of the young men were arguing with a couple of the guards who worked for Global, and one of them was yelling and shaking his fist angrily. I got out of the car and sauntered over, nice and casual, to the apparent leader of the group—the most vocal of the young males.

"Hi, I'm Bryan Vila," I said, holding out my hand.

He glared at me and said nothing.

Venturing a guess, based on some information Jan had given me that morning, I kept my hand out and said, "You must be Jendrick Heine."

Reluctantly, warily, he nodded and shook my hand briefly.

"Can I talk with you just a minute?" I asked, as deferentially as possible. Jendrick Heine was one of the youngest of the Marshallese nobles—the equivalent of a prince, in Marshallese culture—and I didn't want to risk offending him straight off the bat.

He looked at the gun on my hip and said, "What are you going to do, arrest me?"

"No, that's not what I'm here for," I assured him. "C'mon. Let's go talk."

We walked away from the crowd to a quiet place and I said, "Look, my goal here is to keep a lid on things, to try to prevent any more problems, and to keep anyone from getting hurt. What do you want?"

"They can't arrest these people, my family and the others. This is wrong. This is *our* land. This is *our* island. They can't do this," he said.

"I know," I told him. "We're working on it."

"Well, you *better* work on it," he snapped. "Because we're gonna take these people out of here tonight, one way or another. You understand?"

"I told you, let me work on it," I said. "Just sit tight for a while, all right?"

He snorted and strode away haughtily. Forgetting him for the moment, I went inside the jail and met with the head of the Global Security Services detachment, a washed-up stateside alcoholic, and asked him if I could talk to the protesters who'd been detained. He seemed relieved to have someone else there who was willing to take charge of things.

So I went from cell to cell, shaking hands with some folks and bowing to others, talking softly with them, and explaining to everyone that the high commissioner had sent me to help make sure there was no violence and that things got settled in a way that was fair for everyone.

I was just finishing chatting with the last of the prisoners when one of the officers from Global came in to let me know that the Marshallese policemen had arrived and were waiting for me next door, in the back room of the local bowling alley.

I said my good-byes, reassuring the prisoners that I'd be back as soon as possible, and headed on over to the bowling alley, where the twenty Marshallese policemen who'd been sent over from Majuro were waiting. I was relieved to see that Leviticus Savu was the lieutenant in charge of the detail, and that there were a couple other officers I recognized from previous training programs as well. I shook hands with Leviticus, but he didn't even chuckle when—trying to cut the tension a bit—I jokingly reminded him that he still owed me the twenty bucks he borrowed three years before. Leviticus was tight-jawed, and so were his men. They all looked really nervous. Frankly, I could understand why. It wasn't just that they'd been called to police their own people—that's what they did every day on Majuro. The problem was that royalty had been arrested, and they feared that they were going to be asked to stand up against their traditional leaders.

I talked with them about order, about all the ideals they had been taught to uphold as police officers, and about how we were working to try to resolve things and reach a peaceful understanding so the prisoners could be released from jail. I also made it clear that I didn't want them to arrest anybody unless absolutely necessary. But I could tell that they still weren't convinced that everything was going to work out.

Frankly, neither was I. I could hear shouting outside, even through the concrete walls of the bowling alley. I didn't want to get the Marshallese officers involved yet, not until I knew just what was going on, so I left, telling them I'd be back to get them in just a few minutes.

When I got outside, there was Jendrick Heine, along with several other of the young nobles, shouting and yelling to the crowd and trying to get things stirred up. Then I heard the glass breaking.

A large rock had been thrown through the glass front of the

MICRONESIAN BLUES

jail, and suddenly, there was silence. Everyone was quiet except for some crying babies and a couple of young boys who were still playing tag around everyone's legs.

The Global cops were tight jawed, crouched a bit, and ready to get it on. They were rent-a-cops who wanted to be real cops. And after months of being stuck on this tiny little atoll with nothing substantial to do, this was their chance—but I wasn't about to let them take it. It might keep things under control at the moment, but over the long term, more arrests—and more strong-arming by stateside guards—would only escalate tensions here further.

So I told them to stay cool and sit tight, much to their chagrin. Then I headed back to the bowling alley to get the relief started. I was pretty sure I could defuse things by bringing the Marshallese police officers into it. They could talk to the protesters in their own language and reason with them, and pretty soon we'd be able to get things back under control.

Except when I ducked into the back room of the bowling alley, there was nobody there. All the Marshallese cops had split. I went around to the front of the bowling alley—and there was nobody there, either.

"Do you know where the Marshallese officers went?" I asked the American guy who worked the front desk.

"Yeah. They all walked out the front door about five minutes ago," he said casually.

"Fuck," I groaned, racing out the front door and looking both directions to see if there was any sign of them. They were all gone, every one of them. "Fuck," I shouted this time, realizing that I was going to have to somehow handle things on my own.

Putting on my best poker face, I walked over to Jendrick Heine and his men, who were still shouting to the crowd in Marshallese and gesturing toward the front of the jail. Obviously, they were planning to go in and take their people out of the cells.

"Look, Jendrick," I said. "If you don't back off, people are going to get hurt here. Let me just talk to everybody and see what we can work out. Give me some more time."

"Fuck you," Jendrick replied.

"No, fuck *you*," I said quietly, smiling slightly for the benefit of the crowd. "It feels real good to be raising hell, doesn't it? Why don't you show some real leadership and let us work this out without violence?"

Jendrick just glared at me and kept working the crowd. Disgusted, I went back inside the jail and asked the jailer to let me talk to the prisoners again. Specifically, I asked to speak with Imata Kabua, who spoke good English and had seemed like a reasonable person.

"Rocks are being thrown, and things are about to get ugly out there," I told him. "If this situation falls apart, people are going to get hurt. There are women and children and little babies in the crowd. Why don't you order your people to calm down? I promise, I'll do my best to get things settled fairly. But first we need to get things back under control so we can talk."

"What about the money?" Imata asked.

"I don't know anything about the money. I'm just here to make sure people don't get hurt."

Imata paused for a moment and sighed. He looked over at one of the traditional leaders, an old and wrinkled man. The man nodded at him solemnly, and he turned back to me.

"He will talk to the people," he said, gesturing toward the old man. "He will go with you now."

"Thank you," I said, bowing to Imata and then to the old man. I told the jailer what we were doing, and he let the old man out of the cell without argument.

I followed him out of the jail, walking slowly behind him. As we walked, I noticed that although he had the same battered feet as everybody else, and the same faded pants, he carried himself with an air of, well, royalty.

When he came to a stop in front of the crowd they quieted immediately, and he began to talk to them in Marshallese. And he talked and talked. Nobody's in much of a hurry in Micronesia, and politicians are politicians wherever you go.

Finally, he said the Marshallese equivalent of, "And that's it." Then he turned and walked back into the jail.

As soon as he was gone, everyone picked up their stuff, turned around and walked back down to the beach, and it was over. The rent-a-cops standing in front of the jail were obviously shocked. To tell the truth, I was a little surprised myself that it had worked. Unable to disguise the look of relief on my face—I've never been much good at poker—I glanced over at Jendrick Heine. Stony-faced, he just turned and walked off with his cohorts.

III

Late the next day Greg Webber released all of the Marshallese leaders from jail, and they rejoined their people at the beach. The crisis wasn't over, but at least we were back to where we could hold negotiations without the threat of a riot hanging over our heads.

Shortly afterward, I met up with Leviticus Savu and the other Marshallese police officers at the airport just before they boarded the Air Mike flight back to Majuro. He wouldn't look me in the eyes at first, but I persisted.

"Look, Leviticus, I just want you to know I understand," I told him. "I shouldn't have put you and your men in that position. It was stupid of me to think it would work out."

"Thanks, Chief," he said, eyes downcast and still a little sheepish.

"No, really," I told him. "It was an impossible situation, and I'm sorry I brought you into it. But you still owe me twenty bucks."

He finally laughed at that and handed over a twenty. He and his men boarded the plane, and I headed on over to the local officers' club, the Yukwe Yuk (which, roughly translated, means "welcome," or "hello"), where I'd agreed to meet Greg and Dean for a drink.

Dean hadn't arrived yet, and Greg was standing alone at the bar, nursing a beer.

"Hey, Colonel. Nice work today," I said in greeting, referring to the painstaking negotiations that had finally led to the prisoners' release.

"It's a start," he said, signaling to the bartender to get me a beer.

We stood there chatting, both of us weary and glad for the brief respite from the constant tension of dealing with angry people.

After a while, the door of the club opened and we both turned, expecting to see Dean. Instead, in walked Imata Kabua, who had only recently been released from jail, accompanied by Jendrick Heine. Because of their rank in traditional society, they had every right to be here. But their attitude, and the way they paused to look around with sneers on their faces, as if to say, "This is our fucking island, people, and we're in charge," just rubbed Greg the wrong way. He was a colonel in the U.S. Army, goddammit, and he was obviously sick of this shit.

He walked over and got dead in their faces. Before I could even get off my stool, he was nose to nose ranting at them, reminding them that this was his fucking base, and if they didn't fucking like it they could get the fuck out of there, or words to that effect. Apparently, the colonel's diplomatic side had its limits.

I scrambled over and stepped in between them. "Greg, how 'bout if I buy you another beer," I said. "And Senator," I added, nodding to Imata Kabua, "how 'bout the first round's on me, and we just let this ride? We're all pretty tired here, and it's been a long couple of days."

I didn't figure it was going to work, but Greg, jaw muscles bulging, turned and walked back toward the bar. I joined him, and it blew over, just like that.

* * *

There were similar crises over the next six weeks. Day to day, Dean and I bounced from one problem to the next. First there'd be a diplomatic squabble over the language in the status negotiations; then there'd be a cable or radio message from the Pentagon instructing Greg to turn the water off or turn the water back on, or some other sort of micromanaging by the suits in Washington, who didn't have a clue about what things were really like there.

The bottom line was, just as Jan had said when she sent us off on this mission, that the missile tests had to happen, and they had to happen soon. The schedule was counting down, although nobody knew when the exact date was because nobody had clearance to know except Greg, and he wasn't allowed to tell us.

A bright spot amid the whole mess was when Jan sent Bill Stinnett out from Saipan to help. The plan was that he'd spend a week or so there with Dean and me to get the lay of the land, and then I'd finally be able to go home, at least for a while. My one- or two-week emergency had already stretched to more than a month, and needless to say, Susan was not happy.

After Bill arrived, I asked Greg for a chopper, a photographer, and a couple of days for us to take pictures and see if we couldn't educate the idiots in Washington about what conditions were like where we were. I figured if they could actually see the situation, they might back off a bit and stop trying to control our every move.

Bill and I went from island to island with the photographer—a young American woman. She took pictures of the beaches there, of neighboring Ebeye and Roi-Namur, and of each of the other tiny atolls that had to be evacuated before the missile tests could take place. Afterward, we put together the briefing book of pictures with captions and sent it off to Washington by courier. Even that, of course, wasn't easy. Everyone bickered over who was going to pay for the film developing, and then the courier.

But when the pictures finally got to Washington, the folks back home could see for themselves what the atolls looked like and what conditions were like for the protesters living on the beach. And for the first time, they just shut up and let us run things on our own. That's when things started to get better.

The protesters eventually began to head back to Ebeye, and a financial agreement between them and their government was reached in October—four months after the sail-in had begun.

***

At about three o'clock one moonless night I got a phone call from the operations center.

"It's coming in now, sir," the radio operator told me. I had asked him to call as soon as the missile was about to strike.

I ran outside the Airstream, and Dean stumbled out after me. We looked up into the sky and suddenly it was daylight, as the missile that had left Vandenberg less than half an hour before reentered the atmosphere, turning night into day. As the reentry burn faded, there was a moment of near darkness before the dummy warheads split off like shooting stars in several different directions. It was just beautiful. But for those of us who grew up playing duck and cover in grammar school, it was also chilling. Any other place, any other time, I knew we'd be watching what was sure to be the end of the world.

CHAPTER 13

Labor Pains

It was a beautiful November Friday, and I was looking forward to a laid-back weekend at home. Then Gene Stevens from Communications came knocking on my office door.

"Can I talk to you for a minute?" he asked, poking his head in through my open door after he knocked.

"Sure, Gene. What's up?" I asked.

"Well, it looks like we're about to have some more trouble on Palau," Gene said, taking a seat across from me.

"How do you know?"

"Dwight Kitalong has been on the horn all day today to friends of his there and they're all pretty sure it's going to blow again soon," he said. Kitalong, Gene's radio operator, was from Palau.

"Shit," I said with a sigh, as I saw my plans for a relaxing weekend go down the drain. "Any idea what's up this time?"

"It looks like another strike by PAGE is in the works," Gene said, referring to the Palau Association of Government Employees. Salvador Idechong, whom I had met on my first trip to Palau several years ago, had been serving as the spokesman for the group since his recent unsuccessful bid for president of Palau, and his right-hand man, Moses Katosang, was the organization's chairman. "Sorry I don't have more information than that, but I thought you ought to at least know about what I've heard so far."

"Thanks, Gene," I said. "I appreciate it."

Gene left and I went down the hall to tell Jan what he had just told me.

"What do you think we should do?" she asked when I finished.

"How 'bout if I just go down there alone in civilian clothes and nose around a little?" I said. "I think at this point, any stronger show from our office might make things worse. You know how the Palauans resent having us interfere in their business."

Jan nodded thoughtfully, remembering. During a flare-up on Palau the previous March, she had gone down with me to help calm things down. It was a pretty dangerous situation. People were running around with dynamite blowing things up, as usual, and we'd heard rumors that some of the hotheads thought the surest way to finish off Palau's relationship with the United States would be to take out the Hi Com.

Undaunted, Jan had stayed on and done a good job of defusing things. She fit in well with the Palauans because she was such a strong leader. But I'd run my ass off and stayed up almost all night every night making sure she was safe.

"All right," Jan agreed. "How soon can you get down there?"

"The next flight is tomorrow morning."

"Good. Be sure to take the radio with you, just in case they blow up the communications station again," Jan said, referring to the elaborate new shortwave radio Gene had recently helped us put together for these sorts of emergencies. "And call me as soon as you know anything."

* * *

I arrived on Palau on Saturday afternoon. The situation there was strained but still stable, and, just like Dean and I had done on Kwajalein, I spent a lot of time simply walking around and talking to folks to get a feel for what, if anything, was about to happen.

When it did, it was fairly anticlimactic. The majority of government workers went on strike on Monday, but this time—unlike the strike back in September of 1981—the sixty members of the Palau Police Department stayed on the job. With the officers working around the clock to guard public utilities, government offices, and nonstriking workers, civil order was maintained despite increased tensions. Joshua Sadang, the police chief, seemed to have things firmly under control, the officers were doing a good job, and I was really impressed.

Without bothering to set up the radio—there was no need to since no one had blown up the communications station this time—I called Jan from the police station to tell her that things were looking good. We both agreed that I might as well head back to Saipan to avoid giving the impression that we lacked confidence in the local cops' ability to handle things.

A reporter from the *Pacific Daily News* was waiting at the airport to interview me when I got home. Proud of the job the Palau police were doing, I was happy to oblige, praising the officers highly throughout the interview and emphasizing that they were "maintaining civil order superbly."

Of course, I should've known better than to tempt fate like that.

* * *

I got back to the office on Wednesday, reported in to Jan, and spent the rest of the day scrambling to catch up on the work and phone messages I had missed while I was gone. All hell broke loose the next day. Jan called to tell me about it shortly after I returned from lunch.

"Bryan, I need to talk to you," she said tersely.

"I'll be right there," I replied. Figuring something must be wrong—Jan was only terse when she was extremely concerned or extremely angry—I hurried down the hall and into her office.

"What's up, Jan?" I asked as she looked up from the stack of papers on her desk.

"There's been a shooting on Palau," she said, leaning back in her chair and taking off her big black reading glasses. "Apparently the police opened fire on a mob of strikers who were trying to storm the police station. The report we received said one person has been killed, but the radio station shut down in the middle of a broadcast and the phone lines are down, so we can't confirm or get any more information at the moment. I think you'd better get back down there right away—and take someone with you this time."

"Right. But I don't think there's another Air Mike flight to Palau until Saturday, Jan. Do you think COMNAVMAR can help us out?" I asked, referring to the Naval Command on Guam.

"I'll call Admiral DeMars and find out," Jan said.

While Jan put in a call to the admiral on Guam, I called Bill Stinnett and told him what was up. Then I packed up our new communications equipment and weapons, threw some clothes in a bag, and waited. And waited.

II

Even with Jan's influence, we weren't able to get a plane to Palau until early the next morning. Like I had told the folks in Washington, you just can't get from A to B quickly in Micronesia, even in a crisis situation. But at least we did finally manage to get there, and in the admiral's private twin-engine turboprop, no less. It was nearly noon on Friday when we finally began to make our descent toward the big island of Babelthuap.

"Would you mind circling downtown Koror a couple of times before we land?" I asked the pilot. "I'd like to get a better idea of what's going on down there if I can."

"No problem," the pilot, a Navy lieutenant, replied. "You just let me know when you've seen enough."

He took us down as low as he could, passing the airport on Babelthuap and continuing southwest to Palau's capital. As we approached Koror, we could see big clouds of black smoke billowing up from somewhere in the vicinity of the main town square. On closer inspection, we could see a building on fire—I couldn't tell which one—and lots of people running around frantically. I got out my camera to get a better look at the situation through the 200mm telephoto lens and to take some pictures to send back to Washington.

I was about halfway through the first roll of film when my inner ear caught up with me, and I felt the gorge rise up in my throat. I hadn't stopped to think about the possible effects of looking down through the zoom lens while circling in a tight radius. It was only by sheer force of will that I didn't throw up all over the place. I was damned if I was going to puke in front of a couple of Navy guys. But I did ask them to go ahead and take it down.

By the time we landed at the airport on Babelthuap, my breakfast was back down in my stomach where it belonged. Bill and I thanked the pilots for the lift, gathered up our gear, and hauled it down the gangway.

Two Palauan police officers were waiting for us at the airport and greeted us with solemn expressions.

"So, what's going on here, exactly?" I asked. "It seemed like everything was under control when I left a couple of days ago."

"It's bad," said one of the officers. "But it wasn't his fault."

"Whose fault?" I said.

"The chief," said the officer. "Everybody was shouting and angry. They were threatening to take our guns away from us and to take the prisoners from the jail, and he couldn't let them do that. He had to shoot. He had to stop them. But he didn't mean to kill anybody."

"How many people were killed?" Bill asked.

"One, and three are in the hospital," the officer said. "But it wasn't the chief's fault. They were going to take our guns away."

"I understand," I told him, putting a hand on his shoulder. "We'll look into it and see what happened."

"What else is going on out here?" Bill asked. "We saw a fire in Koror."

"Yes, there's been a lot of rioting since the shooting yesterday," the other officer told us.

"Are all the police officers still on the job?" I asked.

"Most of them," he replied.

"Good. Then you have things pretty much under control still?"

"I think so. It's hard to tell what will happen."

More than a little concerned, we got into the two rental cars the police officers had brought and drove them as fast as they would go down the bumpy jungle roads and across the bridge to Koror. The smoke was heavy in the downtown area, both from the building fire and from several trash fires that the demonstrators were burning in the square. People were milling around in large groups. Some were acting surly and threatening, while others seemed wary—frightened even, despite the fact that Palauans usually tend not to show much fear.

Bill and I drove directly to the police station, where we parked and went looking for the police chief, Joshua Sadang.

Joshua was in his office, and he was a basket case. He seemed completely demoralized, and a little out of it.

"What happened, Joshua?" I asked quietly.

"I don't know, Bryan. I don't know," he said, shaking his head.

After a few minutes, it became apparent that Joshua wasn't in any condition to talk to us just yet. I'm not sure he even noticed when we left.

After Bill and I left Joshua's office, we went looking for

Lukas Panuelo, a Ponapean captain who had worked for the Palau Police Department since the early days of the Trust Territory. We found Lukas in his office, and he gave us the details of what had happened. Basically, it was just what the Palauan officers had told us. Angry over the arrest of two strikers, about a hundred demonstrators had gone to the police station where the prisoners were being held to demand their release. Led by Moses Katosang, they had taunted Joshua and his officers, threatening to take their guns and their prisoners. Joshua, shotgun in hand, had stood his ground at the entrance to the police station, with his officers behind him. At some point things had gotten out of hand, and Joshua had pointed the shotgun at Katosang and fired. However, Katosang had ducked out of the way just in time, and the shotgun blast had killed another demonstrator, Pascual Armaluuk, by mistake, as well as injuring three others.

"Did Joshua know the man he killed?" I asked.

"Yes, he's known him since he was a boy," said Lukas. "He's very upset about it."

"Do you think he'll be OK?" I asked.

"I don't know. I hope so," Lukas said quietly.

"Me too. Joshua's a good guy," I said. "Look, do you mind if we set up a communications point somewhere here in the station? The Hi Com really wants to know what's happening, and we can't get through on the phones."

"Sure. You can set up here in my office, if you want," Lukas said.

"That'd be great, Lukas. Thanks," I said. Turning to Bill, I added, "Well, let's see if any of this shit really works."

We went back to the rental car, got out the new shortwave radio and long-line antenna, and carried them into Lukas's office.

"Is there a good place where we can put up this antenna?" I asked Lukas, showing it to him. It looked sort of like a surveyor's tape—one of those big reels you use to measure property—only it had tails going off in two directions instead of just one.

"There's a pole behind the station that might work OK," he said.

We followed Lukas out behind the station, where there was a tall telephone pole with a couple of radio antennas already on it. Looking up, I told Bill, "You know, if we can get the antenna up there, we can run one end over to the police station and the other to that coconut palm over there."

"Yeah, that'll work," said Bill. "But how are we gonna get it up there?"

"Well, it's only been eighteen years since I climbed a telephone pole in the Marine Corps. I think I can still remember how," I said. "Has anybody got any climbing gaffs, Lukas?"

"Sure, I think so," Lukas said.

He went and made a couple of calls, and twenty minutes later one of the policemen pulled up with a pair of climbing gaffs that belonged to his brother-in-law, who worked for the communications department. With more than fifty people watching—in the wake of yesterday's shooting, there was still a fairly large crowd of angry demonstrators hanging around the police station—I strapped them on and racked my brain to try to remember how to use them properly. All I could really remember was to lean way back, step them in briskly, and for God's sake, don't get too close to the pole or they'll break loose.

Feigning a confidence I didn't feel, I tucked the tape antenna under my belt in the small of my back and started walking up the pole. *Chunk, chunk, chunk, chunk.* The breeze picked up as I got above the twenty-foot mark, and the pole started to sway more with my weight. Reminding myself that this was normal—tall poles are *supposed* to sway in the breeze—I kept climbing. *Chunk, chunk, chunk, chunk. Don't be afraid*, I told myself. *Breathe. Don't look down. Just keep on moving up. Chunk, chunk, chunk, chunk.* And then *thonk, thonk, thonk, thonk.* The steady, solid *chunk* of the wood was suddenly replaced by a hollow sound. I paused for a moment, then took another two steps up. *Thonk, thonk.* A *very* hollow sound. Careful not to lean forward, I gingerly took one hand off the pole, reached for the tape antenna, and banged it against the pole. It echoed hollowly. *Shit. Termites.* I had another five feet to go to get the antenna to the top, and we needed all the altitude we could get to get a shot to Saipan. I didn't have much choice but to keep on going. *Thonk, thonk.* A foot at a time, I edged up. *Thonk, thonk.* I could hear the wood splintering as I moved. Finally, I made it to the top. I peered down the top of the pole, and, as I suspected, it was hollow as far down as I could see. And it wasn't thick hollow—it was thin hollow.

My heart in my throat, I tied the antenna to the top of the pole, desperate not to drop it from my trembling hands. After letting the two tapes dangle down to the ground, I slowly started my descent. It was even worse, because I couldn't see where I was going so I just had to have faith and step each gaff firmly into the pole. *Thonk, thonk, thonk, thonk.* Then *chunk, chunk, chunk, chunk* on down to the bottom of the pole.

Finally, feet on the ground, I took off the gaffs. Bill was waiting for me at the bottom, grinning.

"That was pretty impressive," he said under his breath so the crowd wouldn't hear.

"Yeah, you wouldn't believe," I muttered back, my knees turning to water and almost buckling under me as I bent to remove the gaffs.

Bill and I found both ends of the tape antenna and pulled them up and out—one toward the palm tree, and one toward the crown of the police station roof—to the prescribed length for the frequencies we were going to be using. Figuring it'd be easiest to start with the palm tree, I took some parachute cord, tied one end of it to the antenna tape and the other end to a rock, and tossed it up toward the cut-off fronds just under the top of the tree, about thirty feet away. I missed the whole damn palm tree—didn't even come close. There I was trying to exude confidence and competence, and I was throwing like a rookie in front of a bunch of Palauans, who are some of the greatest baseball players in the world. Most of them can throw a stone and knock the eye out of a seagull. And I couldn't even hit a target as big as a tree.

I picked the rock back up, tightened the parachute cord back onto it, and tossed again, determined to hit the tree this time. The rock hit the tree at least, but other than that, nothing happened because it didn't snag properly. Finally, I handed the rock to Bill. He didn't say anything, but he had this sort of amused gleam in his eye because he knew how incompetent I was at such things and I expect he had just been waiting for his shot. He took aim, tossed the rock up with one easy movement, and it looped over one of the lower fronds. In minutes, we had pulled the lead of the antenna up taut, using the parachute cord.

After the first tape was hooked up, Bill and I climbed up onto a chain-link fence behind the police station and onto the rusty tin roof, pulling the other end of the line up behind us. We oriented it properly to reach Saipan, then tied it off halfway up the existing radio antenna mast on top of the police station. When it was secure, we scrambled down and, as casually as possible, walked back through the front door of the police station, turning left past the front desk and down the corridor to Lukas Panuelo's office.

"Is the antenna up?" Lukas asked.

"Yeah, I think we've got it, Captain," I said. "Now let's see if we can get this sucker running."

I plugged the antenna into the transceiver unit, plugged the power cord into the outlet in the wall, and dialed up the frequency we'd arranged in advance for TT to monitor. Then I depressed the microphone button and said, a little tentatively, "TT-1, this is TT-2. Over."

There was a *crackle hiss, crackle hiss* in response, and I repeated, "TT-1, this is TT-2. Say again. Over."

This time I heard Dwight Kitalong come on the line. "Stand by, TT-2."

I waited a few seconds, and then I heard Jan's voice. "Bry-, uh, I mean, TT-2, this is TT-1. Do you have information for us? Over."

"Roger that. Situation tense but stable. Most police still on the job. Crowd estimated at fifty to sixty outside the police station. Over."

"Can you confirm the police shooting? Over."

"Roger. One dead, three injured. Over."

"Has anyone else been hurt? Over."

"Negative. At least not that we know of. Over."

"Do you have additional information? Over."

"Negative. That's all we have at this time. Over."

"Roger. We're standing by. People here—and in Washington—are anxious for updates. Please report hourly. Over."

"Roger that. We'll recontact in one hour on frequency Jump 2. Over."

"Roger. TT-1 out."

"TT-2 out."

Looking out the window, I could see the crowd building outside the police station. They looked angry, and a few people were trying to incite the others who were just standing around. It was pretty obvious that everyone was still upset over the shooting.

I turned to Bill and said, "Well, how 'bout if we go work the crowd?"

"Sounds good to me," said Bill.

"Tom Remengesau would like to see you, too," said Lukas. "He said to ask you to come to his office as soon as you can."

Remengesau, the former district administrator for Palau who had first introduced me to fruit bat at the feast following the Con Con back in 1979, now was the minister of justice for the new republic.

"OK, Lukas. We'll go talk to the people in the crowd for a little bit, and then we'll go on over and see him," I said.

Bill and I left Lukas's office and walked down the corridor and out of the shade of the police station into the bright stark heat of midday Palau, just a few degrees north of the equator.

We both made an effort to be casual. All around us, there were people we'd seen before or talked with or drunk beer with at some time in the past, and as we walked near each of them we made a point of looking them in the eyes and saying "*Alii,*" which is Palauan for "Hello."

Most of them looked back at us and said "*Alii.*" The whole process was about us showing that there wasn't a major riot about to happen here—that this wasn't like last September, where we had policemen deserting their posts and going around with strikers blowing up office buildings and chasing the non-strikers out with sticks of dynamite and bombing and burning the president's office. We were trying to communicate that this was different, and that the police weren't going to participate in, or tolerate, that kind of behavior any longer.

This isn't the kind of thing that anybody teaches you to do in some police academy or textbook. It's just the sort of thing that any good street cop learns early on. You learn that what prevents a riot or keeps people from panicking isn't the fact that you can kick their asses or that you have the power to arrest them or shoot them—it's presence. It's the ability to say, "The authorities are here. Things are under control. Things are *not* going to get out of control." It's what being a police officer is really all about, most of the time, no matter where you are. Some things, at least, remain the same from culture to culture.

After about fifteen minutes of just mixing with the crowd, passing pleasantries with a command presence, and acting like everything was perfectly normal, Bill and I walked over to Tom Remengesau's office, just across the square. During our meeting, we assured him that our role was just to observe, support his officers, and report back to Saipan and Washington.

"So Washington knows, too?" said Tom.

"Yes. Everybody is watching," I said, somewhat pointedly.

"Please tell them that we are doing what we can to reinstate negotiations with PAGE. I think President Remeliik is also going to try and work out a curfew to help calm things down, but he has to get the *ibedul's* approval first," Tom said, referring to Koror's tribal high chief.

"Is there anything we can do to help with that?" Bill asked.

"I don't think so," Tom said a little cautiously. "But maybe you should go see President Remeliik and ask him."

As Bill and I left the minister's building and walked down the steps, I said, "So, do you wanna go on over and talk to Remeliik now, then?"

"Yeah, but we don't have time," Bill replied, looking at his watch. "We were supposed to talk to Jan five minutes ago."

"Shit, I forgot," I said. "All right. Let's head back."

Once again we walked back through the crowd outside the police station, saying *"Alii"* and stopping to talk briefly with those we had met before as we made our way to the front door.

Back in Lukas Panuelo's office, I turned on the radio and fiddled with the knobs to make the frequency jump, then depressed the mike button.

"TT-1, this is TT-2. Over," I said.

"TT-2, go ahead. Over," came the immediate reply. It was Jan.

"The crowd outside the police station is estimated at about seventy. The situation is still tense, but stable. There are some reports of groups of strikers in pickup trucks down at the docks and other parts of town, but we don't know the extent of what's going on there yet. Over."

"Roger. Have you any additional information on the status of negotiations?"

"Tom Remengesau said they're still trying to reinstate negotiations, and the president and the *ibedul* are trying to work out a curfew. Over."

"Have you spoken to the president yet? Over."

"Negative. We're on our way to see him next. Over."

"Roger, TT-2. Please check back in sixty. Over."

"Roger. Will check back in sixty. Jump 1. Over."

I released the mike switch and then reached over to turn off the transmitter, thinking to myself what a miracle it was that we were finally able to communicate with headquarters, even if it was a pain in the ass to have to check in every hour. I was also pretty impressed that I was managing to get the jump frequencies right. I mean, Gene had only had time to give me a crash course in operating the radio before Bill and I left, and I still didn't know what half the dials and buttons were for. Take that switch marked VOX, for example. I didn't know what the hell that one was. I flipped it on just to see, but nothing happened so I turned off the radio and then turned to Bill.

"Well, I guess we better head on over to see Remeliik," I said. "You ready?"

"Sure. Let's go," said Bill.

We headed down the hall and out the front door of the police station, wading back through the crowd before crossing the square to President Remeliik's office. We spent more than an hour with Remeliik, going over much of the same information we had already discussed with Tom Remengesau and offering to help in any way we could.

When the meeting was finally over, Bill reminded me that we were late again for talking to the Hi Com.

"Shit." I said. "I thought it would be great to finally have a way to communicate with headquarters, but this hourly call-in business is a bitch when you're trying to get anything done. It's almost as bad as the micromanaging from Washington when we were on Kwaj."

"You're the one who got us the radio," Bill said.

"Yeah, don't remind me," I grumbled.

We walked back across the square to the police department. There were a lot of people still milling around, and a few angry voices, but as we made a point of walking past them, smiling and saying "*Alii*," they became more subdued again.

We apologized to Lukas for yet another intrusion as we entered his office and turned on the radio for the third time to give Jan our latest report. Not that there was much of anything new to report in the hour since I had last spoken to her.

"Don't you have any more information for us than that?" Jan finally asked. "I'm getting many queries from Washington."

"Well I'd have more fucking information if we weren't running back here every hour to talk on the goddam radio," I muttered under my breath, without depressing the microphone button.

"Say again, TT-2?" Jan said sharply.

Shit. I knew I hadn't depressed the mike button, but somehow the radio had transmitted my last comment. I quickly pressed the microphone button and said, "Uh, negative, TT-1. Radio problems on this end. Stand by. Over."

I released the button again, turned to Bill and said, "What happened?" As I spoke, the red transmission light came on, even though the mike button was still off. That's when it finally dawned on me that the little VOX switch I flipped earlier must stand for "Voice-Operated" something-or-other.

I turned off the VOX switch and said, "Test, test," loudly, without depressing the mike button. There was no response, and no red transmission light came on this time.

With my heart up in my throat, I depressed the mike and said, "This is TT-2. Over."

"Go ahead, TT-2. Over," Jan replied. Her voice had an imperious ring to it that was evident even over the shortwave static.

"We're back on the air. Over," I said.

"Roger. Do you have anything more to report? Over."

"Negative. Over."

"Suggest you report back in three hours. Will that work? Over."

"Uh, Roger, TT-1. That's excellent. Thank you. With a Jump 1? Over."

"That's affirmative. Over."

"Roger, TT-1. TT-2 out."

"TT-1 out."

I turned to Bill and said, "*Oeegulah!*" (*Oeegulah* is an all-purpose Palauan expression that literally means, "Oh, what a pig." There really isn't an English equivalent, although I once had a drill instructor whose favorite expletive was "Great hairy ape shit!"—which is about as close as you can come.)

"Well, she didn't sound too pissed off," Bill said, grinning. "Maybe you got your point across."

"Yeah. Or maybe I'm going to be looking for a new job when we get back."

CHAPTER 14

Tropical Troopers

Bill and I got back to Saipan in late November, exhausted after two weeks of almost nonstop talking and conflict resolution on Palau.

Trying my best not to seem overly apprehensive over the VOX snafu, but fully expecting at least a serious ass chewing for it, I stopped in to see Jan first thing the morning after we returned. But you know, she never said another word about it. It was just one of many examples of her maturity as a manager—or perhaps her lack of a male ego. Although come to think of it, she did send me off to Alaska soon after I returned from Palau.

The Alaska trip was vintage Jan. As we were rehashing the latest Palau crisis—and the situation on Kwajalein before that—she asked if there was anything we could do to ever get ahead of these sorts of problems and to really have an impact on the quality of policing in Micronesia. I said I didn't think we'd ever make any serious progress doing nothing but brief, small-scale training projects.

"So what *would* work?" she wondered aloud.

"Well," I replied, "I've got an idea, but I don't think you'd go for it. There's no funding."

"Try me," Jan said, leaning back in her chair and waiting for me to continue.

"OK," I said. "A few years ago John Karja and I worked

out a ten-year plan that would gradually build up a cadre of local police officers with the skills to run their own training academies. Our idea was to take a group of our best Micronesian officers to the State Trooper Academy in Sitka and put them through full-blown academy training. The next year we'd take a second group out there—about thirty officers each time. After that, we'd start running the academies here."

"With the Micronesians as instructors?" Jan asked.

"No, not at first," I said. "By year three, they'd back up our instructors, doing a few lectures and sort of apprenticing on all the administrative stuff. But they'd gradually assume more responsibility and control each year, until they were finally running the whole thing themselves."

"How much would something like that cost?" Jan asked.

"I've got a tentative budget that John and I worked up back in my office. Let me run and get it."

I hurried down the hall to my office and dragged out my scrawled notes from the vodka-soaked brainstorming session when John and I had come up with the plan. Smoothing them out and struggling to decipher my progressively cryptic calculations, I marveled at the hubris that had prompted me to hang on to them.

Jan and I went over the figures for twenty minutes. Then she paused to look out the window past the tops of the coconut palms out toward Managaha Island.

"Three hundred and fifty thousand," she said thoughtfully. "You're right, I don't think anyone at Interior or State has that much funding available for this sort of thing."

"Nope," I agreed. "Neither does DOD."

"Then I think you had better take a trip. First to Washington—I'll give you a list of people on the Hill to talk with—and then to Alaska to get their OK to use the academy." She looked at me over her reading glasses with half a smile. "Can you leave tomorrow?"

I balked a little at that. I'd only just gotten home from Palau the day before, and Susan and I were still in the "honeymoon" phase that usually lasted for about two or three days after I returned home from a long trip. Things were pretty good between us at the moment, and I was loathe to ruin that by telling her I had to leave again so soon.

Sensing my initial hesitation, Jan asked, "Is there a problem with that?"

"No, no, not at all," I lied. "I just hope the water is still on when I get home tonight so I can at least wash my underwear first."

It was a pretty good recovery because it was all too true. There hadn't been time for laundry on Palau, and I was down to my last pair of skivvies.

Jan snorted and shooed me on my way. My hand was on the doorknob when she added, "It's a good idea, Bryan. Make it happen."

* * *

In Washington, it didn't take me long to get the support of Alaska's congressional delegation—Senators Ted Stevens and Frank Murkowski and Congressman Don Young—and their staff. They all remembered what it had been like to be a territory and to depend on other states for training and technical assistance. With their support and John Karja's deft guidance, my trip to Anchorage was equally successful. I was back on Saipan in time for Christmas, with a signed agreement in hand.

I spent much of my well-deserved break over the holidays trying to make it up to Susan for being gone for so long. I wasn't sure if she had really forgiven me or if she just didn't want Christmas to be spoiled, but either way, we made the most of the respite. Then I hit the ground running right after the new year, with just six months to put the whole program together.

One of the first things I did was recruit Art Griswold to help me run the training. Art was an experienced ex-cop who'd also been an Underwater Demolition Team sailor and a submariner in the Navy back before the Vietnam War. A likeable giant of a man, he'd been the police chief on Yap for the past two years before coming to work as an investigator with TTBI on Saipan.

With Art's tireless help, we selected the officers who would participate in the program, arranged to get all of them to Sitka, and coordinated the details of the Micronesian Police Academy with the trooper academy trainers there.

The way Art and I saw it, one of the keys to making this whole thing work was going to be making sure the Micronesian officers were comfortable during their stay in Alaska. For many of the officers, particularly those who had never traveled outside Micronesia, the unfamiliar environment might prove to be a bit overwhelming. But we figured that as long as we were there with them every step of the way, living among them and participating in the training program, they'd be able to handle the culture shock. The troopers agreed and worked out arrangements for us to stay at the academy and work closely with their trainers during the three-month program.

The downside of this, of course, was that both of our wives were going to have to stay on Saipan for the three months we were out there. Susan and Art's wife, Diane, had become good friends, so at least they'd have each other to grouse to about their errant husbands. Still, we knew they weren't pleased about the situation, so Art and I tried our best not to look too eager about the prospect of spending a whole summer in Alaska on our own.

II

After six months of nearly nonstop preparations for the trip, I experienced a strange, almost anticlimactic feeling as I kissed Susan good-bye and boarded the plane from Saipan to Guam—

the first leg of the long journey to Sitka—shortly before noon on June 4.

That feeling didn't last long. As soon as we transferred to the Island Hopper on Guam, joining the Palauan and Yapese officers who had flown into Guam on the Betel Nut Express and were already on board, there was excitement in the air. Even the Yapese were excited, which was a bit of a change from their usual deadpan demeanor.

Both Palauan and Yapese officers alike were heavily laden with leis and *mar mars*. They flashed wide, betel nut-stained grins and said exuberant hellos as Art and I came on board. The Yapese officers were especially happy to see Art, their former police chief. And I was especially happy to see Teresa Robert, the lone female officer in the group.

Teresa, whom I'd met on my first trip to Yap several years earlier, had been a member of the Yapese police force for about five years now. During that time, she had gained a reputation for being a very good officer and, as I recall, she also had gotten the top score on the English exam that was required for attendance in the Sitka academy. During the selection process, I had been concerned that despite her strong attributes, Teresa might have been passed over by the Yapese leaders simply because she was a woman, and Yap still had a very traditional culture. But they had surprised me with their lack of sexism—hers had been one of the first names on the list of nominees, and she had received unanimous approval from the all-male selection committee.

Art and I settled into our seats near the middle of the plane, and pretty soon the Island Hopper was on its way. Most of the officers were already on their third or fourth beer, so even those who had never been on a plane before that day didn't seem too nervous during takeoff. But it was a different story when we landed on Truk with the usual Air Mike flair—slamming down hard on the runway and screeching to a stop as the oxygen masks jolted down from their overhead compartments. This time, more than a few of the armrests received crushing grips from the first-time flyers in the group.

After all the passengers who were getting off on Truk had deplaned, our Trukese officers were first up to board. Art and I made the mistake of getting off briefly to greet them and found ourselves enveloped in the unavoidable clouds of cheap perfume that the Trukese always spray on each other for good luck before a flight. But it was well worth it to me as soon as I saw two of my favorite officers, Katios Gallen and Masachiro Simina, among those who had been selected to participate in the training program.

"*Ran annim*," Katios said, reaching me first and crushing my hand in his.

"*Ran annim*," I replied, trying not to scream and go to my knees. Shaking hands with a Trukese is always dangerous, but shaking hands with an excited Trukese weightlifter is downright foolhardy.

I shook hands with Masachiro next, bracing myself for the pain, but by now my hand was so numb I probably wouldn't have noticed if he had broken several bones.

Katios, Masachiro, and the other Trukese officers said their final good-byes to the crowds of family and friends who had come to see them off, and pretty soon we were on our way again.

On Ponape, the same farewell ceremony that we had witnessed on Truk was taking place—only with slightly less perfume and slightly more plumeria leis. There were at least a couple hundred people at the airport, most of whom were related to one or more of the officers who were leaving. And there among them were the Kosraean officers—*my* Kosraean officers—coming toward the plane. (Air Mike still didn't fly to Kosrae, so they had had to take a missionary flight into Ponape in order to join us on the Island Hopper.) They looked good—very professional and squared away—and I felt a swell of pride as they boarded.

Our last stop aboard the Island Hopper was Majuro, where we picked up the four Marshallese cops who had been selected for the program. The going-away ceremony on the small atoll was a bit more subdued than those on Ponape or Truk had been. Yet despite the fact that there was considerably less fanfare, I could swear there was just as much perfume and plumeria stench emanating from each of the Marshallese officers as they came on board as any of the other officers had brought with them.

* * *

Sixteen hours later, give or take a few hours for those who had boarded the flight before or after Guam, we finally arrived in Honolulu at about eight o'clock in the morning local time.

It was a big transition. Only about a third of the officers had ever traveled outside Micronesia, and Honolulu is a comparatively big place. So for most of them, it was an amazing experience.

Staying together as a group, we stumbled down the corridor to immigration. From there, it was just a quick trip up the escalator to baggage claim and customs. Or at least, it should've been. Art and I hadn't stopped to think how disconcerting an escalator might be to folks who had never seen such a thing in all their lives. I mean, many of the officers had seen damn few if any two-story buildings before, much less one with a moving staircase. The orderly line from immigration to customs knotted quickly as they struggled between fear of this completely new and strange contraption, and their need to appear competent and fearless at all times. But eventually, their egos got the better of their fear, especially given the fact that men, women, and children of all ages were calmly getting on other escalators all around them, and one by one, they took the plunge.

After we got through the airport red tape, we still had eight hours to spare until our flight to Seattle. As much as I would've liked to keep everybody together in one room to avoid the possibility of losing someone in the Honolulu airport, I knew that wasn't going to work so I had to content myself with a long lecture, punctuated by a few dire threats, about the importance of being at the right gate at least an hour before the flight was due to be called.

Amazingly, everybody made it to the gate on time and we boarded the flight to Seattle without incident, unless you count the fact that the Micronesians had all bought so many stuffed animals, T-shirts, baseball caps, and other souvenirs to take back home to their families that there was barely enough overhead storage space on the plane to hold all their loot.

We had a quick plane change in Seattle. And an hour and a half after that, Sitka came into view on the horizon.

III

As the Alaska Airlines plane glided smoothly to a landing in Sitka, Mt. Edgecumbe loomed nearby, and across the harbor to the east, the town itself was tucked around the spire of an old Russian church. We taxied to a stop in front of the small Sitka Airport terminal, where several of the troopers were waiting to greet us.

We waited until the few passengers who weren't with our group had disembarked. Art and I got off the plane next. At the foot of the stair ramp, we shook hands with the trooper academy commander, Captain Warren Townsend, as well as the first sergeant, Ted Hobart, and his drill instructors, who were standing at parade rest in an impeccable line just behind him.

"How was your trip out?" Warren asked me as the Micronesian officers slowly began making their way down the stairs in their wilted leis and rumpled aloha shirts, lugging their overflowing shopping bags and looking a little uncertain about their new surroundings.

"Not a single glitch," I said.

"Good, good," he replied. "So, how many do we have?"

"Thirty-four."

"All right. We'll take it from here," he said.

After Art and I stepped out of the way, Warren turned to Ted, who immediately brought himself to attention and said, "First Sergeant, take charge of your people."

"Yes, sir," Ted replied. He did a crisp about face and barked a series of commands to his squad of drill instructors. "Detail. Atten-hut. Divide 'em into three groups and get 'em on the bus. Fall out."

The drill instructors rapidly marched to positions about ten yards apart from each other and began yelling at the Micronesian officers. "Over here, over here. Fall in, fall in. You, you, you, you, you, you, get over here now."

The Micronesians just stood and stared at first, bewildered by the sudden shouting.

I turned to Warren and asked, "Should I translate?"

"No, they'll work it out," he replied, with just the barest hint of a grin.

I smiled, remembering my own boot camp experience. The goal of drill instructors everywhere is to make it clear from the first that you don't know squat, and that you've got to learn it fast.

"Over here, over here. You, you, you, you. *Now*," the drill sergeants continued to bark.

The Micronesians, most of whom were jet lagged and a little hung over, finally began to understand what was going on and started to break into groups near each of the drill sergeants.

"Get in a line, get in a line. Move it, move it, move it," the DIs barked, jaws jutted forward, as they marched up and down the ragged line of officers. "Stand at attention. Get your feet together. You look like a bunch of animals. You, get in that herd over there. I've already got enough men. You, move over there. Stand straight. Get your eyes front. Suck in that gut. Get your heels together. Hands along the seams of your trousers."

Some of the officers seemed to understand the drill and did their best to comply, while others looked around them wildly, attempting to copy what the other officers were doing. But somehow, in less than five minutes, three groups of rather apprehensive-looking Micronesian officers stood at some semblance of attention behind each of the three drill instructors.

Ted marched to the middle of the sorry formation, came to attention, and shouted, "First squad, board the bus."

The first squad drill instructor called out, "Right face." Two of the officers did a right face, one did a left face, and the others just stood there. "No, your *other* right," the drill sergeant snapped, pointing in the direction he wanted them to turn. The errant officers scrambled to comply. "Forward, march," the DI commanded. Sloppy and uncoordinated, the formation gradually shuffled toward the bus like a drunken centipede, and one by one the officers got on board.

The second and third squads, who had had the advantage of watching the other squad go first, soon followed suit, and eventually all the officers were aboard the bus. Art and I hopped into the front of a pickup truck full of the officers' luggage with Warren and took off after the bus.

We took O'Connell Bridge across Sitka Harbor to the main part of town, past the red-roofed Pioneer Home and St. Michael's Russian Orthodox cathedral, then turned up the road to the academy, which was lined on either side with tall Sitka spruces, cedars, and salmonberry bushes. Soon after we passed the Sitka National Cemetery, we turned left into the parking lot of the Public Safety Academy. The bus was already parked, and the Micronesian officers were just beginning to stumble down the stairs and back into formation amid the bellows of the drill instructors.

***

It was Friday. The academy training wouldn't begin in earnest until Monday morning, but we had plenty to do to keep busy until then. Rooms had to be assigned, rules and regulations explained, uniforms inspected, and, as I soon discovered during the uniform inspection, athletic shoes needed to be bought. I hadn't stopped to think that while most of the officers had fairly acceptable uniform shoes, none of them owned anything even close to a decent pair of gym shoes.

So first thing Saturday morning, we hauled them all down to Sitka's lone athletic shop, where we were lucky enough to get all but three of them fitted with running shoes. For those whose feet had proven just a little too wide for any of the shoes the store had in stock, the owner made a call to Seattle to place a special order and had it express mailed so we'd have the remaining shoes by Monday afternoon.

Our next unforeseen problem emerged on Sunday morning. Art had just returned from the cafeteria at nearby Sheldon Jackson College, where we had arranged for the officers to take their meals. Leaving the officers to their own devices for a couple of hours (the last free time they were likely to have for a long, long time), he joined me for a cup of coffee in the troopers' staff quarters.

"So, how are they doing?" I asked. Our deal was that Art would take the lead in looking after the officers while we were in Sitka, while I would handle the majority of the teaching and administrative duties.

"Well, they're still pretty rocky right now," said Art.

"Culture shock?"

"Yeah. Plus, I don't think any of them are getting much sleep."

"You mean because they're so excited?" I said.

"No, I don't think it's just the excitement," Art said. "The problem is, they're used to going to sleep when the sun goes down, and that's not till after midnight here. Then they wake up with the sun when it comes back up at three-thirty in the morning."

I laughed and said, "Well, they'll be tired enough once the training begins. I bet they'll sleep all right then."

"Yeah, that oughta do the trick," Art agreed.

"Everything else OK?" I asked.

"Pretty much," Art said. "But we do have this one other problem."

"Oh? What's that?"

"Well, Bryan, I don't think Teri's sleeping in her quarters."

"What? Why not? She's not shacking up with somebody, is she?" I asked.

"No, no, not that," Art said. "But she's been sleeping in the Yapese officers' quarters upstairs. I found out about it yesterday and told her she has to sleep in her own quarters. She said she would, but then she was up there with them again last night."

"Well, I can understand that it must be hard on her—I mean, Micronesians almost never sleep alone, especially the Yapese. But while we're here, she's gotta follow the rules or she'll get kicked out," I said.

"I told her that, but apparently it didn't do any good," Art said.

"Do you want me to talk to her?"

"Yeah, maybe that'd help," said Art. "Lemme go find her."

He went out the door and headed for the rec room, which was just across the hall from the staff quarters. When he returned, Teresa was with him, staring down at her feet.

"Hi, Teresa," I said with a smile. "Come on in and sit down."

"Hi, Chief," Teresa said, taking a seat across from me at the table.

"Art tells me you're still sleeping with the Yapese officers instead of in your own room. Why?" I asked.

"I don't want to sleep alone down there," Teresa replied a little nervously.

"I see," I said gently. "But in this culture, men and women who aren't married can't sleep in the same place, at least not here at the academy. It's against the regulations. The troopers would be very upset with you if they found out. So you're going to have to sleep in your own room from now on."

Teresa hesitated for a moment, then said, "But I'm afraid to sleep down there."

"Why?"

"There are ghosts," Teresa said.

I looked at Art for help. He knew a lot more about Yapese culture than I did.

"Why do you think there are ghosts down there, Teri?" Art asked.

"There's a cemetery next to us. Right over there," Teresa said, pointing.

"Ah," Art said, rubbing his chin thoughtfully with his thumb and forefinger. "Tell you what, Teri," he said after a long pause. "Why don't you go back to the rec room for a few minutes. Bryan and I will talk about this and see if we can work something out."

"OK," she agreed, getting up to leave. After she had gone, Art came over and sat down next to me.

"I forgot all about the cemetery," he said. "I know Teri's Palauan, but she's been living on Yap for a long time now, and she's picked up a lot of their customs and beliefs. The Yapese would never sleep near a cemetery, and they'd especially never sleep *alone* near a cemetery. They're afraid the spirits will come and take their souls while they're sleeping."

"So what are we supposed to do here?" I asked Art. "I mean, if it were up to me I'd tell her to go ahead and sleep in the men's quarters if she wants, but I don't think the troopers are going to go for that."

"You can bet on it," Art replied dryly.

"Wait a minute," I said, as an idea came to me. "Back on Truk, Kimo Panolo dealt with this sort of problem by spraying his officers with perfume before they went out on patrol at night—"

"Yeah, but the Yapese don't use perfume like that," Art interjected. "If we had a traditional Yapese medicine woman here, maybe she could help, but I don't know what to do."

"All right, then. How 'bout if we have some of the other officers stand guard outside her door at night in shifts?" I asked.

"Then *they're* not going to get enough sleep," he said.

"No one's getting much sleep anyway, like you said. Besides, I don't know what else to suggest."

"Me neither," said Art.

"Let's try talking to Teresa again and see what she thinks," I said.

We called Teresa back in and I said, "Here's the problem, Teresa. We really want you to succeed here and we want you to finish the academy. We sure don't want to have the only woman in the program be a dropout."

"I'm not going to drop out," Teresa said firmly.

"We think you'll do a good job, too. But if the troopers find out that you're sleeping upstairs with the men, we'll have to dismiss you from the academy. So somehow you're going to have to deal with this. Art and I talked about it, and we thought it might help if we have some of the other officers volunteer to stand guard outside your room at night. Do you want us to do that?"

Teresa was quiet for a minute, thinking. I could tell by her expression that the idea was appealing to her. But finally, more than a little reluctantly, she said, "No, that wouldn't be fair. I'll try to sleep down there by myself."

"Good for you, Teresa," I said. "You give it your best shot, and if you still have problems, you come and talk to us. OK?"

"OK, Chief," she said, her tone still reluctant.

"And if it helps any, I'm almost certain there are no ghosts here," I added. "That's a national cemetery. Only veterans are buried there, and I'm sure they all had proper burials."

"OK, Chief," Teresa said again before she left, not sounding the least bit convinced.

IV

My alarm went off at five o'clock on Monday morning, as it would six days a week for the next thirteen weeks. Badly in need of caffeine, as I always am in the morning, I stumbled into my workout clothes and then roused Art, who'd been snoring thunderously in the next room.

We stepped out into the hallway just as the drill instructors came storming through to rouse everyone out of their rooms. We'd warned the Micronesians to be ready, to set their alarms and be dressed in their physical training gear by five-thirty. Fortunately, they all were—otherwise they would have been in for a rude awakening, literally.

The DIs hustled the officers down the stairs and out of the building, barking orders all the way, and lined them up out in front of the barracks. It was raining and there was a chill in the air—Sitka weather has been described as "perpetual autumn"—but most of the Micronesian officers made a valiant effort to hide their discomfort as the DIs stalked up and down the ranks, correcting their posture at attention.

As soon as the officers were aligned to the DIs' satisfaction, Ted Hobart approached the group. "Who's the fastest runner here?" he asked in a loud, authoritative voice.

No hands came up, of course, because Micronesians rarely boast.

Ted paused, looked up and down the ranks, and said, "All right, then, how many of you have ever run before?"

This time, all the hands came up.

"No, I mean how many of you have ever run in a foot race before?"

All the hands came up again.

"I mean as adults. How many of you can run fast *now*?"

This time, only three officers raised their hands. Ted handed orange traffic safety vests and flashlights to two of them.

"We're going to go for a short run, people," he announced. "I expect you all to stay in formation. You two with the vests, go to the head of the line. You'll run on ahead to each intersection and stop traffic so the formation can pass through. Do you understand?"

"Yes," the officers said in unison.

"What?"

"Yes," both officers repeated, a little louder this time.

"The first word out of your mouths will be sir, and the last word out of your mouths will be sir. Do you understand?" Ted shouted.

"Yes, sir."

"The *first* word out of your mouths will be sir, and the *last* word out of your mouths will be sir. Do you understand?" Ted repeated, louder this time.

"Sir, yes sir," the officers replied, looking mildly terrified.

"Then get to the front of the line," Ted said, pointing.

"Sir, yes sir," the officers said again before scurrying into place.

"All right. Those of you without running shoes, fall out," Ted said, nodding toward the three officers whose athletic shoes had not yet arrived from Seattle. Looking confused, they remained where they were.

"That means step out of the formation, people," Ted said in a quietly exasperated tone.

Eager to comply, the three officers without running shoes quickly stepped out of line.

"You'll wait here for the rest of the class to return," Ted told them. "Do you understand?"

"Yes," they answered.

"The proper response is 'Sir, yes sir.' Do you understand?"

"Sir, yes sir."

Ted turned back to the rest of the officers and gave the order, "Right, face!"

This time, about half of the officers turned to the right, while the other half stared ahead dumbly, and a couple turned to the left. The drill instructors paced up and down the ranks, none-too-gently straightening people out.

"Forward, march," Ted called out, as soon as everyone in line was facing the right direction.

Following behind the two officers in the orange vests, who sprinted on ahead as they had been told to stop traffic at the upcoming intersections, the officers began to stumble forward in a line, stepping on each other's heels and shivering in the rain. Ted and his drill instructors marched alongside them, and Art and I followed suit.

"Double time, march," Ted called out, as soon we reached the main road.

He and the DIs stepped up the pace into a jogging double time, and the Micronesians quickly caught on and did the same, at least for a while. By the time we made it to the first intersection, about a quarter of a mile down the road, they were already beginning to straggle into a long, disorganized line. Half of them were gasping for breath and holding their sides. Two had to stop to puke by the side of the road. One of the drill instructors fell back to take charge of the stragglers and at least keep them moving forward. Another stayed with the middle group, as did Art, while the third stayed up with the front group, along with Ted and me.

But it wasn't long before even many of the officers in the first group were starting to gasp for air, and we had to turn them all around and head back to the academy. That first day's run was all of half a mile, maybe a little more.

As we stood in front of the barracks, waiting for the last of the stragglers, Ted turned to me and said under his breath, "I thought you said these people had been working out for the last three months to get ready for this?"

"I think most of them *have* been," I said with a wry smile.

He rolled his eyes and said, "This is going to be a lot different than training the Village Public Safety Officers. Half of those guys had been running twenty-mile trap lines in snowshoes before they got here."

"Don't worry. I think they'll pick it up pretty quick," I said.

"We'll see. I just hope it's not all this bad."

"It won't be," I said confidently, remembering my first half-mile run in Marine Corps boot camp. We had all felt like we were dying, too, even though individually, we were all able to run at least that far and then some. Part of the problem is that running in formation is very awkward until you get used to it.

Ted snorted in response, then turned to the group of officers, many of whom were still panting and wheezing, and called them to attention once more. "You have exactly thirty minutes to shower, shave, and dress in your uniforms for breakfast. That means you'll be back down here, in formation, at oh seven hundred. Is that clear, people?"

"Sir, yes sir," the officers replied, most of them finally grasping the required response to the first sergeant's questions.

"All right, then. Fall out."

The Micronesian officers stumbled and limped on up the stairs to their rooms to shower and dress, and Art and I headed to the staff quarters to do the same. They were all back downstairs at seven o'clock, as ordered. Art walked them on over to the Sheldon Jackson cafeteria for breakfast while I had coffee and cereal in the staff quarters dining room with Ted and the drill instructors.

Our next scheduled activity for the morning was a physical fitness assessment. As soon as Art brought the officers back to the barracks, we had them go back upstairs and change back into their PT gear. Then we took them all over to the academy gym.

The physical fitness assessment consisted of several stages. First, the troopers used calipers to measure body fat, taking a pinch at the waist, thighs, and arms. Here, as with the morning run, the troopers did a lot of eye rolling at the results. The Micronesians, on the other hand, seemed quite proud. In their culture, body weight is a sign of prosperity and prestige.

But the troopers' reactions were quite different when we took the officers over to the weight room and began administering the strength tests. More than half the officers were weightlifters, most of them powerlifters, and it soon became obvious that there was more than just fat on those massive arms and thighs.

"Well, at least it's not *all* bad news," Ted mused, as he and Art and I watched five-foot-five Gibson Abraham bench press 300 pounds. "If we can ever get these people running, we'll have 'em in shape before the summer's over."

* * *

As the week progressed, the officers received training in academy procedures, military bearing and appearance requirements, and the rudimentary aspects of drill. They learned to fall in on command, line up in reasonably straight ranks, come to attention, and, for the most part, turn right when a right-face command was given and left on a left-face command.

From there, we moved into the formal course work. Each day began with an early morning run of gradually increasing length, followed by breakfast, three hours of classes, and an hour of physical fitness and defensive tactics training before lunch. After lunch there were more classes and then more fitness training, as well as practical exercises on police tactics that often lasted on into the evening.

But despite the fact that the officers were doing better by the day, they still were dragging badly. It wasn't just the arduous physical training or the sun-related lack of sleep—they were also having difficulty with the drastic change in climate. Early into the training, we had a massive outbreak of colds and flu, which we mainly combated with large doses of vitamin C and a few over-the-counter medications.

On top of these complications, there was one other problem we never would have expected.

Just before lunch one day during that first week, Teresa Robert walked up to Art and me. "Can I talk to you, Chief?" she asked.

"Sure, Teresa. How's everything going?" I asked, figuring she was still concerned about the ghosts, although as far as we knew, she had been sleeping in her own room since Art and I had talked to her on Sunday.

"OK, I guess."

"Are you still sleeping down in your own room?"

"Yes."

"And it's OK now? No ghosts?"

"I think so, maybe. I can't sleep very much, but I stay down there," Teresa said, her tone rather stoic.

"Good for you, Teresa," I replied. "So, what did you want to see us about?"

"I have a problem."

"What kind of problem?"

"With the running."

"Oh?" I said, surprised to hear it because Teresa had consistently kept up with the first group on our runs. "What's the matter? Are your shoes OK?"

"My shoes are good. But my breasts hurt," she said matter-of-factly, cupping her rather ample breasts with both hands and hefting them upward.

"Why?" I asked, rather taken aback by this revelation and not quite knowing what else to say.

"From the running. It makes them bounce too much, and they hurt," she said, bouncing her breasts up and down in front of Art and me to illustrate.

Art and I both managed to act mature and detached, but as American men, the sight of an attractive young woman bouncing her breasts up and down in each hand in front of us was a little disconcerting, I'll admit.

"Don't you have a bra?" Art asked, his face reddening slightly.

"I have a bra on now, but they still bounce up and down. See," Teresa said, demonstrating for us once again.

"Well, how 'bout if we get you a running bra?" I said.

"What's that?" Teresa asked.

"It's a bra they make especially for running that'll, uh, hold them in place better," I said.

"Oh, that's good," Teresa said.

"Art, can you get a running bra for Teresa?" I said, turning to Art.

Art gave me a dirty look and said, "Um, sure. What size do you need, Teri?"

"I don't know."

"Why don't you go ahead and take Teresa down to the athletic shop in town," I suggested. "I think they have them there."

I could tell Art wasn't exactly thrilled with the idea, but he agreed and took Teresa down to the store that afternoon. They didn't have a running bra large enough to fit her, but they put in a rush order to have one delivered from Seattle.

That Friday at noon, as Art was sitting having lunch with the officers at the Sheldon Jackson cafeteria, an announcement came over the PA system.

"Mr. Griswold. Your bra is ready at the sports shop."

Art almost spit his soup all over the table.

We went to pick up Teresa's bra that afternoon, and from then on, she kept up with the best of the runners.

***

Six weeks into the training, there was a remarkable difference. The officers were healthy again, and the morning runs had fewer and fewer stragglers each day. We were up to two miles a day now, and some of the officers had even gotten into running so seriously that they were well on their way toward earning their 100-mile T-shirts.

The Micronesians also were becoming much more confident in their new environment. During what little free time they had, they played basketball out behind the barracks, or explored the town and got to know some of the locals. And on the weekends or in the evenings after dinner, they'd gather in the rec room to study, play pool, or watch television.

All in all, things were going pretty smoothly. Then we hit a minor bump in the road.

It was a Sunday morning. Art and I were sitting in our usual spot in the staff quarters overlooking the rec room, relaxing over coffee. He was reading the local paper, and I was catching up on some correspondence.

"Do you want to go fishing today?" I suggested as I finished my last letter.

"Yeah, sure," Art replied. Art was an expert fisherman and always managed to catch his limit. "Just let me get one more cup of coffee first."

Art got up to stretch and was about to head for the coffeemaker in the corner of the room when he stopped, looking out into the rec room, and said, "Hey, Bryan, I think something's wrong in there. Look at those guys."

I looked. Nobody was watching television. Nobody was shooting pool. A few people were sitting around in the study area, but they weren't reading books. There were hurried, quiet conversations and angry shakes of the head. Art was right. Something was definitely up.

Art and I went into the rec room, where I found Masachiro Simina and asked, "What's going on, Masachiro?"

"Nothing, Chief," he replied, avoiding eye contact with me.

"Don't give me that shit. What's happening?" I asked again.

Masachiro continued staring at his feet and said nothing, so I repeated my question to Katios Gallen, who was standing nearby.

"There's a girl downstairs," said Katios.

"Where? In the reception area?" I asked.

"No. In one of the rooms."

"What's she doing down there?"

"She's crying," Masachiro said.

"Why?" I asked, starting to get worried now. "Did something happen to her?"

"No, not like that," both men replied emphatically.

"All right, then. What's wrong with her?" I said. Both Katios and Masachiro stared down at their feet again and said nothing.

"Are you guys going to tell me or do I have to go down there myself and find out?"

"Well, I think she was downstairs with one of the officers, and maybe some of the other officers didn't like that he was down there with a girl, and so maybe they took all their clothes while they were sleeping," Katios replied.

"Took them where?" I asked.

"I think maybe they threw them away."

"So this girl downstairs is crying because she can't find her clothes?" I said. "But other than that, she's not hurt in any way?"

"No, no, she's not hurt. She's OK, Chief," Katios assured me.

"Who is this girl, anyway? Does anybody know?" I asked.

"She's a student," said Masachiro. "From Sheldon Jackson."

Great, I thought. *That's just what we need. Some student from the local church school shacked up in the trooper academy overnight.*

"Well, get her out of here," I told the officers.

"We can't," said Katios. "She hasn't got any clothes."

"Look, I'll tell you what," I said, getting angry now. "Last week you all had the class on search patterns. I suggest you put what you learned to use. You get your asses out there and find those clothes and get them back to that young woman in the next half hour, or we're going to have to deal with this formally. And if we have to deal with it formally, some people are going to get kicked out of this academy, if the troopers don't shut the whole thing down all together. Do you understand?"

The officers nodded, eyes wide, and raced down the stairs and out of the barracks. Art and I went to the window and watched as the officers broke into teams as they had been taught and began a meticulous spiral search of the area. Just a few minutes into the search, one of the Palauan officers came running up with a bundle of clothes under his arm, much to the relief of the others. The entire group of them followed the officer with the bundle back into the barracks, and about ten minutes later, an embarrassed-looking young woman went scurrying across the parking lot toward Sheldon Jackson College, straightening her clothes as she ran.

Art turned to me and said, "Well, I won't say anything if you don't."

"Sounds good to me," I replied, torn between relief that potential disaster had been averted, sympathy for the young woman, and amusement at the Micronesians' somewhat unorthodox method of enforcing group norms.

* * *

In most any sort of recruit training situation, there comes a time when a sense of esprit de corps emerges, and individuals really begin to work together as a group. For the members of the first Micronesian Police Academy, this time came toward the end of the program and was prompted by a single, catalytic event and the heroic actions of two officers.

One evening during the first week of August, Steven Ngalen from Yap and Sam Ngirchokebai from Palau were walking over to the Sheldon Jackson cafeteria for dinner when a four-year-old boy came running up to them, crying for help. They hurried after him down to the river, where they found his young playmate stranded in water up to his neck, clinging desperately to a downed tree in the fast-flowing river.

The boy was difficult to reach, and the officers' first attempt to rescue him from the bank failed. Finally, Steven waded into the icy river, made his way hand-over-hand along the snag to the frightened boy, and hoisted him up to Sam.

The following week the local paper ran an article about the rescue, and both officers received special recognition from Senator Ted Stevens and Alaska's Commissioner of Public Safety for saving the boy's life.

The rescue made the Micronesians even more welcome among the residents of Sitka than they already had been. But even more importantly, it increased their sense of group pride and accomplishment as they entered their final few weeks of the program. From that day forward, I think, they came into their own.

V

As we neared the end of the training program, things were really going well. Not one officer had dropped out, failed, or been kicked out of the program, which was very unusual for a tough training academy such as this one. Even one Marshallese officer who had to have an emergency appendectomy while we were in Sitka managed to get back on his feet quickly enough to finish the training. And to top it all off, the officers were getting really fit. Most of them had lost fifteen to thirty pounds, and some even more than that.

Once the serious business of final exams and oral presentations was over and it was clear that everyone would pass, the excitement at the academy really started to build as we neared graduation day.

The Micronesian officers were planning a party, and nobody throws a party better than Micronesians. All the troopers would be there, of course, as well as people from the local community. Jan's special assistant, Neiman Craley, was scheduled to fly out for the ceremonies, along with Bob Smoak from the Interior Department, FSM's Division of Security and Investigation Chief Joe Race, and the chiefs of police from each of the islands. In their honor, the Micronesians were planning not only a feast, but a show as well.

Preparations for the event had taken up most of their free time during the past couple of weeks. At my request, Bobbi Grizzard had airmailed us a bunch of palm fronds from Saipan, which the officers used to make traditional island costumes to wear in the show. A lot of rehearsing, which Art and I weren't invited to watch, also took place during their off-hours. And, of course, there was lots of shopping for the feast. We bought beer and rice and chicken to barbecue, and the troopers dipped into their freezers and donated generous portions of moose ribs, venison, salmon, and halibut. By graduation day, we had amassed practically enough food and drink to invite the entire population of Sitka to the festivities.

The graduation ceremony started at about 11 AM at the indoor auditorium at Sheldon Jackson College. The Micronesian officers sat in the front row of the packed auditorium, excited yet dignified. There was a hushed air in the room as First Sergeant Ted Hobart and the three drill instructors marched down the aisle and took their places in front of the officers. As Captain Warren Townsend arrived, Ted called out, "Class. Atten-hut." The Micronesian officers snapped to attention in unison, looking sharp.

"At ease, First Sergeant," Warren said, taking his place at the podium.

Ted turned to the officers and said, "Class, seats."

The officers sat back down in perfect unison. Ted and the drill instructors took their seats as well, and the ceremony began.

As the first to speak, Captain Townsend gave a brief history of the Micronesian Police Academy—including how it had come about, who had funded it, and its importance for eventually establishing a police academy in Micronesia.

"Frankly," he concluded, "I had my doubts when we started this program about how well officers from such a different place would do under our training. Our agreement with the Trust Territory and our own responsibility to the Public Safety Academy required that we make the same demands of these officers that we make of our own people, and given those conditions, I wasn't sure they could succeed. But they stood up to those demands, and they exceeded our expectations. I know I speak for every member of the staff when I say congratulations. We're very proud to have you as graduates of the Alaska State Public Safety Academy."

You could feel the pride beaming from every one of the officers, and you could see it in the faces of their instructors. I felt pretty darn proud myself.

Bob Smoak took the floor after that, although he only said a few words because the long-winded speech he had brought with him from Washington had somehow gotten lost on the way from the airport (with just a little help from me). Neiman Craley then delivered the commencement address, followed by a short valedictorian speech by Thomas Kintaro, who proudly presented the troopers with a large framed map of Micronesia on which we had mounted police patches from each of the islands.

Next came the presentation of special awards and certificates to the most outstanding officers for academic achievement, physical fitness, and other areas. Finally, Lieutenant Colonel Mike Simpson from the troopers' Anchorage headquarters presented Commissioner's Commendations to Steven Ngalen and Sam Ngirchokebai for saving the Sitka boy who had fallen into the river.

Then, like every commencement ceremony everywhere, the officers' names were called, and they marched proudly across the stage to accept their diplomas from Captain Townsend.

After the last of the officers had received his diploma, Captain Townsend took the floor again and announced, "As a final treat, the officers of the first Micronesian Police Academy would like to do us the honor of presenting a traditional Micronesian dance. If you'll all remain seated, the show will begin in just a few minutes."

The lights dimmed as about fifteen officers got up and hurried behind the stage to change into their costumes. Soon after, the lights came up again, and out they stomped in their palm-fronded headbands and grass skirts.

Covered in ocher face markings and painted-on tattoos, they performed a number of traditional dances from each of the islands, including a Trukese war dance, a Yapese men's dance, and a Kosraean stick dance. When the last of them leapt off the stage with a yell, and the backbeat of pounding on the floor with sticks stopped, there was a brief pause before the audience jumped to their feet and gave the performers a standing ovation.

The celebratory feast that followed lasted well into the evening as we gorged ourselves on moose ribs, salmon, venison burgers, and chicken grilled in spicy Chamorro barbecue sauce—all washed down with plenty of Budweiser and Moosehead ale.

Tropical Troopers

* * *

It was a more confident, more fit, and substantially lighter weight group of officers that flew back to Micronesia on the Island Hopper at the end of the summer of 1983. On each of the islands, the returning officers were greeted with great ceremony by their own departments, families, and friends. Amid the hugs and laughter, one comment we heard over and over again, island after island, was a plaintive, "But you're so skinny!"

All in all, that first academy was a resounding success. The Micronesians were thrilled with the results, and we got good press coverage in the *Pacific Daily News* and the *Marianas Variety*.

The next year, Bill Stinnett took another group of about thirty officers up to Sitka for the second Micronesian Police Academy. The year after that, a Micronesian Police Academy was established at the community college on Palau. Several Alaskan troopers flew out to help run it, while many of the Micronesian officers who had been through the training in Sitka served as assistant trainers. By the fourth year of the academy, the Micronesian officers began to teach some of the basic classes, and by the fifth year, they were handling the majority of the instruction themselves.

Ten years in, the academy was completely their own. After decades of short-term training and transient improvements, we had a strategy that worked.

CHAPTER 15

Saipan Sunset

Those first few weeks back in Micronesia were great. Art and I and the newly trained officers were riding high on the wave of approval that had been gaining momentum since our return from Sitka. In addition to the local recognition and media attention we received, the Palau Congress and each of the state delegations to the Federated States of Micronesia introduced resolutions expressing their appreciation for the training program and commending the individual officers who had completed it.

Just as gratifying as the official accolades, though, were the responses of the individual police departments on each of the islands. The success of their officers, who were eager to use their new teaching skills to pass on what they had learned at the trooper academy, brought a newfound confidence—a sense that they were finally on the road to being real, competent police agencies. People saw this as an important and very concrete step toward becoming genuine independent nations.

Then, somewhere in the midst of all the excitement, I received a thick letter from Bob Smoak in Washington. In small-type, single-spaced governmentese, Bob told me that there was an opening in his division in the U.S. Department of the Interior that I would have an excellent shot at if I wanted to apply.

The position was chief of the department's branch of emergency preparedness. Bob wouldn't—couldn't—say exactly what the job would entail, other than that much of it would be classified beyond the Top Secret level. But basically, I'd be responsible for preparing the Interior Department's emergency plans and assuring that its dozens of agencies were ready to meet their responsibilities in the event of either natural or man-made disasters, from catastrophic earthquakes to nuclear war. At the same time, I'd still be a sworn police officer responsible for handling law enforcement issues in U.S. overseas territories, including Micronesia.

On one hand, the thought of working in the bowels of some government bureaucracy was distasteful. On the other hand, it seemed like a good opportunity to dust off my master's degree in public administration and start moving up the ladder. I was also tempted by the allure of big-city amenities and the promise of long-term career potential that had never been possible working for the Trust Territory, and I was pretty sure Susan would jump at the chance to get back to "civilization."

Saying yes was a tantalizing idea. But first—even before I told Susan—I needed to talk it over with Jan.

It was almost four-thirty—the end of the official workday at TT headquarters, although few of us ever paid much attention to the clock. I set Bob Smoak's letter down on my desk and dialed Jan's two-digit extension.

"High Commissioner's office," Bobbi answered promptly.

"Hi, Bobbi. Is Jan there?" I asked.

"Yeah, Bryan, but she's got a meeting in just a minute," Bobbi told me.

"I just need to talk to her for a second," I said.

"OK, I'll put you through."

"Hello, Bryan. What can I do for you?" Jan answered a couple seconds later.

"Hi, Jan," I replied. "I just got an interesting offer from Bob Smoak. Have you got time to discuss it later on today?"

Jan paused for a moment, then said, "Why don't you come up to the house for drinks around six-thirty?"

"That'd be great, Jan. As long as *I* get to make the martinis."

"You never use enough vermouth!"

We chuckled over this longstanding joke, then rang off.

I fiddled around with some more paperwork for the next hour and a half, although I was too intrigued by Bob's job offer to get much of anything done. Finally, at about quarter after six, I went down to the parking lot, got into my rusty little sedan, and headed up the now familiar driveway to Jan's house at the top of Capitol Hill. I parked behind the house, got out, and knocked on the kitchen door.

Jan, on the phone as usual, waved through the kitchen screen, gesturing for me to let myself in. I walked in and waved "hi" back. Jan smiled and pointed toward the bar, and I went over and mixed two deep-dish martinis—Jan's with one-third vermouth, mine with just a whisper. As I handed Jan her drink, she gave me a exaggeratedly grateful look before holding the telephone receiver away from her ear momentarily and rolling her eyes at it, as the person on the other end of the line—most likely some long-winded bureaucrat—continued to ramble on.

When Jan finally got off the phone, we perched ourselves on a couple of comfortable chairs on the lanai, looking out over the sparkling lagoon and the big fluffy clouds and the brilliant blue sky and the picture-perfect tropical sunset in the making.

Jan took a sip of her martini and said, "Well, *that's* better."

"All that vermouth will rot your liver," I replied.

"Why don't you just drink straight gin if you're not going to make a proper martini?" Jan tossed back.

We paused and smiled for a moment, old friends sharing oft-traded barbs.

"So, what's going on, Bryan?" Jan eventually asked.

"Well, Bob Smoak's offered me a job at Interior as chief of emergency preparedness," I said.

"Oh?" Jan replied. "And what does that mean, exactly?"

"Frankly, I don't know," I admitted. "Bob couldn't tell me most of what the job would entail because it's all classified—"

Jan interrupted with a loud snort that spoke volumes about what she thought of the secrets of Washington bureaucracies. Then she asked, "What about the law enforcement issues here?"

"He said I'd still have that hat as well," I explained. "I wouldn't be able to do the hands-on, day-to-day things here, of course, but I'd be overseeing law enforcement to a certain extent from Washington. I've been thinking about it, and maybe I'd even be able to do more good for Micronesia from there because I could keep the political side of things rolling a bit better."

"Maybe," Jan agreed, somewhat reluctantly. "So, does that mean you're planning to take the job?"

"I don't know, Jan," I admitted. "I've enjoyed Washington a lot on my trips out there, and it sounds like an interesting job. At least what I know about it so far. But I really wasn't planning to leave here until you do. Until we were finished here."

"Well, that could be any time now," Jan said. "If the Palauans could get things settled, that is."

"Do you think that'll ever happen?"

"God, I don't know," Jan said with a rueful laugh. "They don't seem to be able to agree on much of anything, do they?"

There was a long pause as we both sipped our martinis and watched the growing sunset. Finally, slowly and pointedly, Jan said, "I'd hate to see you go, Bryan. But if you want this job, and if you think you'd like working back there, I think the best thing for you to do would be to take it. We'd miss you, but we'd manage all right."

"Thanks, Jan," I said. "I want to think about it some more, but you know, I'm kind of inclined to go for it."

"How long do you have till you have to give them an answer?"

"Well, Bob said the position's coming open real soon, so he

wants my answer in a couple of days," I said. "I'll let you know as soon as I make up my mind."

"OK," said Jan. "You know my door's always open."

I smiled and nodded, and we sipped the last of our drinks in silence.

"You ready for another one?" I asked.

"Why not?" Jan replied.

I made us another pair of lopsided martinis, then went back out and sat down next to Jan on the lanai, where we watched the sun go down together.

* * *

That night, I went home and talked it over with Susan. Jan was right, we both agreed. The Trust Territory government was already beginning to wind down, and it probably wouldn't be too much longer before it was dismantled entirely. Departments were being consolidated, and staff were being laid off or shifted to the new Northern Marianas government offices. Old friends like Denny Lund had already left, and more were sure to be leaving soon.

Me? I originally had planned to come to Micronesia for two years, and six had already passed. Part of me still wanted to stay. I was comfortable and happy there. I had good friends. I had respect and status, even if on a micro-level. I met with kings and presidents and governors and went to diplomatic receptions with visiting dignitaries. And I had the power to make things happen, like the Micronesian Police Academy in Sitka.

But at the same time, I was getting itchy. With the launching of the academy, my creative role in Micronesia was largely done. The Micronesians already were increasingly able to handle their own law enforcement problems and would continue to become even more adept as the academy program progressed. That meant that even if the TT government lasted another two—or even ten—years, there would be less and less chance to saddle up and go be a cop. More and more, my job would be about training and administrative duties, and politicking and looking for funds.

Going back to the States would also be good for Susan and, I hoped, for our marriage. Susan was weary of island life—of everything from real hardships like typhoons to minor aggravations like not being able to get her hair styled the way she wanted it anywhere. I figured going back to the States would make her happy, and maybe even help us put our marriage on track. The challenges of living in a foreign culture far from home and family were hard enough on a marriage. My constant travel added loneliness, anxiety about personal safety, and the threat of infidelity to the daily inconveniences Susan had to face. On average, I'd been gone three weeks out of every month for six years. It was time to get home.

II

Almost as quickly as things had happened when we first made the decision to come to Micronesia, Susan and I were on our way to Washington, D.C. Actually, Susan went on to the States ahead of me. She wanted to spend a few weeks with her family in Seattle while I found us a place to live in the D.C. area and got us settled in. So, after taking her to the airport a few days before my flight was scheduled to leave, I cleared out my office, packed up our now faded and disreputable-looking household effects, and sold our car. And all too soon, it was my last day on Saipan.

After a teary going-away party at TT headquarters—replete with flower leis, *mar mars*, a cake, and the obligatory framed certificate—I found myself standing awkwardly with Bill Stinnett outside Saipan's fancy new air terminal.

"Who'd a thought, huh?" Bill said quietly.

"Yeah, it's been a good run, hasn't it? Hard to believe it's over," I said.

Bill held out a plain manila envelope. "This is for you. But wait to open it till you're on the plane, OK?"

"Sure, Bill. Thanks."

I took the envelope in my left hand and held my right hand out to Bill. He grasped it, then reached up and grabbed my forearm, and I his, in a firm grip.

I shook my head and said lamely, "Well, I won't be too far away."

"Yeah—just the other side of the world."

"But if you need me—"

"Yeah, I know," Bill said, letting go of my arm and giving me a grin as I boarded the Air Mike plane for what might be the last time.

I buckled up, sat back, and glanced out the window, waving good-bye once more to Bill before opening the thin envelope he had given me.

I chuckled to myself at the contents. Leave it to Bill to come up with something original. It was a poem, simply titled "Bye." It began,

So long, B
you've paid your dues
But better you than me
just send back the news

Now some stories of old
but just a few
Some can't be told
or it'd be the end of you

I remember Ponape
your assistance so able
On jailbreak day
you broke the autopsy table

The poem continued at length, through stanza after stanza of fractured (some might say tortured) verse—most of which elicited a laugh or a groan. It finally ended with,

I'll now cut the bullshit
it's getting late
Guess this is it
and it's truly been great

Choking back a tear, I put the poem back in its envelope just as the engines started up, and the plane begin to taxi. I watched out the window as we raced down the runway and took off, and Saipan and its pristine beach—the beach my father had stormed onto as a young man and almost died on forty years earlier—receded below me.

Yeah, it truly had been great, like Bill said. My six years in Micronesia had been everything I could have hoped for in an adventure, and then some.

Thinking back, I was stunned to realize just how little I'd known about training cops in another culture when I'd first arrived. I'd waltzed in—a confident young cop who'd worked some of the toughest beats in American policing—figuring, "I know how to do this. I know how to train police. I'll figure the rest out as I go along."

There'd been a lot to figure out. Not just the little day-to-day flexibilities and improvisations that are essential to policing in any foreign culture, or the logistical nightmares involving equipment, transportation, and manpower. Challenging as those problems were, they were nothing compared to understanding the bigger picture of cross-cultural policing which, for me, began to come into focus for the first time.

In Micronesia, I had soon learned, police officers weren't just anonymous cops working a beat; they were somebody's son and grandson, and maybe the nephew of the guy down the street or the brother of the drunk on the corner. They were truly a part of their communities—so much a part that compassion and kindness were as natural to dealing with people on the job as they were when interacting with their own families.

It made me realize that what had been wrong in L.A.—why I'd always felt like a member of an occupation force as a police officer there—was that I and most of my fellow officers there *hadn't* been a part of the communities we served. We had lived in nice, middle-class suburbs an hour-and-a-half drive and a world away from the ghettos and barrios we'd worked in. We'd been outsiders.

But insiders, not outsiders, make the most difference in any culture or community. In Micronesia, that had seemed so obvious. Perhaps it was the smaller scale of the place, or my lack of preconceived notions. Perhaps it was because it was impossible *not* to become a part of the community, given the intimacy of island life. In any event, I discovered the importance of participating in the local culture wherever I went. That meant drinking *sakau* on Ponape, chewing betel nut on Yap and Palau, gently holding hands with my burly cops on Kosrae, and shaking hands with a crushing grip on Truk. It meant avoiding conflict in the Marshalls, and joining in heated arguments on Palau. It meant knowing when to speak softly, and when to bellow in a deep, strong voice.

In short, I discovered the importance of building bridges that go both ways. Every day, I learned as much from the Micronesians as they learned from me. And the more I came to appreciate that—the more I came to genuinely respect their culture and their way of doing things in the world they lived in—the more effective I became as a police trainer.

I'm not saying I didn't screw up. I screwed up all the time. I learned to apologize in nine different languages. But like most of the Americans I knew in Micronesia—at least those of us who stayed despite all the hardships—I came to truly care about what I was doing and the people I worked with.

It wasn't just a job or even just an adventure. I gave my whole heart to Micronesia, and in return I made friends and memories that will last a lifetime and took home lessons about policing I'll never forget. And maybe, just maybe, I did some good there as well.

The End

Postscript

So, I've told you my stories—my adventures and misadventures, my successes and screw-ups. Most of them, at least.

I suppose I could just leave well enough alone and end the book here. But I'm a college professor now, and I can't let all that schooling go to waste. Not when I see the same mistakes still being made over and over again when it comes to the way the United States approaches police training in developing nations. Not when I see obvious solutions based on both practical experience and academic knowledge. As someone who's been there, I think I have an obligation to speak up.

In the thirty years since I was a police trainer—hell, in the more than 100 years since we first started training police internationally back during the pre-World War I "Banana Wars" in Central and South America—it seems to me that very little has changed. All too often we simply take American cops or military troops, drop them into the middle of a foreign culture with little or no special training, and leave them to figure things out on their own.

That's what happened to me. Ultimately, it worked out all right—but I was lucky. I was in an island "paradise" instead of a war-torn region. I had experienced people like Denny Lund and Jim Grizzard to help take me by the hand and show me the ropes. And I had six years to learn how to get the job done.

But most police trainers today who go to Iraq—or Afghanistan, Bosnia, Kosovo, Liberia, East Timor, or some other global hot spot—are on one-year contracts or less. They're given very little advance preparation. Most know little to nothing about the culture or the language of the country where they'll be training cops. There typically aren't enough of them, so each trainer is assigned way too many new recruits. And sometimes, as has been the case in Iraq, the situation on the ground is so dangerous that they're forced to wait in a safe zone for weeks before they can even begin training.[1] Given all these obstacles to success, I'd be willing to bet that by the time most trainers are just starting to hit their stride, their contracts are up and it's time to head back home, or on to the next assignment.

My heart goes out to all of them. It shouldn't be like this. We ought to know better by now. But apparently we don't.

For example, David H. Bayley, a Distinguished Professor in the School of Criminal Justice at the State University of New York at Albany and a leading expert on international policing, has noted our inability to learn from experience when it comes to international police training.

"Foreign assistance in the justice sector is not designed as a 'learning' operation," says Bayley. "Evaluations are few, experience in the field is not studied systematically for 'best practice,' people returning from overseas missions are not debriefed for insights into improvement, and agencies do not share assistance experience."[2]

The good news is, it looks like the U.S. government is finally starting to understand the critical role competent, independent, uncorrupt police forces play in maintaining stable nations. As a result, police training in emerging democracies is now considered a higher priority than ever before.

As evidence of this, Bayley points out that U.S. assistance in this area has increased substantially during the past two decades, beginning in 1986 with the establishment of the International Criminal Investigative Training Assistance Program (ICITAP). By 2004, U.S. training assistance for police from more than 120 countries was up to about $634 million per year. The United States has also contributed a large number of officers to the United Nations' Civilian Police force (UNCIVPOL) in recent years, in addition to our efforts to reconstruct local police in places like Afghanistan and Iraq.[3]

What can we do to help guide this new focus on international police training in the right direction? I certainly don't have all the answers, but based on my own experiences in Micronesia—as well as three subsequent decades during which I've followed America's international police training efforts via the news and in academic circles—I have a few ideas on the subject. And while each situation is different, which means there's no "one size fits all" solution, there are many common truths about building police forces in less-developed countries that apply in any foreign culture. Thus, the lessons I learned in Micronesia ought to be useful for cross-cultural police development any time, any place.

I'll try not to get too professorial on you, so bear with me. This stuff is really important to all of us, from cops to military personnel to Peace Corps volunteers to public policy-makers to concerned citizens everywhere who share a desire for a safer, more stable world.

Lesson One: Halfway measures don't work. The way I see it, once we commit to providing a developing nation with police training assistance, we need to make sure we send in enough people to get the job done right. And, in addition to adequate logistical support, we need to provide trainers with sufficient advance preparation to be as effective as possible while working in a foreign culture.

But typically, this hasn't been the case. Police training in Iraq is a prime example. Early on, before the war, the Justice Department backed a plan to deploy thousands of American police trainers to Iraq after the American invasion. But that recommendation fell on deaf ears at the White House and the Pentagon, which initially sent just a dozen advisers to help rebuild the Iraqi police force, according to the *New York Times*. Moreover, "After Baghdad fell, when a majority of Iraqi police officers abandoned their posts, a second proposal by a Justice Department team calling for 6,600 police trainers was reduced to 1,500, and then never carried out. During the first eight months of the occupation—as crime soared and the insurgency took hold—the United States deployed 50 police advisers in Iraq."[4]

These alarming statistics are put into perspective by Bing West, former assistant secretary of defense under Ronald Reagan and a highly respected combat journalist who made fourteen extended field trips to Iraq between 2003 and 2008.

"On paper, 1,500 retired police from the United States and Europe were to be the trainers," says West. "By October [2003], twenty-four police trainers had shown up in the Green Zone. Two retired cops were dispatched to Anbar, a province the size of Wyoming where tribal Sunnis in a dozen cities were launching 200 attacks a month. The math worked out to one police adviser per one million Iraqis."[5]

Additional U.S. police trainers eventually were sent to Iraq, but never in numbers anywhere close to the Justice Department's initial recommendations, even after the United States declared 2006 "the year of the police."[6]

Worse, those who *are* sent typically don't receive much advance preparation for the job, just like it was back in the seventies when I first went to Micronesia. I scoured the library for information, but all I'd been able to find was a couple of old *National Geographic* articles that offered a bit of history and background on Micronesia. With no Internet back then and just six weeks to quit my job, sell my house, pack up all my belongings, and move halfway around the world, that's the best I was able to do.

DynCorp International, a defense contractor that currently recruits the majority of U.S. civilian police trainers for Iraq, Afghanistan, Kosovo, and numerous other countries, provides at least some advance preparation for its employees, according to Robert M. Perito, former deputy director of ICITAP who has been responsible for police training programs in Haiti, Bosnia, Kosovo, and East Timor.

"DynCorp . . . offers a nine-day, predeparture Police Assessment Selection and Training Process that includes a battery of psychological, medical, and firearms tests; training in police skills and defensive tactics; and training modules on the United Nations, peacekeeping, human rights, living abroad, and the history and culture of the country to which the officers will be assigned," says Perito.[7]

It's a start—it's better than what I got—but still, that's a lot of information to cram into just nine days. Robert Cole, a retired East Palo Alto police officer who accepted a one-year assignment as a police trainer in Iraq with DynCorp in 2004, was given a bit more advance preparation, but not much. He and eighty-seven fellow team members attended a three-week "boot camp" in Fredericksburg, Virginia, before heading to Iraq. However, perhaps understandably since they were about to enter a war zone, the program was focused more on survival training and defensive tactics than on cross-cultural police training issues.[8]

Lesson Two: Choose the right agency for the job. Over the years, we've often called on military troops with no civilian policing experience to train local cops in foreign lands. Hell, they wear uniforms, they know how to use guns, how different could it be, right? Wrong. Most of these folks have done their very best, but they're simply not the right people for the job. Many top experts agree.

For example, according to *The Iraq Study Group Report* coauthored by former U.S. Attorney General Edwin Meese III, the wrong U.S. agencies have been assigned to train the new Iraqi Police Service. Rather than the State Department, the Defense Department, and private contractors, all of whom have been given responsibility for police training at some point since the war began, police training in Iraq should be under the jurisdiction of the Justice Department, which "has the expertise and capacity to carry out the police training mission." The Defense Department, says the report, "is already bearing too much of the burden in Iraq."[9]

Major General Joseph Peterson, who was in charge of the Pentagon's plan to train the Iraqi police force as of May 2006 (and was the third general assigned to the task since March of 2004), would likely agree with this view. Peterson "conceded that he was a peculiar choice for the job since he had never created any organization from scratch, much less a police force of nearly 190,000.

"'I'm an armor officer, which doesn't qualify me for anything but combat,' General Peterson said."[10]

Moreover, the new U.S. Army/Marine Corps *Counterinsurgency* field manual emphasizes working *with* police trainers to help build police forces in post-conflict regions, but acknowledges that civilian police training is not normally a military activity.[11]

It shouldn't be. I've been a Marine and I've been a cop, and I can tell you that there's a big difference between the way the military does things and the way the police do things. The fact of the matter is, policing is an art that depends on being able to persuade people to do the right thing, and it relies upon the threat of force only in extreme circumstances. But military tactics typically depend on force—mostly because there's little room for persuasion in a traditional war zone.

As West more eloquently puts it in his excellent book, *The Strongest Tribe: War, Politics, and the Endgame in Iraq*, "Western armies lack the doctrine, training, and inclination to do police work. The problem in Iraq (and in Afghanistan) was that the nature of the combat demanded police skills on a scale that the police program run by the State Department could not handle."[12]

Of course, civilian cops can't handle everything on their own, especially during an insurgency. The "one ranger, one riot" attitude that police officers typically employ works pretty well during civil disturbances—like it did for Bill Stinnett and Dean Aguilar and me during the problems on Palau and Kwajalein—but not when there's a war on. That means that in post-conflict areas like Iraq that are still experiencing insurgencies, police trainers and military personnel should work together to each do what they do best.

Lesson Three: Choose the right people for the job. Nothing is more important to the success of foreign police training programs than the people we select to be trainers. Proficiency and credibility as a cop are obviously critical. So is previous success training other officers. But a trainer's personality and character are also key to gaining trainees' respect, and people everywhere naturally tend to learn more from people they respect.

In addition to these essential skills and qualities, police trainers need to be ready and willing to rise to the challenges that come with living and working in a less-developed country. Water, power, communications, food, medicine, and other things we take for granted in the States are iffy commodities in many parts of the world. And hard as it may be to believe, I met many Americans in Micronesia who didn't know this.

I remember one criminal justice development consultant who came to Ponape from Los Angeles. On the way to his hotel from the airport, he wanted me to stop at a drugstore so he could get sterile solution for his contact lenses. When I explained that there were no drugstores on Ponape—he'd have to fly all the way back to Guam for contact lens solution—he was just flabbergasted. At least he stayed and finished the job he came out to do. In Micronesia, it wasn't all that uncommon to recruit someone for a position and fly them out, only to have them flat-out refuse to get off the plane once they saw that "paradise" had rusty tin roofs and rough-looking people.

Beyond being prepared for the hardships of expatriate life, successful foreign police trainers must have a genuine regard for the people and the culture they're working in, and appreciate that there can be more than one legitimate world view. Too often I've seen Americans saunter into a less-developed nation with condescending attitudes that say, "Your way of doing things is all wrong, and I'm here to show you how things are *supposed* to be done." Good trainers know that a much more effective way to sell new ideas to people and help bring about change is to show respect for their culture and their ways of doing things. Then they can work with them to make improvements, incorporating new ideas with the old ways whenever possible. (Of course, there are some instances when the old ways *must* be discarded because they violate human rights—I'll address that issue in Lesson Seven.)

Other essential qualities of effective cross-cultural police trainers include flexibility, creativity, and initiative. I say "essential" because without a lot of creative problem solving, we never would have gotten much of anything done in Micronesia. For example, on Ponape when the pinkeye epidemic hit and threatened to shut down the training session we had worked for months to put together, Ted Burkin and I strong-armed the local doctor to get the medication we needed for our trainees. If we got to an island to conduct a firearms training session and discovered that the local police department's weapons weren't fit to use, we'd cannibalize what they had to cobble together at least a few that were adequate for familiarization training. And when we needed to create a shooting range for target practice, we'd borrow a bulldozer and flatten down a bit of jungle to make one.

POSTSCRIPT

We were pretty good at improvising in Micronesia, but the Alaska State Troopers who came out to help us train on a regular basis were real masters. In fact, they embodied all the qualities any successful expatriate police trainer ought to have. They were used to working with indigenous peoples and treated them with respect. They understood what it took to succeed in remote places where the nearest backup was days away. They were used to living in the communities they policed. They were tough and not afraid of a little hardship (or a lot of it). And they were really good, professional cops to boot. If today's troopers are anything like those I knew thirty years ago, they're exactly the sort of folks we should be hiring as international police trainers. Unfortunately, I doubt that many of them would be willing to sign on—from what I hear, there's no salmon fishing in Iraq—but you never know. By mid-February, 120 degrees in the shade might start sounding pretty good to a trooper stationed in a cold, dark Alaskan outpost.

Lesson Four: Choose the right people to train. It probably goes without saying that police development efforts work best when we choose the right people to train. Then again, based on recent reports from Iraq, perhaps this isn't as obvious as I would have thought.

For example, according to the *New York Times*, American, British, and Iraqi officials said that the rush to rebuild the Iraqi police force after the American invasion lacked proper controls. As a result, "In recent background checks, police investigators found more than 5,000 police officers with arrest records for crimes that included attacks on American troops, American officials said."[13]

Moreover, L. Paul Bremer III, a retired career diplomat and counterterrorism expert appointed Director of Reconstruction and Humanitarian Assistance for Iraq on May 11, 2003, told the *New York Times* that police training efforts in Iraq were focused more on increasing the quantity of officers than on quality. "They were just pulling kids off the streets and handing them badges and AK-47s," said Bremer.[14]

Admittedly, recruiting new officers in Micronesia was a bit different than rebuilding a police force in a war zone, but it seems to me that arming and training the wrong people is worse than doing nothing at all.[15]

In addition to hiring qualified, competent police recruits (preferably ones without criminal arrest records), we need to carefully consider whom we select for more advanced police training. These are the people who have the potential to become police trainers and executives themselves, so the goal is to choose officers who are most likely to become both good leaders and positive change agents in their communities.

But choosing the right officers in a foreign culture isn't always as simple as selecting from among the best and brightest officers, like we do in the States. Not all cultures share our meritocratic ideals. In many places throughout the world, including Micronesia, if you're not from the right clan or the right caste or if you don't have the right family connections, you're never going to be successful as a leader.

We understood this in Micronesia, and took it into account when selecting officers for advanced training at the Micronesian Police Academy on Sitka. First we identified our top officers— those who were qualified for the program and would get the most out of the training—and of these, we chose officers who had strong political connections and respect within their communities to become our cadre of future trainers.

This wasn't exactly egalitarian, but it was culturally appropriate to the part of the world we were in, and it worked. The Micronesian Police Academy continued for the next ten years, until U.S. funding for it ran out, and eventually the Micronesians we selected for the program were successfully running the majority of training programs themselves.

POSTSCRIPT

Lesson Five: Don't underestimate trainees. As Bayley notes, "Providers of assistance must guard against condescension in their relations with local police. The fact that a country needs foreign assistance does not mean that its people, including government officials, are unintelligent, backward, or incompetent."[16]

It's easy for American trainers to underestimate local police in less-developed settings, especially at first. They tend to be less professional looking than American cops, poorly equipped and less thoroughly trained. However, just because they look a bit scruffy or don't know how to come to attention properly doesn't mean they're not real cops, many of whom were serving the needs of their communities long before foreign trainers arrived on the scene to assist them.

I learned this the hard way on my second day as a police trainer in Micronesia, when Kimo Panolo and I sprang our stateside role-playing scenario on the unsuspecting officers at the training session on Ponape. Even though this was a police academy, we forgot that we were training experienced cops, not rookies. Kimo's Trukese officers lacked formal training and had never been exposed to role-playing exercises before, but they certainly knew what to do when one of their own was attacked. It's a good thing they weren't armed, or I'd have been dead.

The Ponape jailbreak is another good example of a time when I underestimated the local cops. They had been left with almost no weapons, no police vehicles, and no communications equipment, so I just naturally assumed they'd need our help. We all did. But by the time Bill Stinnett, Jim Grizzard, and I landed on Ponape the next morning, fully armed and ready to take on the bad guys ourselves, the local police were already in hot pursuit of the escapees in a borrowed pickup truck. Armed with only their .22s from home and the police captain's snub-nosed .38, they chased the suspects down, returned fire when fired upon, and won. These officers had no previous experience dealing with a situation of this magnitude. Yet they rose to the challenge, they protected their community, and they showed great valor and initiative in the process.

Of course, there were incidents where the local cops *did* need our assistance—like when we arrested several members of the Kichy-Lokopichy clan on Wonei, quelled labor riots on Palau, and coaxed the sail-in protest to a peaceful resolution on Kwajalein. Learning not to underestimate local officers didn't mean assuming that they were ready yet to handle every difficult situation that arose on their own—after all, there was a reason we were there to provide training assistance. But it meant adopting a different attitude toward them. It meant respecting them like the real cops they were, and treating them as partners in the training process.

Lesson Six: Tailor what you teach to your audience. If you give people training that fits them like a bad suit, it'll never get used. Training needs to be custom-tailored so the topics are relevant to trainees, the examples you use fit with things they already know and understand, and the level of discussion is accessible. For example, trying to explain a fancy term like "curtilage" to a bunch of Micronesian cops who spoke very little English, like the FBI agents were doing at the first training session I attended on Ponape, was a waste of everybody's time.

On Kosrae, some words and ideas didn't even translate. The concept of "safety" was completely foreign to them, to the extent that there wasn't a word for it in Kosraean. In their world, things happened—sometimes good, sometimes bad. When bad things happened, you responded to them. But the notion that there were things you could do to help prevent bad things from happening made no sense to the Kosraeans. It was as if I was trying to tell them it was possible to control the weather.

Preventive maintenance was another concept that baffled the Kosraeans. They'd typically drive their police jeeps until they ran out of oil or water and the engines burned up, rather than checking the fluids on a regular basis and filling them when they got low. Putting gas in the jeeps they understood, at least most of the time, because it was akin to feeding livestock. But on a tropical island where the basic necessities of life were abundant and little work, attention, or maintenance was required to grow or collect food or provide adequate shelter, checking the fluid levels in a machine seemed to them like a silly thing to do.

Finally, in an informal setting over beers one evening, I managed to walk them through the logic behind preventive maintenance and found examples that made sense to them. It wasn't enough to just feed a jeep—like you would chickens or pigs—you had to check it over like an open-ocean canoe, I explained. Otherwise, it would likely fall apart at the worst possible time. Once I got the point across in a way that helped them understand why it was so important, we set up policies and procedures for tracking vehicle maintenance, and we never had a problem with it after that.

Another way to tailor training programs to better fit trainees is to choose equipment that fits their environment. For example, if you're going to provide firearms training in departments that can't afford enough ammunition to burn the 2,000 rounds per officer most American cops shoot during academy training—not to mention the additional ammo necessary for regular requalification—you need to rethink how you do things. In Micronesia, we focused our efforts on familiarizing the officers with handguns rather than trying to bring them up to a level of proficiency they'd never be able to maintain without constant practice. And on Kosrae, I ultimately convinced the police to opt for shotguns, which don't require much practice, in lieu of sidearms. Similarly, in the Middle East, the preferred weapon is the AK-47. Why? Because it requires little practice, it doesn't jam, and it doesn't care if it gets dirty or full of sand— most of the time, it just works.

Of course, any good police development effort begins with a basic needs assessment to find out exactly what the trainees and their communities hope to get out of foreign assistance. In Micronesia, I spent many days eating and drinking and chatting with town elders, community groups, police officers, and others to find out what was important to them and identify their goals before actually beginning the work of training, just like police trainers in Iraq today need to sit through endless tea ceremonies to learn what kind of assistance is needed from them.

Lesson Seven: Respect local customs without compromising core values or human rights. Unfortunately, at some point in prolonged training efforts, local customs and culture inevitably clash with trainers' core values and professional ethics. Such conflicts test trainers' leadership and political skills by requiring them to build a solid understanding of the moral, legal, and practical issues at stake, and then find workable, ethical compromises.

In Micronesia, just like in many parts of the world today, it wasn't easy melding old ways of maintaining social order with those that grew out of new constitutions, new penal codes, and increasing contact with the outside world. My job was to help them strike a balance that worked. That balance required respecting local customs and giving full consideration to local practices, but it didn't mean giving up my own core values. Sometimes a trainer has to stand up and say, "That was the old way. It's unconstitutional now, and you're a criminal if you do that."

For example, the new prohibition against coerced confessions was especially hard for some of the older cops in Micronesia to understand, particularly those on Palau. They'd first become police officers when Micronesia was under Japanese administration prior to the end of World War II. In those days, suspects always confessed, even if it took hours of kneeling on a broomstick, a beating, or even dangling from a bridge to convince them to do so.

POSTSCRIPT

As a former ghetto cop, I understood the temptation to resort to street justice and coerced confessions. But as a trainer, I was trying to bring the best of what American law enforcement had to offer to the people of Micronesia. That included respect for human rights and respect for their new Constitutions. Torture obviously wasn't a part of Micronesian police culture that we wanted carried over into the new era. Officers either caught on to the change, found a new job, or ended up in jail.

Lesson Eight: Learn the language. I can almost hear the folks who have been recruited to train police in Iraq or Afghanistan saying, "Are you nuts? I don't have time to learn the language. I'm only going to be there for a year." Bullshit. Becoming fluent in the language would be wonderful, but learning even *some* of the language—hello, good-bye, I'm pleased to meet you, please, thank you, where is it, how much does it cost, I'm sorry—is better than nothing at all.

I've heard stories about police trainers in Iraq stuck in hotels or barracks for weeks on end when the insurgency heated up, because it wasn't safe enough to go out into a war zone to start training. That's gotta be a terribly frustrating situation. Having been a private in the Marine Corps, I know about the boredom of being stuck in a barracks someplace. But instead of spending all that downtime exercising, reading, playing videogames, or watching DVDs, it seems to me it would have been a wonderful opportunity to learn the language. Four or five weeks of immersion training can take a person a long way. If you can just learn enough of the language to converse at a child's level, you can begin to understand the nuances of social interaction, you can connect with people better, and you can take care of business much better than if you simply rely on a translator.

Micronesia was especially challenging because there were nine different languages to learn. Obviously, I couldn't become fluent in all of them, especially in the places where I spent limited time. But I always made sure to learn the basics everywhere I went.

On Kosrae, where I spent three months as the chief of police, I knew going in that only half of my new officers spoke any English. So, using flashcards, I taught myself about 100 key words and phrases. I also relied on local folks like Isaac Aloka, the young man who lived next door to the Kosrae Hilton, and my police officers to help me learn more of the language, and within three months I was fairly fluent.

Learning the language not only makes training more effective, it says to local folks that you respect them and care enough about them to make the effort. Most people anywhere you go—whether it's Kosrae or Iraq or France or Thailand or Katmandu—really appreciate that.

Lesson Nine: Mind your manners, and participate in local culture. In addition to learning the local language, having good manners and participating in the local culture go a long way toward helping expatriate police trainers become effective change agents.

The best way I found for learning good manners in Micronesia was to simply ask people to help teach me. Often, I'd informally recruit someone to be my local guide to culture and manners. On Kosrae, as you may recall, I enlisted my entire police department in this effort.

Most people were more than happy to tell me about their culture and customs and the way they did things. But getting them to tell me when I did something wrong was more difficult, because most Micronesians are extremely polite and tend to avoid conflict, which means they were reluctant to let me know when I was committing a faux pas.

So I made lots of mistakes at first. For example, on Ponape, I was invited to dinner at the home of one of my trainees. His whole family was there, and he was the only one who spoke any

English. When it came time for dinner, his mother served me an enormous plate full of tough boiled chicken and starchy yams. I had remembered reading somewhere that in lots of cultures it was considered rude not to finish everything on your plate, so I made a valiant effort to eat it all as the family watched. But about halfway through, I just couldn't manage another bite. I apologetically handed the half-full plate back to my hostess, only to discover, as she passed it on to the next person, that the plate of food had been meant for everyone, not just me. They seemed pleased that I had apparently enjoyed it so much, but I felt terrible—and more than a little embarrassed—as I watched everyone else split the meager remains.

And then there was that fart on Yap. And countless other screw-ups, far too numerous to mention here. Micronesia was especially difficult to figure out because there were twelve very different cultures, and what was considered perfectly acceptable in one was often considered an abomination in another. Everything from the appropriate volume of speech to the firmness of a handshake to whether you were supposed to greet the elders or the young people first varied from island to island, and it was hard to keep it all straight.

But I tried my best to fit in and to learn about and participate in the local culture whenever possible. So I drank *sakau* on Ponape, I squatted in the dirt and chewed betel nut until my jaws ached on Yap, I ate fruit bat on Palau, I bellowed in a deep voice and endured crushing handshakes on Truk, and I went to church on Kosrae.

I had six years to work my way through the cultural maze in Micronesia. Foreign police trainers on one-year contracts really have to hit the ground running. Fortunately, there's the Internet now, and you can find out about anything almost as quickly as you can move a mouse. So there are ways for modern trainers to get information about the culture and customs of the countries they're headed to that didn't exist thirty years ago. The CIA's

World Factbook (https://www.cia.gov/library/publications/the-world-factbook/index.html) is a good place to start. So are the State Department's website (www.state.gov), U.S. Embassy websites, or the government websites of the countries themselves. Wikipedia (www.wikipedia.org) is another excellent resource, and on-line bookstores are a convenient way to search for books on international customs and culture.

But even with all this information available at one's fingertips, trainers still have a lot to learn on the ground. For example, I doubt there's a book or a website that tells what to do when all the officers providing security for a police station in an embattled area of Iraq lay down their weapons and drop to their knees when the call to prayer comes, leaving the station vulnerable to attack.[17] These are the kinds of things cross-cultural police trainers need to work out on their own with the people they're training—developing compromises and solutions that take the cultural and/or religious foundations of client countries into account. It's not easy. Building bridges between cultures is one of the most challenging aspects of international police training, but it's also one of the most important keys to success.

Lesson Ten: Change takes time. According to Bayley, "There is universal agreement among scholars as well as foreign assistance practitioners that democratic reform takes a long time—five years at least, more likely ten or more . . . . Germany and Japan are the most successful examples of directed democratic police reform in the recent past. Yet observers agree that it wasn't until the 1960s, almost twenty years after World War II, that the spirit of democratic policing as opposed to its form became institutionalized in practice in both countries . . . ."[18]

In other words, change takes time, and fundamental change takes even longer. Which means the best way to ensure enduring change in a developing nation is to ensure a funding stream for continued police training over the long term. If you can't keep

the training going for at least twenty years—that's one genera-
tion of officers—you may be wasting your time, because all it
takes is two or three years without funding for everything to
start coming unraveled.

Unfortunately, this has been the case in Micronesia during the
past fifteen years or so, since U.S. funding assistance for the Micronesian Police Academy we established in 1983 ended in 1992.

During its first ten years in operation, the academy was a
big success—the responsibilities of the Micronesian trainers
were gradually increased until they were running the academy
on their own, and the academy was relocated from Sitka to
Palau. But beginning in 1992, when U.S. funding ran out and it
became the responsibility of each of the newly independent Micronesian nations to pay for the academy themselves, police
training became a hit-or-miss operation, conducted only when
budgets permitted. As a result, police training is once again a
struggling enterprise in what are now the Federated States of
Micronesia, the Republic of the Marshall Islands, the Republic
of Palau, and the Commonwealth of the Northern Mariana Islands. Things are progressing, but very slowly. Without adequate funding, there's only so much that can be done.

We need to remember this when building similar institutions
throughout the world today. We routinely plan cities, highways,
and military weapons systems twenty years or more into the future, and we need to give similar consideration when developing
police in foreign nations. It's not enough to get them started on
their way, and then leave them to work things out on their own.
We need to be in it for the long-term to ensure that all our efforts don't go to waste.

Conclusions: The world has changed rapidly and fundamen-
tally during the past two decades—perhaps more so than during
any two decades in human history. We have shifted from a
world dominated by ponderous, strongly demarcated nations

into a world where ideas, goods, and people flow ever more freely. The aftermath of September 11 has led to even more changes as we transition from wars on terror to the slow process of democratic nation building.

As Bayley notes, "[W]e are in a period of unprecedented effort to expand democratic institutions around the world, with the explicit recognition that reform of the police, and of the larger criminal justice system, is a critical component."[19]

In fact, since the 1990s, the United States and other nations have provided police reform and development assistance to Iraq, Afghanistan, Kosovo, Bosnia-Herzegovina, East Timor, Macedonia, Serbia and Montenegro, Sierra Leone, Liberia, Haiti, Cambodia, El Salvador, Guatemala, Mozambique, Namibia, Nicaragua, Panama, Somalia, South Africa, Sudan, and the Palestinian Territories.[20]

And while we haven't always done things right from my perspective, or made an effort to learn from our mistakes as we should, we *have* done some good and made some important improvements.

But we can do better—particularly in post-conflict regions. For these areas, I strongly support Perito's recommendations for a U.S. Stability Force composed of military units, armed civilian constabulary forces, civilian police trainers, lawyers, judges, and corrections officers. These elements, he says, are essential for maintaining public order and preventing security gaps in post-conflict regions, and for supporting the development of democratic governments.

"As postconflict stability operations have shown, civilian constabulary, police, and law enforcement units deployed in a timely, fully equipped, and well coordinated manner provide an invaluable asset to U.S. military operations," says Perito. "The civilian units help establish police and judicial authority from the outset, thereby freeing the military to concentrate on performing other duties. Most important, they help create the vital foundation for the rule of law from which the other aspects of political, economic, and social reconstruction can go forward in an environment conducive to achieving success."[21]

Getting back to my area of expertise, it seems clear to me that all international police training is much more likely to succeed if we choose the right people as trainers and choose the right people to train, treat them with respect, and tailor training programs to fit them. Even more importantly, police trainers must learn to bridge cultural barriers. Those bridges are built, and rebuilt, each day in a foreign land by respecting the enormous challenges faced by cops in less-developed settings, and by honoring local languages and customs while remaining true to core values. Finally, once we make the commitment to provide police training assistance to a developing nation, we need to follow through with adequate personnel and logistical support, and we need to continue to provide that support over the long term, until they become fully functional without our assistance.

In plain English, just as there's no sense planting a tree unless you're going to keep watering it long enough for the roots to grow deep, there's no sense doing a half-assed job planting the ideals of democratic police. And democratic police—competent, ethical, reliable, democratic police who are committed to protecting people, enforcing the law, and respecting fundamental human rights and liberties—are key to sustaining stable, democratic nations.

I've worn a lot of hats in life—Marine, ghetto cop, international police trainer, federal agent, graduate student, professor, federal policy-maker, and now professor again. At sixty-two, an age I never thought I'd live to see (hell, when I was in the Marine Corps I never expected to make it to twenty-one), I can take the combined sum of all this experience and education and say, without reservations, that I'm right about this. If by some slim chance it turns out I'm wrong, I'll do more than eat my hat. I'll eat another fuzzy little fruit bat—fur, teeth and all.

NOTES

[1] Cole, Robert and Jan Hogan. *Under the Gun in Iraq: My Year Training the Iraqi Police*. New York: Prometheus Books, 2007, p. 25.

[2] Bayley, David H. *Changing the Guard: Developing Democratic Police Abroad*. New York: Oxford University Press, 2006, p. 131.

[3] Bayley, p. 8.

[4] Moss, Michael and David Rohde. "Misjudgments Marred U.S. Plans for Iraqi Police." *New York Times*, May 21, 2006.

[5] West, Bing. *The Strongest Tribe: War, Politics, and the Endgame in Iraq*. New York: Random House, 2008, p. 21.

[6] Moss and Rohde. May 21, 2006.

[7] Perito, Robert M. *Where is the Lone Ranger When We Need Him?: America's Search for a Postconflict Stability Force*. Washington, D.C.: United States Institute of Peace Press, 2004, pp. 91–92.

[8] Cole and Hogan, p. 57.

[9] Iraq Study Group, *The Iraq Study Group Report: The Way Forward–A New Approach*. New York: Vintage, December 6, 2006, p. 54.

[10] Moss, Michael, with David Rohde and Kirk Semple. "How Iraq Police Reform Became Casualty of War." *New York Times*, May 22, 2006.

[11] Headquarters, Department of the Army. *Counterinsurgency, FM 3-24*. December 2006, pp. 6-20, 6-21.

[12] West, p. 369.

[13] Moss, with Rohde and Semple. May 22, 2006.

[14] Moss and Rohde. May 21, 2006.

[15] It's beyond the scope of this book or my expertise to say how to handle a horrible situation like the chaos that occurred in Iraq after the American invasion in 2003—which is largely what led to such disastrous problems with the Iraqi police.

However, for some excellent suggestions for how we might prevent similar future problems, I highly recommend Robert Perito's book, *Where is the Lone Ranger When We Need Him?: America's Search for a Postconflict Stability Force* (Washington, D.C.: United States Institute of Peace Press, 2004).

[16] Bayley, p. 99.

[17] Cole and Hogan, p. 112.

[18] Bayley, p. 90.

[19] Bayley, p. 6.

[20] Compiled from Bayley, pp. 6–7, and the U.S. Department of State, Office of Civilian Police and Rule of Law, *General Information Fact Sheet* (www.state.gov/documents/organization/115512.pdf, downloaded 6/22/09).

[21] Perito, pp. 328–329.

About the Authors

Bryan Vila, Ph.D., is a professor of criminal justice at Washington State University and founder/director of its Hazardous Operational Tasks Simulation Laboratory. His research interests include cross-cultural policing, police fatigue, and criminology theory. He has published more than fifty articles on these topics as well as four books, including *Tired Cops: the Importance of Managing Police Fatigue*.

Since receiving his Ph.D. in 1990 from the University of California, Davis, Bryan has held tenured faculty positions at the University of California, Irvine and the University of Wyoming. Prior to joining WSU in 2005, he directed crime control and prevention research at the U.S. Department of Justice.

Before he became an academic, Bryan served as a law enforcement officer for seventeen years—including nine years as a street cop and supervisor with the Los Angeles County Sheriff's Department, six years as a police chief helping the emerging nations of Micronesia develop stable and culturally appropriate law enforcement agencies, and two years as a federal law enforcement officer in Washington, D.C.

Cynthia Morris has been working as a writer, editor, and publicist for twenty-five years. She is the co-author (with Bryan) of two previous books, *The Role of Police in American Society* and *Capital Punishment in the United States*. She and Bryan are currently working on the sequel to Bryan's 2000 book, *Tired Cops*.

Cyn's solo writing projects (in progress) include a science-based thriller titled *73 Seconds* and a series of American history–themed quotation puzzles titled *American Acrostics*. She has also written and edited numerous articles, reports, and grant proposals for individuals and organizations, including the Institute for Law and Justice in Alexandria, Virginia, and the National Strategy Information Center in Washington, D.C.

Prior to becoming a full-time author/editor in 1995, Cyn was an award-winning science writer/public information officer at the University of California, Irvine for ten years.